Teaching Reading in Middle School

By Laura Robb

SCHOLASTIC

PROFESSIONAL BOOKS

NEW YORK · TORONTO · LONDON · AUCKLAND · SYDNEY
MEXICO CITY · NEW DELHI · HONG KONG

Dedication

With love for Lloyd, Evan, and Anina.
With thanks to all my students for teaching me.

Cover photograph by Vicky Kasala
Cover design by Kathy Massaro
Interior design by LDL Designs
Photographs by Bonnie Forstrum Jacobs
Photographs on pages 9, 29, 31, 61, 87, 89, 94, 143, 145, 183, 187 by Vicky Kasala

ISBN 0–590–68560–0

TABLE OF CONTENTS

Acknowledgments 4

Foreword by P. David Pearson 6

Introduction 8

Chapter 1: The Research That Shapes a Middle School Reading Program 11

Chapter 2: Organizing a Reading Workshop 29

Chapter 3: Strategic Reading in the Middle School 55

Chapter 4: Discover What Students Know About Reading 87

Chapter 5: Strategy Lessons That Prepare Students to Read 115

Chapter 6: Modeling During-Reading Strategies 133

Chapter 7: Modeling Post-Reading Strategies 153

Chapter 8: Ways to Connect Students to Books 183

Chapter 9: Organizing and Guiding Strategic-Reading Groups 201

Chapter 10: Cross-Grade Projects Support Struggling Readers 227

Chapter 11: Assessment, Interpretation, and Evaluation 243

Closing Reflections on Guiding Students' Reading 275

Bibliography 279

Appendices

    Appendix A: Learn About Students' Reading Lives 285

    Appendix B: Open-Ended Discussion Questions 289

    Appendix C: Responding to Literature 296

    Appendix D: Assessment Forms 301

    Appendix E: Guidelines for Writing Readers Theater Scripts 308

Index 311

ACKNOWLEDGMENTS

A book is like an opera. To produce an opera, many people collaborate behind the scenes and on the stage, creating a memorable experience for the audience. Guiding the performers and helping them find their voice is the opera's conductor.

To shape a book, a team of people—editors, teachers, peers in the profession, and designers—collaborate, each bringing a unique eye and talent to the raw manuscript. An editor, like an opera conductor, encourages and guides an author as he or she discovers a book's vision, and harmonizes the suggestions from diverse people in order to publish a book that remains true to the author's ideas, experiences, and research, while meeting the needs of a wide audience.

Wendy Murray, executive editor of Scholastic Professional Books, has been my conductor throughout the process of writing of this book. Because of Wendy's vision, I am writing the acknowledgments for *Teaching Reading in Middle School* and not the original book, which was conceived on a smaller scale. After Wendy read the first manuscript, she encouraged me to expand the book, delve deeper into my teaching, weave in the research on teaching middle school students, and write without worrying about length. The freedom that Wendy gave me was a wonderful gift, one that allowed me to pursue this topic without wondering whether or not I should include material. An editor like Wendy, who nurtures and cares for her writers, is rare, and I am indeed fortunate to work with her.

Terry Cooper, editor-in-chief, supported my wish to reach classroom teachers and professors of education with a more comprehensive look at teaching reading, and established a new line in her publishing program "Theory and Practice Books" to give the book a niche. To Terry, my thanks for believing in me, always being there with great suggestions, always making time for conversations about teaching and learning, and for helping the vision become reality.

To Steve Clegg, fifth-grade teacher at Quarles Elementary School in Winchester, Virginia, I deeply appreciate your willingness to try to iron out reading and classroom management strategies with your students.

To John Lathrop, head of Powhatan School, my sincere thanks for supporting my writing and research. To Ann Robb, Lynn Esslinger and Kathleen Hobbs, colleagues at Powhatan, thanks for all you do to create productive and successful reading workshops. You have provided me with many student conversations as well as feedback on ways you constantly fine-tune mini-lessons, think-alouds, and strategic reading lessons.

I am grateful to all the teachers at Keister Elementary School in Harrisonburg, Virginia, and teachers in Winchester City Public Schools who helped revise strategies and learning experiences.

Teaching Reading in Middle School

You are all an important part of this book.

And to my daughter, Anina, who teaches sixth and seventh grade at a public school in New York City, thanks for the frequent telephone conversations and faxes of students' work. You constantly informed me about how your struggling learners responded to reading strategies, guided practice, and journal work.

The input I received from all those who read the manuscript in its various stages—Suzy Stroble Kaback, Jeannine Reynolds, Adam Berkin, Myra Zarnowski, Joanna Davis-Swing, Rita Randozzo—was invaluable. Your comments and questions helped me revise the text with renewed energy. How grateful I am for your honesty and the long hours you devoted to my manuscript. A special thanks to Lauren Leon for creating a design that is innovative, making the reading easier and more enjoyable.

Finally, my deepest thanks to my husband, Lloyd, who never complained as I worked evenings and weekends to meet the deadlines. Thanks for believing in me, for helping me find the time by more than sharing daily chores, and for reading, rereading, and commenting on every draft of the book.

—Laura Robb

FOREWORD

With the publication of *Teaching Reading in the Middle School*, Laura Robb has given us all a great gift. In this book, she tells a compelling tale about how a teacher can combine several key ingredients to craft a middle school reading program that can turn lives around, that can reverse the cycle of failure experienced by so many struggling readers in our middle schools. The recipe is clear—you combine a large chunk of knowledge about how kids learn to read, mix in some careful planning, add a lot of hands-on trial-and-error experimentation in your classroom, and finish it all with a solid dose of concern for the lives of the kids in your care. The result is also clear—students who had given up on themselves as readers and learners come to realize that being a successful, strategic reader is a goal within their reach.

Robb's book is grounded in three independent, but ultimately complementary, scholarly traditions in literacy education. First, she draws on the account of strategic reading that underlies the model of learning to read that we find in Reading Recovery (and in the writing of Marie Clay) and in the model one finds in recent accounts of classroom learning put forward by Gay Su Pinnell and Irene Fountas, two of the leading figures in the Reading Recovery movement in the United States. The essence of the model is that the most fundamental task of readers is monitoring reading for making sense. At every step of the reading process, readers must learn to marshal all of their existing knowledge to judge whether the meaning they have constructed for a text makes sense. Activities that promote sense-making can be found in each and every chapter of this book.

Second, Robb explains many of the concepts from the account of strategic reading that emanates from the instructional research on comprehension and metacognitive strategies that came out of the 1980s and early 1990s. Here her intellectual ancestors are Michael Pressley, Scott Paris, and several other instructional researchers whose work was prominent in that period. From this expansive research tradition Robb adopts and adapts not a general "strategy," but a host of very specific "strategies." She teaches teachers how to help their students predict and verify outcomes, create visual images from a text, locate the really important stuff, synthesize information across texts, connect the text to their lives, decide whether to keep reading a book, and find details to answer specific questions. A very explicit goal in Robb's model is to make sure that each and every middle school student gets the opportunity to develop expertise over each and every important comprehension and metacognitive strategy associated with expert reading.

Third, she draws good teaching from the more process-oriented approaches associated with Reader's Workshop and whole language. Central to her entire approach is creating a workshop atmosphere in one's classroom. Quite sensibly, she prefers block scheduling so that a workshop session can transcend the bounds of 45-minute class periods so typical of middle schools, but she also shows us how to make it work even within those boundaries. Another cornerstone of her model, one that is most likely the legacy of whole language, is the mini-lesson—that short, snappy, highly focused burst of energy directed toward helping a specific set of students fine-tune their ability to apply a specific reading or writing strategy.

The very best thing about this book, the feature that teachers will appreciate most, is its eminently useful character. Chapters are organized to help teachers implement the strategies and techniques in the way they would use them in their classroom. Readers—classroom teachers, teachers-in-training, staff developers, teachers of teachers—will appreciate the formatting. There are lots of call-outs and text boxes to highlight specific strategies, convenient summaries, step-by-step procedures for implementing complex routines, and classroom-based examples—complete with transcripts of conversations between students and teachers.

Ultimately what Robb realizes, and what she is able to communicate to the rest of us so compellingly, is that in order to help students become strategic, independent readers—readers who can recognize and solve their own problems—teachers must provide them with two equally important ingredients: (1) opportunities to engage in authentic reading activities, the type that real readers encounter in everyday experience, and (2) a deep and broad infrastructure of reading strategies to use when they take advantage of those opportunities.

There is a lot of talk these days in our professional forums about research-based practice. Governmental agencies demand that schools submit proposals for programs based upon scientific research. Districts demand that schools select a research-based model of reform. We have national panels commissioned specifically to tell us what the research says about teaching various aspects of reading. But if we are ever going to achieve research-based practice, then more than anything we need rich and detailed accounts that link important research to classroom practice and that show what that practice looks like when teachers do it well. Laura Robb's book goes a long way toward providing middle school teachers with a clear account of how to make research-based practice a classroom reality.

—P. David Pearson
John A. Hannah Distinguished Professor of Education, Michigan State University

INTRODUCTION

"You teach middle school students?" the high school teacher asked, his voice registering total disbelief. We were attending a workshop for at-risk readers and chatting during our morning coffee break. "One year was all I could take," he added. "They're noisy, unsettled, more interested in each other and searching for themselves than in learning. I like high school seniors because they're adults, and motivated to study."

It's precisely because middle school students have high energy levels and are in search of themselves, their beliefs and values, that I enjoy learning with them. They bombard adults with challenges and questions while they seek support and identity from peers, all the while trying to discover an answer to, "Who am I?" On their journey to define themselves, they constantly test the adult world by breaking rules and appearing unconcerned with adult goals and values.

Some adults view middle school students' behavior as outrageous, rebellious, and annoying. A sense of humor, however, allows me and my fellow schoolteachers to deal with students such as seventh grader Jon, who arrives at school with the hairdo of the day, or eighth grader Tara, who rebels against the rule of "no earrings" by clipping a large, dangling earring onto her left nostril. "No one said anything about noses," she says, challenging me.

These moments of rebellion notwithstanding, middle school is a time of significant academic, emotional, and social growth. Most middle schoolers relish the opportunity to be actively involved in research, reading, writing, talking, and thinking about topics that are relevant to their lives.

These phrases, *actively involved* and *topics that are relevant to their lives,* are at the core of successful middle school classroom practices. Setting up our teaching so students are active learners, and giving them choices in how and what they study, make mandated curricula palatable to them. We also need to offer our young adults elective choices such as foreign language, art, chorus, band, dance, creative writing, and journalism. Whether elective or mandated, classes engage students when they build on, rather than resist, students' high energy levels and curiosity about themselves, others, and the world. During the middle school years, teachers can inspire students' desire to read and think by teaching strategic reading and offering students books they can read.

Students enter middle school with diverse levels of reading and problem-solving skills. A class of 25 sixth graders can have a reading range from third to eighth grade. Meeting the reading and emotional needs of such a diverse population is the primary challenge of every middle school teacher.

What do I do with students who can't read the textbook?

How do I find time to work with struggling readers?

How do I help students reading three years below grade level feel good about reading easier books?

What can I do with students who hate to read?

I've had to confront questions like these throughout my career, and the teachers I coach ask them, too. Important goals of this book are to provide suggestions that will enable you to:

- Teach strategic reading across the curriculum.
- Present mini-lessons that deepen students' knowledge of how specific reading strategies work and can support their reading.
- Develop learning experiences across the curriculum that are relevant to middle schoolers and can improve their reading process.
- Support struggling readers with frameworks that improve reading.
- Create an environment that motivates and involves students in their reading.
- Provide students with standardized test-taking strategies.
- Explore the importance of choices for middle school students.
- Discover book selection strategies that enable students to read at their independent and instructional levels.

- Organize teaching time in a block schedule or a 45-minute period.

To develop strategic readers and bring books and middle school learners together is an overriding purpose of this book. When you offer students strategies that bond them to books and stimulate thinking and wondering, you plant the seeds that germinate lifelong readers—readers who turn to books because of the knowledge, pleasure, and entertainment reading brings to their lives.

Chapter 1

The Research That Shapes a Middle School Reading Program

"Why should I change my reading program? I like it."
—Sixth-Grade Teacher

It was 10 o'clock, the first morning of a weeklong summer class on reading strategies that I was giving for middle school teachers. My goal that first day was for teachers to understand the relationship between prior knowledge and comprehension. After presenting an overview of the class, inviting teachers to introduce themselves and anonymously pose written questions for us to investigate, I asked them to activate prior knowledge using brainstorming for the article called "The Sifting Sands of Factorland" by Ian Steward (*Scientific American,* June 1997). No one had prior knowledge about complex factoring—that's exactly why I selected the article. Despite this, I asked teachers to read it and answer five questions. Groans and disgruntled comments of, "I can't make sense of this; I don't know a bloody thing about the world of integers; I'm not doing it," echoed across the room.

Good, I thought, as I asked, "How do you think prior knowledge affects comprehension?" The group's comments revealed a rift. Most agreed that without prior knowledge, comprehension was limited and reading felt like a chore. A few insisted that the problem was with the article—it was too difficult—beyond their reading level.

Before releasing the 35 teachers for a midmorning break, I asked if they had any questions. Julie, a seventh-grade reading teacher in the second year of her career, said, "Yeah, I've got one. I don't know what teaching reading means in my grade. I never learned what to do in college, and I still don't know what to teach my students to help them improve." Several people nodded in agreement.

During the next hour, teachers vented their frustrations over:

✦ having only a 45-minute period to teach reading;
✦ not knowing how best to group 30 students with a wide range of reading abilities;
✦ feeling ill-equipped to reach students who "hated" and shunned reading;
✦ not knowing how to assess progress;
✦ not knowing what to do with the rest of the class while working with one group;
✦ finding time to read literature worth thinking and talking about.

What luck, I thought. Two hours into the seminar, and I've already raised the discomfort level of many and angered a nucleus of teachers who adamantly defended placing students in books beyond their instructional level, believing students would rise to the challenge and enlarge their vocabulary.

When teachers (and that includes myself) feel discomfort and anger, it's a sign that old beliefs have been shaken. That's good. Discomfort often precedes change and growth. However, my greatest concern was that these teachers had no framework for and no theory about how middle school children read to learn and learn to improve reading.

By listening to these teachers, I discovered that many of them framed their reading instruction around three activities:

✦ **Round-Robin Reading:** Students take turns reading the story or chapter out loud. Accuracy in oral reading is the focus. Follow-up activities center around teacher-made comprehension questions.

✦ **Curriculum Read-Alouds:** The teacher reads required books to students that are too difficult for most of them. Students have copies of the books and follow along during the read-alouds, then answer teacher-made comprehension questions.

✦ **Prepared Skill Worksheets:** Students complete skill sheets on vocabulary, finding the main idea, making predictions, and sequencing events. The worksheets do not relate to books students were reading, nor do teachers attempt to connect the practiced skill to real reading materials such as novels, magazine articles, and the newspaper.

While teachers sipped coffee and chatted during their break, the challenge before me appeared across my mind in boldface print: To offer these teachers learning experiences and professional materials that would enable them to rethink and revise their notion of reading instruction in the middle grades—first steps to a long but exhilarating process of meaningful change.

The reading program I suggest integrates three elements that interact and address the emotional, social, and academic needs of middle school students, who search for their adult identity and yearn for independence and control over their lives. A productive reading program for middle schoolers considers and makes use of research in these areas: 1) strategic reading; 2) motivation and involvement; 3) a workshop environment.

This chapter presents the teaching implications of the research on strategic reading, motivation, and reading workshop for middle school. The ideas that follow will be developed in later chapters.

STRATEGIC READING

Marie Clay (1979), an educator who developed the Reading Recovery program and has conducted extensive research on emergent and beginning readers, described a complex network of unobservable, in-the-head strategies that readers use to make sense of print. Though students' reading processes are hidden from teachers, we can observe, note, and analyze students' patterns of error while they read a short passage out loud (Barr et al., 1990; Gillet and Temple, 1990). We can also enter students' minds through conferences (Robb, 1998), by observing their behaviors during silent reading and book discussions, and by reading students' written responses to literature.

The route to teaching strategic reading, then, is a two-way street. It involves discovering as much as we can about students' reading processes, *and* making our own reading process visible for them. Modeling during mini-lessons how a strategy such as activating prior knowledge works is an important first step toward students owning the strategy and applying it automatically to a variety of reading materials (Pearson et al., 1992). Along the way to this automaticity, students practice and use the strategy, participating in whole- and small-group guided-practice sessions (Robb, 1995) while teachers monitor how students employ strategies during small guided-reading groups (Fountas and Pinnell, 1996) and one-on-one reading conferences (Bomer, 1998; Robb, 1994, 1996). Fountas and Pinnell call this "reading for strategies" because teachers are helping students solve problems with strategies as they read texts. That's how students can gain a repertoire of in-the-head strategies. By middle school, students refine and deepen their application of strategies in strategic-reading groups.

Pearson et al. (1992) recommended a comprehension curriculum structured around seven strategies that thoughtful readers use. *All readers, from emergent to proficient, use combinations of the strategies that follow as they read to make meaning and remember.*

Seven Key Reading Strategies

Activate Prior Knowledge: In 1938 Louise Rosenblatt published *Literature as Exploration* and showed that readers use prior knowledge, information, and experiences stored in the mind to make meaning from a text. According to Rosenblatt, during reading a reader integrates this personal knowledge with the author's words, creating an original text. To every text, a reader brings his/her personality, present mood, and memories, making each person's experience of a text almost as unique as a fingerprint. Rosenblatt suggests that what readers bring to a text affects their ability to comprehend the author's words.

Years later, researchers like Marvin Minsky (1975) and Richard Anderson (1984) gave Rosenblatt's observations of readers' behaviors a name: *schema theory*. Schema theory implies that each child brings a unique set of experiences and knowledge, called *schemata*, to reading. As we read, we use our schemata for birthdays to understand a birthday celebration in China, and our schemata for feeling ill and weak to understand the new word, *enervate*.

The research of schema theorists supports the importance of teachers initiating getting-ready-to-read strategies. Doing the "prep work" before students read a book or study a topic also enables teachers to discover and reflect on what students know about a topic. If students' background knowledge is limited, building additional knowledge prior to reading will improve comprehension and engagement.

2 Decide What's Important in a Text: Proficient readers are not bogged down or discouraged by the myriad details and information in texts. Using their prior knowledge and determining a purpose for reading helps them to separate unimportant information from key points.

3 Synthesize Information: Good readers silently synthesize and summarize sections of a text as they read. This strategy involves selecting key points and organizing them under general topics. It's a complex process that moves beyond retelling, an important strategy for emergent, beginning, and struggling readers, since synthesizing involves determining the main idea of a passage or chapter and choosing points that relate to that idea. Brown, Day, and Jones (1992) highlighted five operations readers use as they synthesize and summarize:

1. Remove irrelevant data.
2. Remove repeated information.
3. Categorize information into lists, such as "fruit" for peaches, tomatoes, apples.
4. Try to locate topic sentences in the text and use these for their internal summaries.
5. Create topic sentences when they can't find any in the text.

4 Draw Inferences During and After Reading: Reading between the lines (Calkins, 1991; Robb, 1994) to determine a character's motivation and personality, to discover themes, and to identify the main points in informational texts is what comprehension is all about. In most curricula, inferential thinking is delayed until students become proficient readers. However, Anderson and Pearson (1984) believe that students should be taught to make inferences beginning in the primary grades.

5 Self-Monitor Comprehension: All readers bump into perplexing passages. Proficient readers can pinpoint confusing passages and vocabulary, and are able to tackle them on the spot. They view discovering meaning in difficult passages as a challenge they can meet.

Struggling readers, on the other hand, tend to skip over difficult passages and unfamiliar words, unaware that the information is important. This results in diminished comprehension and an inability to recall details in retellings, frustration with reading for meaning, and low-ered self-esteem (Schunk and Zimmerman, 1997; Sweet, 1997).

6 **Repair Faulty Comprehension:** When good readers identify a confusing part, they have a repertoire of fix-it strategies to access, such as rereading or using context clues and prior knowledge, which enables them to comprehend. Struggling readers' fix-it strategies are undeveloped, and they lack the ability to independently "unconfuse" themselves.

7 **Ask Questions:** Proficient readers pose questions before, during, and after reading. This questioning allows good readers to assess what they already know and to set guidelines for what they need to learn in order to enlarge their knowledge (Gillet and Temple, 1990). Making this thinking process explicit for students by encouraging them to pose questions can set purposes for reading and deepen students' involvement in fiction and nonfiction, as they keep reading to satisfy their wondering. Predicting is a form of questioning that engages readers in fiction as they ask what will happen next, then read on to confirm and adjust.

Nonfiction texts also raise questions in readers' minds as they confront new information and try to link it to what they already know. For example, when reading an article about the Great Depression, engaged readers try to construct meaning by applying their knowledge of unemployment, poverty, and homeless people.

Two More Strategies to Consider

8 **Build Vocabulary:** Pearson et al. (1992) point out that these seven strategies, taught alone, do not make a complete comprehension program. I agree, and have added vocabulary-building and developing fluency to the strategy curriculum. A primary task of teachers who learn with middle schoolers is to enlarge their reading vocabulary (Barr et al., 1990; Gillet and Temple, 1990). In content subjects such as history and science, dozens of unfamiliar words bombard students each week—words they need to extract meaning from as they read. Moreover, Barr et al. stress that most middle school students' comprehension difficulties are due to inadequate vocabularies. Therefore, word study before, during, and after reading should be integrated into the middle school curriculum. (For more on building vocabulary, see my book *Easy Mini-Lessons That Build Vocabulary,* Scholastic, 1999.)

9 **Develop Fluency:** Middle school students who read in a halting, word–by–word manner, who struggle with phrasing, expression, and reading in meaningful chunks, are at great risk of being turned off by reading. Their lack of fluency impedes recall and comprehension, making reading an unpleasant, unrewarding chore. And to middle schoolers concerned with peer acceptance and looking cool, disfluent reading is an embarrassment. It's safer for these students to avoid completing assignments than to risk exposing their "flaw" (Cunningham and Allington, 1999).

Teachers can improve these students' fluency by designating a private, quiet area of the classroom as a place where students can try repeated readings, tape-record stories for a primary classroom's listening center, and practice reading poetry or a Readers Theater part with drama and emotion (see page 308).

INTEGRATING VOCABULARY INSTRUCTION

Daily vocabulary instruction throughout the year is an unrealistic goal, given the limitations of instructional time that middle school teachers have. I solve this problem by alternating teaching vocabulary-building strategies with responding to literature in journals, spelling, and grammar. For six to eight weeks I emphasize vocabulary, then move to modeling journal responses, spelling, and, finally, grammar. Within a 36-week school year, there's plenty of time to rotate in-depth studies of these topics.

However, if students' work reveals that I need to remain on one topic, I'll extend our mini-study. Don't lock yourself into rigid time frames. Observe your students, read and reflect on their work, then set priorities. Maintaining a flexible stance is the hallmark of interactive teaching that responds to students' needs (Clay, 1993).

HOW A STRATEGY-BASED CURRICULUM INFLUENCES YOUR TEACHING OF READING

The goal of organizing instruction around reading for strategies is to provide opportunities for middle school students to practice, use, and apply a wide range of strategies to reading problems encountered while completing school assignments and during independent reading. Here are some ways you can enlarge and exercise middle school students' repertoire of in-the-head strategies:

+ Model, through mini-lessons and during read-alouds, how these strategies work for you.

+ Record mini-lessons on chart paper so students can refer to them again and again.

+ Offer opportunities for students to practice and discuss strategies using materials at their independent level. Easier materials allow students to focus on understanding the strategy instead of struggling with the text. I use the SMOG formula (see page 191) to level books for this purpose.

+ Group students for guided reading according to their needs. Once students show you that they can apply a strategy, reorganize the group and continue to move students forward.

+ Reserve time for short, focused, one-on-one reading conferences during which you can observe students reading and help them explore strategies that can help them comprehend confusing passages and words.

+ *Accept that for all readers, practicing and internalizing a strategy takes time.* Reserve as much time as middle school students require. Moving them forward too fast, expecting students to use a strategy independently after a couple of practice sessions, will only confuse them and decrease their chances of ever owning the strategy. You'll find that some students will be ready to move on, while others will need continued scaffolding from you and/or a peer.

MOTIVATION AND INVOLVEMENT

Research shows that as children progress through school, their interest in reading for pleasure, and their motivation to read to learn, diminishes (Ruddell and Unrau, 1997). This research compels middle school teachers to reflect on these questions: *What kinds of student-teacher interactions increase motivation to read? What reading goals, values, and beliefs foster high levels of motivation among students? How do teachers become aware of these beliefs? Do choice and appropriate reading materials affect students' motivation?*

According to Schunk and Zimmerman (1997), students' belief in their ability to learn to read proficiently, and to set specific, short-term goals for an assignment, motivates them to work hard, become involved in an assignment, and successfully complete it. For example, a student who rereads just the first two chapters of a novel when asked to identify the main character's personality traits at the beginning of the story fares better than a student who can't set a manageable goal, and is overwhelmed at the idea she must reread half the book.

Success, in turn, increases a middle schooler's belief in her ability to improve reading, continue to set productive goals, and remain involved in the book. Moreover, involvement (Schunk and Zimmerman, 1997) and interest in reading increase when students' pleasure comes from completing books, improving, and learning rather than an outside reward such as a free pizza or money for grades.

Ultimately, motivation to read for school, and the belief that "I can do it well," hinge on the readability of the books teachers offer middle school students. Schallert and Reed (1997) state that when students read books that are too difficult because of unfamiliar vocabulary or lack of background knowledge, involvement with the story and characters is impossible. Because the struggle to decode unfamiliar words becomes overwhelming, comprehension is blocked and students' desire to achieve shuts down.

All Children Deserve School Libraries

According to the research of Sherry Guice et al. (1996), children who attend schools in low-income neighborhoods have 50 percent fewer books in their libraries than schools in wealthier communities. Children who attend schools in these communities are the ones who need the *best* stocked libraries.

It's necessary to fight for two things in schools that have large populations of disadvantaged children who arrive at school with limited literacy experiences:
1. Create a library schedule where children can check out books before and after school, and during the day.
2. Increase the number of high-quality books so the very children who need them most have opportunities to read.

Since the depth of reading comprehension and recall is related to motivation, belief in self, and text readability, then classroom environment, the nature of book choice, and teacher-student interactions have a great impact on students' achievement and involvement in reading.

Who Selects Books for Students to Read?

In some school districts, teachers inherit sets of textbooks and trade books that supervisors have purchased, and they must use these whether or not students can read them. Being forced to instruct with books that are too difficult for students has resulted in a practice in which teachers read aloud and students follow in their books. *This strategy improves students' listening; it does not improve students' reading.*

Steve Clegg and I level books for fifth graders.

Other districts invite grade-level teams to choose books for a range of instructional and independent levels and pay for these selections from a school's budget. My son, Evan, principal of Warren County Middle School, in Front Royal, Virginia, annually allocates money for instructional and classroom library books for the English Department. Additional dollars for books come from fund-raisers conducted by the parents' association.

Since the reading levels and abilities of students change throughout the year, and at the start of each year with a new group, it makes sense for schools to reserve money for the purchase of books that meet the needs of students. Many teachers use bonus points from book club orders to purchase appropriate titles.

Another way to broaden teachers' choice of books is to have a book storage room where books are shelved according to grade and reading level. Sharing books this way is an excellent practice, for it allows teachers to select an easier title and place a group of struggling readers in a book they can read.

HOW MOTIVATION RESEARCH
AFFECTS YOUR CLASSROOM

Here are some practical, research-based suggestions to incorporate into your reading program that can deepen middle school students' involvement in reading.

Build Students' Confidence: Help students believe in their ability to successfully complete assignments. Make sure assignments are reasonable and can be completed in the time you've suggested. Throughout the process, offer students feedback that lets them know what's working well and how they can make adjustments for success. Positive statements like those that follow are powerful motivators: *I noticed you had a great interpretation of… The point you made in your reading journal about courage is very interesting—I'm going to share with the class so they can hear it. You're reading up a storm. I'm glad you like fiction—I'd like to see you try a nonfiction book next, though. I'd like to see you put sticky-notes where you are having trouble staying involved. We can look at those places and figure out what's causing this problem.* Listen carefully to the feedback that students offer.

Offer Learning Models: For example, through teacher demonstrations show students how you identify a book's themes by sifting through a story and composing general statements based on the characters, setting, and conflicts in the book (see pages 172–173). Invite student experts to share their process of discovering themes.

Present Goal-Setting and Self-Evaluation Strategies: Explain how to set small, short-term goals, such as reading 25 pages and jotting notes on sticky-notes about the setting. Consistently point out to students that reaching doable goals prepares them for class, enables them to participate in discussions and group work, and improves their comprehension and recall. You might have to confer with individuals and model short-term goal setting until each student internalizes the process and can work independently.

Be a Careful Observer: Watch students during mini-lessons, group discussions, and sustained silent reading, noting their level of involvement. Observing students'

continued on next page

…HOW MOTIVATION RESEARCH AFFECTS YOUR CLASSROOM

behaviors allows teachers to "see into students' minds" and form hypotheses about how students are using reading strategies to comprehend (Goodman, 1985; Powers, 1996).

Use Books at Students' Instructional Levels: Friendly, readable texts can lead to a pleasurable reading experience because the learner comprehends and becomes involved. A study conducted by Schallert, Reed, and Goetz (1992) showed that involvement in and comprehension of nonfiction texts increased when these books contained many stories and vignettes. This research poses a great challenge to schools and classroom teachers, who must find nonfiction and fiction for instruction that meet a wide range of reading levels and interests. (See pages 192–196 for lists of great books.)

Identify What Students Can Do Well: Discover each student's strengths through strategy interviews, conferences, and observations, through reading students' responses to literature, and by listening to pairs of students and groups discuss books. Guided practice, strategic-reading groups, one-on-one interventions, and independent reading improve what students do well and foster progress in reading. Raise students' awareness of what they do well by giving them positive feedback.

READING WORKSHOP

During the Middle Ages and the Renaissance, aspiring artists learned to paint by joining a master painter's workshop. Here the novice learned techniques, such as perspective and mixing colors, by observing the master and more experienced artists. Painters developed by being immersed and participating in real painting experiences.

Reading workshop (Atwell, 1987, 1999; Calkins, 1991), like an artist's workshop, immerses students in reading experiences that closely simulate the experiences of adult readers. The reasons students read resemble the reasons adults read: to research, to learn, to keep abreast of current events, for a job, for pleasure and entertainment. Like the master painter and his expert assistants, the teacher and proficient readers in a workshop model for the "apprentice readers" what good readers do to make meaning. The extended blocks of time in a reading workshop (see pages 49–50)—one to one-and-a-half hours—allow teachers to organize a variety of authentic reading activities.

Independent reading in a fifth-grade workshop.

Workshop structure, which should center around fine literature (Strickland, 1987), offers students choices in reading and activities (Kohn, 1993). It provides opportunities for students to work with peers and observe how those who "get" a strategy apply it.

A typical day in my eighth-grade reading workshop might include several of these experiences:

Read-Aloud: by the teacher. [Could be a poem, short story, myth, fable, magazine or newspaper article, or part of a novel or informational text.]

Gathering: to review schedule, answer questions.

Mini-Lesson: presentation by the teacher or a student expert to the entire class or a small group, followed by a brief question/answer session.

Guided Practice: students have many opportunities to practice a reading strategy collaboratively, with an easy, short text.

Meaningful Reading Experiences: students read independently, discuss books, and respond to them in journals.

Guided Strategic-Reading Groups: while other students work in groups or pairs or alone, the teacher works with students who need more support in learning a strategy.

Conferences: one-on-one meetings with students about their reading.

Choices: students choose reading books from the school, classroom, home, or community library, based on interest and readability.

Reader's Chair: spotlights students as readers while they present book talks to small groups or to the entire class.

Closing: Teacher's final comments that showcase what worked—groups or pairs conferred productively; partners supported each other during guided practice. Reserve three to five minutes for copying homework.

Reader's Chair

Talking about books is a shared language experience between two or more people. As they exchange stories or story together (Wells, 1986), they can make personal connections to the text and gain insights into literary structures and their own reading process (Rosenblatt, 1978). During Reader's Chair, the primary focus is on the reader, the book, and the reader's thinking as he or she composes oral texts and receives immediate feedback from peers and teachers.

Reader's Chair builds on talk as a means of comprehending and honors reading and the reader much the same as the Author's Chair (Calkins, 1991) honors writing and the writer. Through Reader's Chair, students and teacher can talk about books completed and books-in-progress (Robb, 1994). Sitting in a special chair reserved for the speaker, the reader makes a brief presentation that can involve personal connections to the story, new information, and observations about setting, characters, events, and illustrations. After a presentation, the class questions the reader who calls upon two to three peers.

Schedule two to three sessions a week; students can reserve share time on a bulletin board sign-up sheet or on the chalkboard. Because time is precious in middle school, teachers can integrate Reader's Chair into workshop for one marking period—more if their workshop block allows.

If your class is new to such reading share sessions, start Reader's Chair with a demonstration. Open with think-alouds that discuss how you collected ideas and feelings. Point out that you're not looking for a retelling, but for selecting material that relates to the purpose of your talk. Then in a brief monologue, present a book talk that focuses on genre or a character you related to or disliked, why you chose the novel, or literary techniques such as flashback, foreshadowing, or irony. To emphasize a point, the reader can also read aloud a short passage.

On chart paper, keep a running list of book talk ideas as a student resource. You'll find that students' suggestions will far exceed your list of ideas. Here's what a list begun in January in my eighth-grade class looked like at the end of February:

- ✦ How this book changed my thinking.
- ✦ What I learned about people, families, friends.
- ✦ Why I chose this genre.
- ✦ How literary foils helped me understand characters.
- ✦ Why setting was important.
- ✦ Problems characters faced that I related to.
- ✦ Why I reread this book.
- ✦ A mystery you'll never figure out until the end.
- ✦ A minor character I related to.
- ✦ How this book changed my thinking about...
- ✦ Read a moving passage and explain how it relates to the themes.

The power of Reader's Chair emerges from students speaking candidly to peers. The interest and pleasure in reading that they transmit to classmates is the best advertisement for books. The eighth-grade Reader's Chair monologue that follows illustrates how students can learn to focus on new information and personal reactions to theme and events.

> California Blue *by David Klass is what I'd call realistic fiction. The story takes place in a small mill town where people make their living by cutting down trees in the forest. This book taught me a lot about the difference between butterflies and moths and also why it's important to preserve a new species. Besides the scientific information, this is the story of John, a high school runner who loves biology. John struggles to form a relationship with his father who was a football hero at John's high school. John and his dad always argue and fight, even when John learns that his father is dying of cancer. I understood that learning about a serious illness was not enough to patch up the fact that John felt his dad didn't accept his being different. John was different because he wanted to go to college and wasn't a football hero like his dad and brother, Glenn. When John tells that he is the one that found the butterfly, named Rodgers California Blue at a town meeting, peers and adults attack John because they fear the mill will close. The struggle of working through the issue of keeping the forest safe for this new species and also keeping the mill going affects John and his father. I learned that intense situations, even though they are painful, can change people.*

Reader's Chair is a natural way to introduce a class to many different genres. You, as a participant, can also enlarge students' range of reading, by presenting a talk on a genre that many students haven't tried. Most important, Reader's Chair honors the reader while placing great value on independent reading.

Reading Workshop: Some Basic Routines

Workshop is an ideal environment for high-energy middle school students who love to chat and socialize, are working toward independence in reading, and yearn for more responsibility. In a workshop setting students learn to budget time, complete assignments in many subjects, meet deadlines, and interact productively with peers and their teacher. Because students become skilled at working independently during part of workshop, you can use this time to support struggling readers by scheduling individual or small-group conferences (Bomer, 1998).

Here are some teaching tips that can make a workshop hum:

+ Provide a structure for your workshop by including these basic routines during each meeting: teacher read-aloud; mini-lesson; whole-class gathering and closing.

+ Involve students actively in their learning by inviting them to negotiate the following with you: due dates; number of journal responses; number of books to complete each month; reading experiences to work on during each workshop.

+ Teach students how to create open-ended discussion questions so their book conversations are relevant to their lives and experiences (see pages 127–129).

+ Build a classroom library with books on a wide range of reading levels to meet the varied needs and interests of your students. Use bonus points from book club orders to enlarge your library and/or request that your school's parent organization raise money for books. Some principals apply for grants for books. In 1999 Jane Gaidos, principal of Robinson Elementary in Woodstock, Virginia, received a grant for $6,000 for teachers to purchase books in kindergarten to grade two.

+ Record your mini-lessons on large chart paper so students can

Grants for Books

School districts receive federal dollars, such as Title VI literacy funding. Many districts invite principals to write grants to use this money as long as the dollars spent relate to literacy development. In addition, Dennis Norris has published a book about getting grant money that can assist teachers who are searching for ways to build classroom and school libraries. (*Get a Grant: Yes You Can!* Scholastic Professional Books, 1998)

refer to the demonstrations as they practice and apply a strategy.

◆ Vary the way you group students, organizing them according to interests, a specific project, an author study, friendship, genre studies, etc.

◆ Teach students how to work independently so you can confer with individuals and guide the reading of small groups of students (see pages 209–213).

◆ Make self-evaluation a key component of assessment. (A discussion of self-evaluation and assessment tools is in Chapter 11.)

As You Read On

The chapters that follow build on the best practices in reading I've just outlined and also consider the unique developmental stage of middle schoolers. As you read on, you will:

◆ Discover how to organize and schedule a productive reading workshop in Chapter 2.

◆ Explore the purposes of strategic reading and review in-the-head strategies students employ before, during, and after reading in Chapter 3.

◆ Consider several ways to learn about your students' attitudes toward reading and levels of competency in Chapter 4. The more you deepen your knowledge of students, the better equipped you'll be to get them involved with reading.

◆ Review key mini-lessons that activate students' prior knowledge and experiences before reading in Chapter 5.

◆ Learn how to present demonstrations that help students self-monitor during reading in Chapter 6.

◆ Explore mini-lessons that invite you to reserve time for thinking, questioning, journaling, and critical analysis of literature after reading in Chapter 7.

◆ Explore interactive teacher read-alouds and learn how to choose books at students' independent and instructional levels in Chapter 8.

◆ Visit middle school classrooms and observe a workshop in action in Chapter 9. Learn about flexible grouping for instruction and observe how I teach small groups and individuals to read for strategies.

◆ Observe how cross-grade projects can help struggling readers improve in Chapter 10.

◆ Study a variety of practical ways to assess and evaluate middle school students' reading progress in Chapter 11.

Pause and Reflect on:
Examining Your Reading Workshop Each Year

At the close of each school year, jot notes that highlight workshop needs, then reflect on these in August when you're about to launch reading workshop with new students. Here's what I wrote in June 1999:

✦ Need more time for choice activities.

✦ Don't ever skip a read-aloud

✦ Find more short stories to read aloud.

✦ More conferences with struggling readers to monitor their progress—find the time!

✦ Get more fantasy and science fiction in class library.

Each year I struggle with the issue of time. While I know I'll never feel I have sufficient time, I keep discouragement at bay by setting two goals in the forefront of my mind: to improve students' reading and to deepen their involvement with books. Throughout the year I revisit these goals as students and I negotiate our use of the time we have.

🌿 Chapter 2
Organizing a
Reading Workshop

"I like all the different things we do in workshop and most of the time I'm liking what we do." —Sixth Grader

It's a mid-October morning and 26 eighth graders enter my reading-writing workshop. Chatting, pairs and groups of students find their way to desks arranged in five communities. As all students silently settle in, taking out their response journals and books, I begin reading aloud Roald Dahl's short story, "The Landlady." Then I present a 15-minute mini-lesson on generating words that accurately describe a character's personality. We move immediately into guided practice, during which groups of students practice the strategy for 15 minutes, using a short story they've already read. I circulate among groups and jot down notes, pausing to observe and/or converse with individuals.

Next, students have 40 minutes of choice time (see page 42). I write three choices on the chalkboard and review them quickly: 1) read silently; 2) finish the journal entry on the problems the main character faced in the short story you read; 3) using brainstormed notes, write a self-evaluation of your reading progress.

I list on the chalkboard the names of students in reading groups and individual students I plan to meet with to practice a strategy presented earlier; everyone else is expected to choose an activity and dive in.

Today four students and I spend 20 minutes practicing selecting the details that help them

WHAT THE RESEARCH SAYS ABOUT INDEPENDENT READING

Allocating ample time for actual text reading, and ensuring that students are actually engaged in text reading during that time, are among teachers' most important tasks in comprehension instruction—for both able and struggling readers (Fielding and Pearson, 1994). Citing research by Anderson et al., 1988, and Leinhard et al., 1981, Fielding and Pearson assert:

Recent research has debunked the misconception that only already-able readers can benefit from time spent actually reading, while less able readers should spend time on isolated skills instruction and workbook practice. A newer, more compelling argument is that the differing amounts of time teachers give students to read texts accounts for the widening gaps between more able and less able readers throughout the school grades (Allington, 1983).

discover the themes of the short story "The Landlady." Then, we practice expressing the story's themes with general statements (see pages 172–173). Next, I hold two one-on-one conferences with struggling readers, while the rest of the class selects and works on one of the choice experiences.

During the first conference, Jolene and I practice using context clues to figure out the meanings of tough words. During the second conference, Juan rereads each couplet of Arthur Guiterman's poem, "Ancient History," until the reading is fluent and expressive. Tomorrow, as part of a cross-grade project that the fifth-grade teacher and I arranged, Juan will read aloud the poem to the fifth-grade class. The teacher and I organized this exchange to provide authentic opportunities for fifth and eighth graders to read aloud to each other. One week an eighth grader reads aloud to fifth graders; the next week a fifth grader reads to the eighth grade.

I hope this glimpse into my workshop illustrates why so many middle school teachers favor this environment. It provides students with the time they need to select and read books that interest them. All the other acts—modeling strategies during mini-lessons, guided practice, meeting with groups and individuals—support the main act: *students reading.*

Nancie Atwell, in her groundbreaking book, *In the Middle* (1986, 1998), connected the goals and environment of writing workshop (Calkins, 1991 and Graves, 1983) to reading workshop. For Atwell, the purpose of reading workshop is for students to choose and read books during class—books at their independent levels—books that students *wanted* to read. In notebooks that Atwell called "dialogue journals," students wrote letters about their books and Atwell or classmates responded. The exchange of letters, one-on-one conferences, and mini-lessons enabled Nancie Atwell to develop a wide range of literary tastes among students, and to demonstrate reading strategies and ways to reflect on books that nudged her students to think more deeply about their reading.

Reserving a block of time for independent reading is one of the most effective ways to improve reading.

Other Important Benefits of Workshop

✦ Because workshop is a mixture of teacher- and student-led experiences and offers choice time (Atwell, 1986; Robb, 1994), it's the ideal environment for middle grade students to develop the responsibility they crave.

✦ Having long stretches of time for reading workshop enables students to practice and apply reading strategies at school (Robb, 1994, 1995).

✦ Chunks of time build on the social needs of middle schoolers and allow flexibility in arranging strategic-reading groups (pages 203–209), book discussions, paired readings and retellings, and sustained silent reading. Moreover, *talk* (social interactions around a text) provides opportunities for students to interpret, clarify, and exchange ideas, resulting in deeper comprehension of texts (Gambrell, 1994).

Why Flexible Grouping Matters

Teaching reading should not be confined to whole-group interactions (Goodman, 1996; Edelsky, Altwerger, and Flores, 1991). To meet the needs of elementary and middle school students, educators recommend a mixture of whole-group, small-group, one-on-one, and individual learning events. Regie Routman (1990) and Don Holdaway (1980) describe class schedules that include *whole-group events,* such as gatherings, shared reading, teacher read alouds, discussions, sharing students' projects, book talks, and mini-lessons. Gambrell and Almasi (1994) and Diane Lapp et al. (1997) point out the benefits of *small-group events,* such as book discussions and dramatizations. Atwell (1998) includes mini-lessons and conferring as important small-group events; Bomer (1998) highlights the benefits of one-on-one interactions to help readers practice and apply fix-it strategies. *Individual events,* such as silent reading, journal entries, self-evaluation, and choice in reading (Atwell, 1987; Hansen, 1987; Routman, 1990) are also included in this workshop model.

For me, the Russian psychologist Lev Vygotsky's view of teachers and peer experts as mediators (1978) holds the most sway in validating the flexible, ever-changing grouping of students in workshop. Vygotsky believed that children learn best in social situations where they work alongside more competent adults and peers. During whole-group discussions, and as heterogeneous groups of children talk about books, developing readers can observe how proficient readers go about summarizing, synthesizing, posing questions, and so forth. Over time, observations and guided practice, combined with scaffolding from teachers, help struggling readers develop their own strategy models.

Workshop upholds another important Vygotskian idea: the "Zone of Proximal Development," or ZPD, the area between what children can accomplish independently and what they can learn with the help of an expert. Your job and mine, then, is to discover what students can do on their own and what they can accomplish with support.

Each day, teachers who interact with their middle school students observe them at work, confer with them, and read their journal entries. The information gathered enables teachers to decide how to group children for reading instruction and when to move each child forward (see Chapters 9 and 11).

This chapter will acquaint you with practical ideas for organizing and managing a workshop, meaningful reading experiences for middle school students, and sample schedules. Chapters that follow will explore these ideas in the context of different middle school classrooms.

Strategic-Reading Groups

A component I've added to middle school workshop is strategic-reading groups, which builds on the dynamic model presented in *Guided Reading,* by Irene Fountas and Gay Su Pinnell, and Michael Opitz's *Flexible Grouping in Reading.* To instruct these small groups, teachers use their knowledge of students' reading process and application of strategies; groups change as students begin to show they can apply a strategy independently.

In the context of these groups, reading becomes an interactive social event that helps each student move forward within Vygotsky's zone of learning. Students do not get trapped reading books and completing tasks that are too difficult for them to accomplish. You'll learn more about organizing and leading strategic reading groups in Chapter 9. (See pages 198–199 for tips on matching books to students.)

THE TEACHER READ-ALOUD: A WORKSHOP ANCHOR

Each year in February or March, I invite my eighth graders to evaluate reading workshop. "You never skip read-aloud, even if the schedule's been shortened," is a unanimous observation, and I wear it as a badge of honor. Read-aloud is sacred. Schedule changes may shorten workshop time, but I never skip the read-aloud, and my students know that I won't answer questions or review the day's schedule until I finish reading. Sharing poems and books with the class nurtures me as well as students; it sets the tone of our workshop and enables students to quietly prepare for work.

When I'm pressed for time, I'll read poetry, short myths, legends, folktales, a newspaper or magazine article, a picture book—selections that I can complete in five to eight minutes. I'll alternate these selections with short stories, which are perfect for introducing students to narrative structure and a variety of themes. In two or three days, I can complete a short story, giving students and me a common literary experience to discuss. Together, we can share our personal responses to the story and examine elements such as character, plot development, setting, and climax.

I find reading a novel frustrating for me and for students when a holiday interrupts the story's flow, so I wait until January to read a longer book, when the schedule usually remains constant through March. I'll choose a novel or biography and read a chapter or part of a chapter each day.

I refer back to these short selections when I introduce and model a variety of journal entry prompts that students will use (see pages 38 and 39 and Appendix pages 296–300), when I make reading-writing connections, and when I discuss an author's style or a literary technique.

The read-alouds I offer students introduce them to new genres and reinforce their experiences with literary language. It's an opportunity for me to extend a theme (such as fairy tales or peer pressure), build prior knowledge about a topic before students read, and model reading with

SOME READ-ALOUD TIPS

- ✦ Always read the book before you share it with your class to make sure it's appropriate for your students.

- ✦ Reserve a minimum of 5 to 10 minutes for read-aloud. 8 to 10 is ideal for me.

- ✦ Be dramatic, become a ham. Students enjoy hearing readers adopt the voices of different characters. Remember, you're modeling good read-aloud techniques.

- ✦ Share books you love, and you'll transmit enthusiasm for reading to students.

- ✦ Select a variety of literary genres and authors throughout the year.

- ✦ After completing a read-aloud, make the book available to students. Many will want to reread sections, look at photographs or illustrations, or reread the entire book.

expression and fluency. Through read-alouds, I can draw students into the world of story and communicate meaning and emotion through the beauty of language (Robb, 1994; Freeman, 1998).

Essential Workshop Reading Experiences

As you construct a workshop, choose reading experiences that enable you to interact with students and monitor their progress. The reading experiences that drive my workshop are:

+ **Teacher Read-Alouds:** daily read-alouds introduce students to a variety of genres, improve listening and recall skills, and enable the teacher to think aloud and model reading strategies.

+ **Strategy Mini-Lessons:** demonstrate reading strategies and how they can help solve reading problems. These can be whole or small group or for the one student who needs more explanation.

+ **Guided Practice:** the whole class practices a strategy with the teacher after a mini-lesson. Students who require extra support continue to practice in small groups on other days.

+ **Independent Free-Choice Reading:** while students read, teachers can hold short one-on-one conferences, giving students individualized support on selecting readable and interesting books.

+ **Strategic-Reading Groups:** pairs or small groups of students with similar needs work with the teacher on understanding and applying reading strategies.

+ **Literature Discussion Groups:** small heterogeneous groups talk about books they've read that relate to a theme and/or author study.

+ **Vocabulary-Building and Word Study:** vocabulary instruction occurs before, during, and after reading. Students study the meanings of prefixes, suffixes, and roots.

+ **Conferring:** teachers hold brief one-on-one meetings with students to observe and support how they apply strategies to reading.

Note: With the exception of the teacher read-aloud, these activities do not have to occur every day, especially within a 45-minute class.

Resources for Read-Alouds

In addition to tapping the expertise of your school and community librarians, consider these resources to discover read-alouds that work!

Books Kids Will Sit Still For: The Complete Read-Aloud Guide by Judy Freeman, Bowker, 1990.

More Books Kids Will Sit Still For: A Read-Aloud Guide by Judy Freeman, Bowker, 1995.

The Read-Aloud Handbook by Jim Trelease (4th ed.), Penguin, 1995.

Making Facts Come Alive: Choosing Quality Nonfiction Literature K–8 by Rosemary A. Banford and Janice V. Kristo, Christopher-Gordon, 1998.

MANAGING A READING WORKSHOP

An important aspect of managing workshop is offering students consistent routines that balance teacher-led, student-led, and choice-reading experiences. During the opening weeks of school, I focus on these two strategies:

1. Discover the kinds of reading support students need, then organize small strategic-reading groups (see pages 92–93, 203–206).
2. Teach the class how to work in groups, pairs, and alone without the support of a teacher.

Teach Students to Work Independently

It can take from four to six weeks for students to learn how to work on specific tasks without your guidance. Teach them how to:

✦ organize their response journals and have them practice three or four responses with your guidance before asking them to work alone (see pages 38–39 and Appendix pages 296–300);

✦ create their own discussion questions (pages 127–129);

✦ set up behavior guidelines for book discussions (page 41–42);

✦ engage in paired reading and retelling (pages 145–146); and

✦ negotiate the ground rules for independent reading.

Investing the time to teach your students how to work alone allows you to support everyone in small-group and one-on-one meetings. From time to time, during the closing of a workshop, you'll need to address behavior glitches that arise.

Offer Meaningful Reading Experiences During Choice Time

Students can work successfully in small groups, pairs, or alone when they're truly engaged. It's the busywork, such as fill-in-the-blanks worksheets or copying definitions from a dictionary, that lures students to misbehave out of boredom or rebellion against nonmeaningful work. Your students will be engaged by these activities, providing you first teach them how to approach each one:

✦ **Independent Reading:** students read a free-choice contract book (see pages 198–199) for 15 to 30 minutes at school. *I ask students to read an additional 30 minutes each night for homework.*

✦ **Paired Reading:** partners read and retell sections of a text to one another.

- **Paired Questioning:** partners read passages and question one another.
- **Listening to a Book:** students listen to a book on an audiocassette in a listening center.
- **Complete a Journal Entry:** see suggestions on the next page.
- **Write a Book Review:** see guidelines on pages 38–39.
- **Readers Theater Scripts:** groups create and practice reading aloud scripts based on books they've read (see Appendix page 308).
- **Practice a Strategy:** students, solo or in small groups, use books at their independent reading level to cement their understanding of a strategy.
- **Work on Research:** students read about *their topic* using various sources (see below).
- **Peer Conferences:** pairs or small groups discuss how they apply a reading strategy or share journal entries.
- **Group Dramatizations:** small groups select a section or chapter of a book to dramatize, using voice and gestures to reveal character.
- **Student-Led Book Discussions:** Organize heterogeneous groupings, mixing ability levels and gender. Sometimes you'll organize students around interests, choices, achievement, knowledge of a subject, or by chance (see pages 43–45).
- **Complete a Portfolio Entry:** Portfolios in my class are a collection of eight to ten pieces on students' friends, interests, and selections from writing folders and journals that students

RESEARCH WORK DURING WORKSHOP

Often, research is associated with content-area subjects where students write term papers and reports. Term papers and reports are not part of my reading/writing workshop. However, composing articles and essays, writing poems and narratives are important to the writing workshop. If a student is planning a persuasive essay against using animals for cosmetic testing, making schools safe from violence, or spending too many tax dollars on our space program, they will research information that supports their arguments. When students write articles, similar to those found in magazines such as *Sports Illustrated, Zoobook, Boys' Life,* or *Cricket,* they complete research in order to collect accurate data for their pieces. For poems and narratives, students might have to learn more about setting, an animal, a planet, etc. Library books, magazines, interviews with experts, and the Internet are resources students use to collect information.

choose and self-evaluate. Self-evaluations include: my favorite piece, most enjoyable topic, the piece that illustrates progress in content, in mechanics, in paragraphing, etc.

Easy-to-Introduce Journal Responses

For me, response journals inform me about students' levels of comprehension, their ability to connect books to their lives, and how well they can select story details to support an idea. First, model how you set up a journal page and go about responding to each suggestion; then, reserve time for students to practice before moving them to independence. Use prompts such as the seven listed on top of the next page. Post these on chart paper. Prompts should invite students to dig deeper into a book, stirring them to make emotional connections, explore the significance of the theme for them, and unearth students' feelings about characters (see Appendix pages 296–300).

GUIDELINES FOR WRITING A BOOK REVIEW

To help students dig deeper in reflecting about a book they've read—and to avoid the surface plot retellings that come with traditional *book report* assignments—teach students how to write a book review. Book reviews, found in newspapers and magazines, are an authentic method of evaluating fiction, nonfiction, and poetry. Bring in a bunch of them, from an in-depth analysis you might find in the *New York Times Book Review* to a pithy one in *People* magazine. Read them aloud, photocopy them, and let students study them. What do the reviewers accomplish in the course of their pieces? Is there a standard format? List what you find on a big piece of chart paper, and from there, develop your own guidelines. Here are the book review guidelines eighth graders and I developed:

1. At the top of the page: write your name and the date.
2. Skip a line and write: Title, Author, and ISBN.
3. Paragraph 1: Summarize the plot in two to four sentences. In your summary, identify the genre: fantasy, sci-fi, realistic fiction, biography, historical fiction, journal, photo-essay, etc.
4. Open this paragraph with a lead that grabs our attention:
   a. Pull a short quote from the book.
   b. Point out a terrific part.
   c. Tell why the book was tops or why you found it blah.

- Identify the main character, list several problems he or she faces, and explain how the problem was solved. If the problem wasn't solved, explain why and tell how you might have solved it.
- Summarize and evaluate two or three decisions the main character made.
- Select an important quote from the story (one to three sentences), explain how you connected to the quote, and show how the quote relates to a theme, conflict, or character in the text.
- Choose a minor character and show how he or she was important to the plot, main character, or themes.
- Select three key events and show how each provided insight into a character's personality.
- List several things that you value or that are important to you. List your favorite character's values. Compare and contrast lists, pointing out similarities and differences.
- Visualize a scene or a character and use illustrations or words to help others see your mental images. (See Appendix C–1 to C–5 for ways to organize journal responses.)

---

5. Paragraph 2: Do you or don't you recommend the book? Give reasons to back up your opinion. The suggestions below will help you develop points to support your position. Address two or three in your review.
   a. Was it a page-turner? Why?
   b. Was it hard to concentrate on the story? Why?
   c. Did you connect to a character or event? Why?
   d. Do you enjoy this genre? What about this book made you like the genre?
   e. Did you enjoy the style of writing? Give an example.
   f. Were there surprises in the story that held your interest? Briefly tell one.
   g. Did every chapter end with a cliff-hanger? Give an example.
   h. Was it boring? Why?
   i. Did your mind wander when reading? Why?
   j. Was the plot unbelievable? Why?
   k. Who would enjoy reading it? Why?
6. Maximum length: One handwritten page or three-quarters of a typewritten page, double-spaced.

Use the sample book reviews on the next page, composed by students in grades six and eight, as models for your students to study.

Ernesto C.
April 22, 1999
Tinker Vs. Des Moines by Doreen Rappaport
ISBN: 0-06-025117-4

You can be the judge and the jury in this book that is a trial of students' rights.
Five students in Theodore Roosevelt High School decide to wear black armbands.
The armband s are a sign of mourning the dead in the Vietnam War. Teachers do not
approve of the armbands and order the kids to take them off. Students would not
listen, and the school ordered them suspended until they took off the armbands.
Because the kids thought the school was violating their first amendment rights, they
took their case to court.

This book is great for giving a good understanding of how the court system
works. I liked being the judge and jury because I gave my opinion and felt like a
lawyer and someone on the jury. If you're a person who likes to make decisions, this
book is for you. You'll be able to decide who is guilty and who is not guilty.

Sixth grader's book review.

Rebekah   October 11, 1999

Albion's Dream, Roger Norman
ISBN 0-385-30533-8

Eighth grader's book review.

Have you ever wished that you had
magical powers? In this fantasy
book Edward and his cousin Hadely are
learning what it is like the hard way.
Edward found an old game in his
uncle's attic. When they play it correctly
they control what happens, but if they don't
it controls them and everyone else.
I believe this was a terrific
book. It had lots of adventure and
plenty of twists. This book has many
surprises also. One of them, was realizing
that the new school doctor was the face of
the death card in the game. Now he is
death in real life. This book was also
a page turner. You keep wanting
to read more to find out what
effect the game will have on life
and if Doctor Death will take the game.
This was a terrific book and
anyone who loves mystery,
adventure, and suspense will
enjoy it.

SETTING AND MANAGING GROUP BEHAVIOR GUIDELINES

Early in the year, take the time to establish guidelines for productive, independent group work. I always include students in this process, for they are more apt to follow guidelines and goals they helped create.

Ask students to suggest behavior guidelines that will help groups discuss books, complete projects, or confer. I require that students state guidelines in positive sentences so they understand what they can and should do.

Record students' suggestions on the chalkboard. Add one or two of your own. Then ask students to select five key guidelines and post these on a chart.

Tips for Productive Group Work

+ Review behavior guidelines frequently, as students need reminders.

+ Create a signal for immediate quiet, such as flicking the lights.

+ If students are rowdy, give them one warning.

+ If unacceptable behavior persists, stop the activity, explain why, and tell students you'll try group work on the next day.

PREVENTING DISRUPTIONS

While you're working with a group of students, others will have questions that need answering. Post the following four guidelines and periodically review them with students.

1 Pause and think for a minute. Try to discover ways to solve the problem on your own. Reread the class chart that lists strategies that have been modeled and practiced.

2 Ask members of your group for help.

3 If group members can't help, ask another student, one who is not working with the teacher.

4 If none of the above works, turn to another task until the teacher is free to help.

Sixth Graders' Behavior Guidelines

....

- Come prepared. Read the materials, and bring your pencil and journal.

- Listen when others speak. Talk softly.

- Value different ideas, for there are many possible answers or solutions.

- Contribute and prove your ideas with examples from the book.

- Ask questions when you don't understand.

Managing Choice Time

During the final 40 minutes of each workshop, I always offer choices for independent, pair, and small-group projects (with the mainstay being independent reading) and write them on the chalkboard. Students can choose to engage in one activity or budget time to work on all three.

This choice time frees me to meet with groups and individuals and provide support for students who need more than mini-lessons and several practice sessions to move forward. I usually meet with one group of students who all need help on a strategy and conduct one-on-one conferences with two students.

I've found it's best to offer a limited number of choices—two for grades five and six; two or three for grades seven and eight. See the list on pages 36–37 for some effective choice activities, or generate them from class reading and writing projects, such as researching inventors or collecting and illustrating poems.

Sometimes you'll want to hear a soft hum during choice time, other times silence. In one eighth-grade class, silence always deteriorated into chatting. One day, totally frustrated, I handed out paper and asked students to define silence and explain why it might be important to work in a silent environment. Several students defined silence as *talking in a very, very, very low voice.* I chuckled, but took the time to help them revise their definition—and hold them to it!

The amount of choice time students have depends on the time your school has reserved for workshop. In some schools, reading and writing is taught by one teacher; in others the subject is split between two different teachers. Since students learn about writing from reading, and write for a reading audience, I cannot separate these and prefer that the same educator teach both.

STUDENT-LED DISCUSSION GROUPS

Student-led discussion groups take many forms, and occur both during choice time or once a day when you've reserved part of a workshop for them. These groups of four or five students may discuss a section of a novel, short story, myth, fairy tale, or nonfiction selection that they have recently dealt with in a strategic-reading group. More often, though, they discuss reading materials at their independent levels, in literature circles and book clubs.

Rich, strategy-building discussions don't just happen. You have to seed them in such a way that students apply what they've learned during mini-lessons, guided practice, and small strategic-reading groups to their discussions. Often I'll suggest a focus for book discussions that relates to our work. I might ask students one week to "Be able to find the page(s) that support predictions and record these in your journal," or "Select a dialogue, reread it, and discuss what it teaches you about the characters' personality and plot," or "Work with your group or partner to use the text to figure out the meanings of words you've jotted on a sticky-note." If I'm having difficulty listening to all groups in a week, I invite students to summarize their discussions in journals which I can read later.

Suggestions for Organizing Student-Led Discussion Groups

Teaching students how to lead and participate in productive book discussions eventually frees you to work with individuals, pairs, or small groups who require additional scaffolding. During this time, you can also support groups who struggle with valuing diverse ideas, referring to their books for evidence, or focusing on the discussion. What follows are ideas for managing and planning, as well as guidelines for the group's leader and prompts students can use to move book conversations forward.

Workshop Is Flexible

It's easy to juggle time in workshop and accommodate research and special projects. You can temporarily reduce the number of conferences and strategic-reading group lessons you schedule. The workshop elements that remain constant, providing a comforting structure, are the read-aloud, mini-lessons, guided practice, and reading homework.

Some Open-ended Questions for Discussing Fiction

+ How does the title connect to the book?

+ Did you connect your life to any characters or events? Discuss.

+ Who is the protagonist and what problems does he or she face?

+ Does the protagonist make sound decisions? Explain.

+ How do events and other characters affect the protagonist?

+ Are there humorous, sad, or suspenseful parts? What words, phrases, or characters' actions create these moods?

+ How does the protagonist change from the beginning to the end?

Some Management Tips

+ Set behavior guidelines with students.

+ Offer books that are at the comfort or independent reading levels of students so they can comprehend the texts and engage in meaningful talk. Students can all read the same novel; each student can read a different book or groups can read the same title that relates to an author study or a common theme such as peer pressure, human rights, war, peace, etc. (see pages 172–173 for more on understanding theme).

+ Consider the consequences of being unprepared for a book discussion. In my classes, unprepared students read the pages in class before joining their group.

+ Agree on a cue to alert students that noise levels are escalating. When I flick the lights, students stop talking and listen.

+ Tell students the reading and writing choices they will have after they complete a discussion and journal work.

+ Decide on the number of student-led book discussions you will have each week. The number will change and depend on other reading experiences that you offer students. *During the year I hold student-led book discussions from two to three times a week.* When the class is involved in a special event such as writing and performing Readers Theater scripts, I might have to temporarily suspend book discussions to gain time.

+ Show students where to turn in completed journal entries. A plastic tray, crate, cardboard box, or shelf work well.

+ To show everyone what a meaningful discussion looks like, place a group of four or five students on center stage in front of the room. Invite them to discuss a story or several chapters in a book. Prompt students with questions when necessary. Ask the class to discuss what worked well, then set one goal that can improve the discussion. Have other groups, in turn, take center stage and discuss a story or part of a book.

Students Write Story-Specific Questions

During workshop, teach students to write story-specific questions (see pages 128–129). When you do this, students can discuss issues that are relevant to their lives and experiences.

On this page are discussion questions two groups wrote for a Jean Craighead George study. As each group completed its book, they traded novels and questions with classmates, freeing me to observe students, listen to their discussions, and read journal responses.

The Summer of the Falcon
Raveley, Susan, Christy

1. Why do you think June gets upset when Zander runs away for the first time, but she is calm when he flys away at the end? Explain your answer.

2. What do the Jesses symbolize?

3. When and why does June finally begin to act like a lady?

4. Why did June lie to her uncle about feeding Zander?

5. Read the last 3 paragraphs. Why do you think June doesn't cry when Zander flys away?

1. Why do the twins make a "helmet" for Zander? Why is it important?

2. Why were the Jesses nessesary?

3. What happens if a falcon stays cold for to long?

4. Why does a falcon train to hunt and a sparrow does not?

5. Why was it really nessesary for June to train Zander?

Julie of the Wolves

1. Immy Byrd
2. Christy Bryant
3. Susaph Carter
4. Natalie Swope
5. Jason Lorenzetti

Questions
1. Compare Amorok to Kapeugen
2. What does the airplane near the end symbolize?
3. How would you attempt to survive without the wolves?
4. Compare and contrast Julie's life with Daniel to her life with the wolves.
5. Predict how Julie will attempt to get to San Francisco if she is without the wolves.
6. Do you think Julie will make it to San Francisco? why or why not?

Some Open-ended Questions for Discussing Nonfiction

✦ Why did you choose this topic?

✦ What new or unusual information did you learn?

✦ Did the book raise questions that you would like to investigate? What are these? How will you explore these questions?

✦ Has this book changed the way you think about this topic? Explain.

✦ Reserve time to circulate once groups move from center stage demonstrations to student-led discussions. Listen and validate students' conversations or offer questions that maintain the momentum of the discussion. Spotlight what worked well. Note groups who might benefit from extra teacher support and work with them.

Planning Suggestions For Teachers

✦ Help students decide on how many chapters they'll read before discussing. I encourage students to read two to four chapters.

✦ Ask students to create their own discussion questions (see pages 128–129) or offer open-ended questions that you have practiced with them. Emphasize the importance of finding evidence in the book to support responses.

✦ Have students summarize a book discussion in their journals bimonthly. Read students' summaries to assess how much students recall.

✦ Invite students to evaluate their participation in discussion groups. Ask them to consider these questions: Was I prepared? Did I contribute? Did I use the book to support my ideas? Did I listen to and value the ideas of other students? Did I stay on task?

Guidelines for the Group Leader

✦ Rotate this position so all students can experience leading.

✦ Open by asking, "Has everyone completed the reading?"

✦ Ask one of your group's questions. Move to other questions after everyone has expressed their ideas.

✦ Use prompts (see below) to keep moving the conversation forward.

Prompts That Move a Discussion Forward

Put these prompts on an overhead or large chart paper and periodically review them with students.

✦ Can you give support from the story?

- ✦ Does anyone have something to add?
- ✦ Does anyone have a different idea?
- ✦ Can you connect this book to other books?
- ✦ Can you connect a character/event to your life?
- ✦ Did the discussion raise a question? What is it?

Five-Day Sample Reading Workshop Schedules

Too many middle school teachers are restricted by 45-minute periods called "English." Administrators expect them to cover reading, writing, spelling, vocabulary-building, and grammar during those

The Wave #13

	Character	Epiphany
1)	David	When he found out how bad the Wave was
2)	Ben	Christy convinced him to stop the Wave
3)	Robert	At the last assembly, realizes that no one is equal no matter what
4)	Everyone in Wave	At the last assembly (Hitler)
5)	Mr. Owens	When the Jewish kid gets beat up
6)	Laurie	When she was reading the letter
7)	Christy	After that kid get beat up, After Ben started acting funky
8)	Brian	After the football game
9)	Brad	Seating kids at game

Eighth graders summarize their discussion of the epiphanies characters had in *The Wave* by Todd Strasser.

brief sessions while meeting the needs of 30 to 35 students. Far better is the block scheduling that many schools have adopted, where teachers have one and a half to two hours to immerse students in a meaningful reading and writing workshop and scaffold students who require additional support.

If you're bound by 45-minute periods for reading and writing, spelling, and grammar, I suggest that you hold reading workshop one week and writing the next week. Over 10 days, your students will have had reading workshop five times and many opportunities to practice strategies and read. If you have reading workshop daily for 45 minutes, the schedule might look like the one that follows.

SAMPLE 45-MINUTE SCHEDULE FOR
FIVE READING WORKSHOPS

Since it takes students five minutes to settle down and organize materials,
I've scheduled only 40 minutes.

SESSION 1

- ✦ Teacher read-aloud (5 min.)
- ✦ Mini-lesson (15 min.)
- ✦ Student-led book-discussion groups meet; teacher works with one group (15 min.)
- ✦ Homework assigned, closing (5 min.)

SESSION 2

- ✦ Teacher read-aloud (5 min.)
- ✦ Mini-lesson and whole-class practice (15 min.)
- ✦ Independent and/or group choice activity; teacher meets with one group (15 min.)
- ✦ Homework assigned, closing (5 min.)

SESSION 3

- ✦ Teacher read-aloud (5 min.)
- ✦ Mini-lesson (10 min.)
- ✦ Student-led book-discussion groups meet; teacher works with one group (20 min.)
- ✦ Homework assigned, closing (5 min.)

SESSION 4

- ✦ Teacher read-aloud (10 min.)
- ✦ Independent and/or group choice activity; teacher meets with one group (25 min.)
- ✦ Homework assigned, closing (5 min.)

SESSION 5

- ✦ Teacher read-aloud (5 min.)
- ✦ Mini-lesson and whole-class practice (20 min.)
- ✦ Student record keeping (10 min.)
- ✦ Homework assigned, closing (5 min.)

Both teacher and students must be highly organized to complete this schedule. Groups
receive teacher support three times every ten days since reading workshop alternates
with writing workshop. These short periods may heighten teacher anxiety and students'
frustrations as everyone tries to stay on the rigid time schedule.

SAMPLE 90-MINUTE SCHEDULE FOR
FIVE READING WORKSHOPS

Blocks alternate, three days one week and two days the second week. Three days are for reading workshop, two for writing. Then the blocks switch to three days for writing and two for reading. Eighty-five minutes of time has been scheduled, allowing five minutes for students to get ready.

BLOCK 1
+ Teacher read-aloud (10 min.)
+ Whole-class gathering to review schedule (5–10 min.)
+ Mini-lesson (15–20 min.)
+ Student-led book-discussion groups meet; teacher works with two groups (30 min.)
+ Independent choice activity; teacher confers with students (20 min.)
+ Homework assigned, closing (5 min.)

BLOCK 2
+ Teacher read-aloud (10 min.)
+ Whole-class gathering to review schedule (5–10 min.)
+ Mini-lesson and practice (30 min.)
+ Group and/or independent work; teacher works with two groups (30 min.)
+ Homework assigned, closing (5 min.)

BLOCK 3
+ Teacher read-aloud (10 min.)
+ Whole-class gathering to review schedule (5–10 min.)
+ Mini-lesson (15–20 min.)
+ Vocabulary-building and word study (15 min.)
+ Groups and/or independent work; teacher works with two groups (30 min.)
+ Homework assigned, closing (5 min.)

BLOCK 4
+ Teacher read-aloud (5 min.)
+ Whole-class gathering to review schedule (5–10 min.)
+ Independent choice activity; teacher works with two groups (30 min.)
+ Record keeping or portfolio work, or conferences (20 min.)
+ Vocabulary-building and word study (15 min.)
+ Homework assigned, closing (5 min.)

BLOCK 5
+ Teacher read-aloud (10 minutes)
+ Whole-class gathering to review schedule (5–10 min.)
+ Mini-lesson (15–20 min)
+ Vocabulary-building and word study (15 min.)
+ Student-led book-discussion groups meet; teacher works with two groups (30 min.)
+ Homework assigned, closing (5 minutes)

See note, next page.

NOTE: A preview of each day's workshop is presented at whole-class gathering. A block provides time for questions, projects, and reading and responding to literature on a regular basis. During the five blocks that span two weeks, you can conduct a minimum of two group meetings each session, gaining more time to monitor and support students. There's also room to juggle time, so that one day you might extend the mini-lesson to include whole-class practice of a strategy; on another day you might eliminate gathering and spend 10 minutes conferring or sharing journal entries. What follows is a guideline for placing your daily schedule in the context of the first seven weeks of school. Beginning teachers might need to adjust these suggestions and add an extra week or two to each one, for when everything is new, it takes longer to negotiate reading experiences with students.

PLANNING WORKSHOP TIME: A SAMPLE CALENDAR

Here is a suggested time line for implementing a reading workshop and carving out time to reach all the readers in your class.

Weeks 1, 2, and 3: Set the stage for your reading workshop.

During these first weeks, you'll set the tone of your class. As you establish basic routines and get to know your students, you'll also build trust and community.

✦ Introduce and use class routines such as mini-lessons, choosing books, maintaining reading logs, and book contracts (see page 306 for more about logs and pages 198–199 for contracts).

✦ Set behavior guidelines for students reading and writing about books independently.

✦ Get to know your students' reading interests and abilities.

✦ Assess students' reading through one-on-one conferences.

✦ Read aloud every day and think aloud to demonstrate how you apply strategies.

✦ Create and post guidelines for productive group activities.

✦ Establish and post procedures for students seeking help.

✦ Work as a whole class on discussing a core book or a basal story, guided by this standard: evidence to prove a position or answer a question must come from the book.

Weeks 4 and 5: Introduce independent choice work.

Now is the time to teach students how to engage in some meaningful reading and writing experiences and utilize negotiated behavior guidelines to be productive during choice time. These are crucial weeks, for students are learning how to work independently.

- Teach students one or two kinds of journal responses (see pages 38–39 and Appendix 296–300). Model a sample response on chart paper or the chalkboard.
- Review guidelines for independent reading, writing, and seeking help.
- Offer students two choices, such as sustained silent reading or working on a journal response, during independent work time. Set aside an area in your room for silent reading, so students can concentrate while others work quietly.
- Begin reading with a small group that has a common problem. But don't do this until most students demonstrate that they can work independently for 15 to 20 minutes.
- Assess students by having them read a passage during a conference while you mark their errors patterns (see pages 248–253).

Weeks 6 and 7: Introduce group work.

When you start working with groups while the rest of the class chooses activities during this choice time, you'll probably have to stop several times to remind students of behavior and work expectations. Even after you've established a productive workshop, middle school students will lapse into social talk; this is part of their persona. I prefer being proactive by briefly reviewing goals and guidelines prior to each choice time.

- Review behavior guidelines for group work and seeking help.
- Organize students into heterogeneous pairs or groups of four or five based on interests, author or theme study, gender, or research project (see pages 203–206).
- Invite pairs and small groups of students to discuss a story, poem, or several chapters of a book.
- Observe students as they work in pairs or groups. Praise and point out everything that works. Select one or two needs such as lowering noise levels, staying on task, or listening while a classmate speaks. Then create group goals.
- At a gathering, post and review group goals until students have achieved them.
- Continue to note what worked well, using positive feedback to reinforce your expectations.
- Teach pairs or small groups how to apply reading strategies to their books. Do this during independent workshop times or when other groups are meeting.
- Move students to another group once they comprehend and can use a strategy independently.
- Continue scheduling one-on-one reading conferences.

Can I Construct a Workshop with 35 Students?

My daughter, Anina, teaches reading and writing to sixth and seventh graders in a small middle school on the third floor of an elementary school located on the West Side in New York City. Anina's first year at this school was her third year of teaching middle school students. That first year, Anina had 39 sixth graders, and she was unable to organize a reading workshop.

"Though I had a model of workshop learning from my elementary school experiences and our discussions," Anina told me, "with a crowded classroom, no middle school or classroom library, and students who had no cooperative learning experiences, I felt that workshop was not possible."

That year Anina selected some workshop experiences to bring to students: She taught students to work in pairs, for group discussions were loud and rowdy; she read aloud every day and also presented strategic-reading and writing mini-lessons; she reserved time for guided practice and responding to literature in journals. Instead of strategic-reading groups, Anina conducted one-on-one five- to ten-minute conferences with students and mini-conferences when she circulated (Robb, 1996). Her crowded classroom had no space for literacy centers or a conference area. Her goal for the year was to find books students could read independently and help them learn to read quietly for 15 to 20 minutes a day. Sometimes Anina checked books out of the public library, and students read these in class only. To build a much-needed classroom library, Anina purchased books from book clubs and asked me to contribute titles and search for bargains at yard sales. "It was difficult," she told me, "accepting that I was not reaching every child in the classroom. Sometimes that frustrated and depressed me, but there were too many students who needed daily help with learning to read. I couldn't adequately meet the needs of so many."

The next year, Anina had many of her sixth graders in a seventh-grade reading-writing workshop. The principal in Anina's school worked diligently to reduce the number of students in classes, recognizing that to improve students' reading and test scores, teachers had to have more time to interact with and assess each child.

With 26 students instead of 39, Anina had room to create centers and teach students to use them, set up a classroom library, offer choices, and teach small groups how to successfully discuss books. "I think," she told me recently on the telephone, "that doing a modified workshop the first year was a great way to start thinking about which elements to bring to so many students. And more than half the class struggled with reading." Anina still holds many more one-on-one meetings than paired or group conferences. "One-on-one gives me a chance to meet *each student's* unique needs," she said.

Halfway through Anina's fourth year, she introduced an author study with five groups, each group reading a different Gary Paulsen title. She and I discussed creating guidelines: Anina and students negotiated daily and weekly goals for the number of chapters to complete, the strategies to practice and record in journals, the focus of group discussions, and the kinds of journal entries to complete. She wrapped up the study with a comparison of themes, settings, and characters in Paulsen's books. "In my mind, I set aside seven to eight weeks," she told me, "but students needed more time." And that's fine, for the only way a teacher can make decisions about learning is by observing and responding to the lessons students teach.

Required to teach the business letter form, Anina invited students to write her a letter explaining what they had learned in the first six weeks. "I was curious to see if my students could write about their learning," she said. The example that follows illustrates how, with smaller numbers, Anina was able to reach the readers in her classroom and improve their knowledge of the prediction strategy and story structure "in half the time I struggled with the same topics last year."

> Dear Ms Robb,
> During this marking period you've taught me alot personally. Ms Robb you've taught me about using show expressions instead of telling someone you're going to do something. You taught me how to predict & how to support my predictions, how to make story structure chart "that helps me out because it make me understand more about the story is about pt I got the story structure right, metaphor poems and the different between similes and metaphors. You also taught me more but I just can't think of anything right now.

A student reflects on her learning

Pause and Reflect on:
Your Comfort Level with Workshop

To organize a productive workshop environment takes two to three years. If reading workshop is new, give yourself the gift of time and avoid unnecessary frustration and anxiety. Here are some guidelines to think about:

The First Year: hold a gathering to preview workshop; get to know your students; practice planning and presenting mini-lessons; teach students how to work independently; offer students two or three choices during workshop; organize strategic reading groups.

The Second Year: take error analyses of students' reading and add these to literacy folders (see pages 248–253); think aloud during your daily read-alouds; reserve time for one-to-one reading support; build a classroom library with books at a wide range of reading levels.

The Third Year: practice taking observational notes and add these to students' literacy folders; introduce student-led book discussions; teach students how to self-evaluate their progress and work (see pages 260–269).

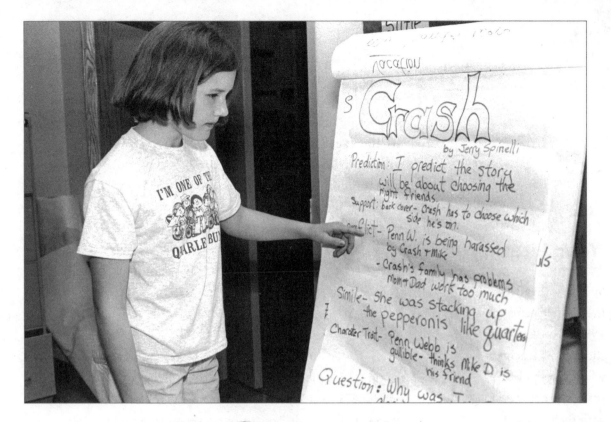

🌿 Chapter 3

Strategic Reading in the Middle School

"This year I started to enjoy reading because I'm learning how."
—Fifth Grader

In *Discover Your Own Literacy* (Heinemann, 1990), Donald Graves shows how teachers who explored their reading processes along with their students gained insight into their interactions with texts and used this knowledge to support students. As teachers explore their own reading, writing, and learning, they can better understand students' strengths and needs because teachers and students share the same process.

The more I reflect on my reading process, the better I can pinpoint and understand the strategies I use to make meaning before, during, and after reading. Like my middle school students, the experiences I bring to a text greatly influence my level of comprehension, enjoyment, involvement, and ability to deal with confusing words and passages. Part of our job as reading teachers is to get in touch with our own literacy history, and to integrate what we've learned from our experiences into the ways we teach.

WHAT I'VE LEARNED ABOUT MYSELF AS A READER

I grew up in a neighborhood of brick apartment buildings in the Bronx in New York City. My friends and I played in a fenced-off, cement-covered area adjacent to our seven-story building. No grass, no flowers, no trees, no swings, no monkey bars—nothing but two long, wood and wrought iron benches filled that space. I know we went through periods of boredom—and we hated being bored. In fact, every time I'd whine to my grandmother, "I'm bored—I don't have anything to do," she'd firmly tell me: "Take your head and bang it against the wall three times." Now, I'm not sure my grandmother was into magic numbers and events happening in threes, but I bet she believed that after the third time my head met the kitchen wall, some idea would finally occur to me—and I'd stop nagging.

So how did we spend our time? And without TV, computers, video games, and VCRs, we did have time. Some days we'd trade movie-star pictures; others we'd play detective or hide and seek. Most often we'd walk to the apartment house down the block where the New York City Public Library had a small branch in the basement of the building. There sat the librarian, Mrs.

Schwartz, guardian of books. She was a magical cure for all our boredom woes. Mrs. Schwartz was a tiny woman, always smiling. She smelled musty, as though she'd absorbed the scent of books and dusty bindings and yellow, dog-eared pages. She welcomed us into her book kingdom and let us sit next to the metal cases and sift through stacks of titles and check out what I'm sure was more than the legal limit. Sometimes she'd gather us around her, and we'd listen to her read a chapter from *The Secret Garden* by Frances Hodgson Burnett or *The Snow Queen* by Hans Christian Andersen retold by Amy Ehrlich. "These are great books," she'd whisper, waggling her finger at us just in case we didn't get it. "They'll stand the test of time—your grandchildren will be reading them." How right she was!

After a visit to the library, we'd cram our bodies onto the playground benches and spend days reading our books. Those were not silent occasions. When one of us was stuck on a word, we'd nudge another to help us figure out how to say it or what it meant. My friend Sandra would talk about a terrifying part and then read it aloud. A few moments later, Carl's giggles would finally transform into rollicking laughter, and we'd stop reading our books and listen to Carl read the funny passage. No one minded these interruptions—we welcomed them because they were spontaneous and meaningful. In my memory, I'd tuck away a title I wanted to check out and read.

Today, when I tell my students this story, they give one another knowing looks that silently shout, "WEIRD." Truthfully, I'm glad I was weird. I'm thrilled that my friends were weird, too. To an outsider looking in, that cement playground—our reality—was bleak, unfriendly, and definitely unstimulating.

Not so. Books led us in all directions and helped us step into other lives as we traveled to unknown ports and visited with royalty, robbers, beggars, elves, fairies, and strange beings from other galaxies.

And then my friends and I entered adolescence and added a new dimension to our reading: romance magazines. My parents had little tolerance for my new literary taste, and forbade these magazines. As you know, the forbidden tantalizes adolescents. So I'd tuck the contraband *True Romance* inside *Life* magazine, which my parents read, and hide them under sweaters in my dresser drawer. That brief foray into love stories didn't change or diminish my reading tastes—it was a stop along the way to becoming an adult reader.

WHAT REFLECTING ON MY READING LIFE TAUGHT ME

Because I teach reading, and am intensely interested in how and why we become readers and develop rich, personal reading lives, I continually reflect on those years in the Bronx and my present reading life. In a sense, I try to recreate in my workshop the authenticity of reading on that bench with my brother and friends. Think about your own reading memories, con-jure up where you were when you were reading happily, and see where these recollections take you. Let them inform what you do as a teacher.

For me, thinking about my reading process helps me better understand my students and provides me with a large menu of mini-lessons. Here are some things I've discovered that I want for my students:

◆ I read for different purposes and therefore the literary quality of the books I select varies greatly.

◆ When I have long stretches of time to concentrate, I choose a classic or a challenging contemporary book. I need time to savor the prose, and to reread difficult parts.

◆ On vacation, or on a long airplane flight, I take a mystery, historical fiction, or a magazine—light, easy reading fare. Such quick reads are similar to watching an action movie—enjoyable while I'm into the book, probably not remembered several months later.

◆ I also read professional books and magazines on a regular basis. Some of these I can skim quickly; others require rereading, note-taking, and reflection.

◆ The stack of "to read" books on my desk is a result of recommendations from friends, reading book reviews, and browsing in bookstores.

◆ I like to read near the fireplace in the winter or curled in a comfortable chair. Never would I dream of reading for pleasure at a desk, sitting against the back of a hard plastic chair.

◆ Struggling through a difficult-to-understand book is not a pleasurable experience.

◆ If I'm not enjoying a book, I put it aside without any guilt and choose another.

◆ I'm constantly having silent conversations with myself as I read. I'm commenting on a character's decision, making and confirming predictions, raising questions, telling characters what to do or say. I even dream about characters and place myself in their world.

◆ I try to figure out the meanings of unfamiliar words by using context clues. I rarely turn to the dictionary while reading. I'm more likely to jot down a word and the page it appeared on, and use the dictionary after I've stopped reading.

♦ I can't wait to tell someone about a book I'm enjoying. Even better is discussing my book with someone who has also read it.

♦ While reading, I pause to think about a character or an event and reread a part that I don't want to leave.

The more I deepen my awareness of how I apply my in-the-head strategies to reading, the easier it is to think aloud and share my reading process. During read-alouds and mini-lessons, when I reveal the thoughts and pictures in my mind, I'm showing students how I apply strategies such as making inferences about a character's motivations, raising questions, and coping with confusing passages.

Often during professional development study groups, when I discuss the importance of teaching reading strategies, a teacher will comment, "I learned to read with skill sheets; why isn't that good enough for my students?" Many of us who completed skill sheets never connected them to *real* reading. Skill sheets were classwork that couldn't change or transform our thinking the way a book or a magazine could. I want students to understand the difference between skills and strategies and the relationship between developing proficiency and personal reading lives to strategic reading.

THE DISTINCTION BETWEEN SKILLS AND STRATEGIES

In the past, educators and publishers designed basal reading programs around a specific set of skills, taught sequentially, that they believed students needed control over in order to become proficient readers. Workbooks and black line masters isolated skills and invited students to practice dividing words into syllables, identifying the main idea from a paragraph, or drawing inferences about a character from a brief dialogue. Workbook reading selections had no connection to the stories in the basal. Today the quality of stories in basals has improved because the books include works by outstanding children's authors. Workbooks, however, still contain isolated drills with no connection to the selections in the basal.

Many skill drills in workbooks are similar to the strategies that Pearson and I have identified, such as using context clues to figure out the meaning of new words or pinpointing the main ideas of a story. What's missing? Connections between practicing a skill in a short passage and how that skill works with real, continuous texts such as fiction, biography, non-fiction, magazines, and newspapers.

I grew up on a steady diet of skill sheets, matching words and their meanings, filling in the blanks in cloze passages, checking off the main idea statements that applied to the passage on the page. No teacher elevated the skill to the level of strategy by linking workbook practice to real books and providing opportunities to independently apply a strategy to new and varied reading materials. My mind separated my personal reading life from school, and I never connected school exercises to reading curled in an overstuffed chair in our living room or on the beach with my friends.

Pearson et al. emphasize three important differences between skills and strategies (1992). Strategic reading means that the learner has a conscious, in-the-head plan for comprehending, while skills are used without conscious planning. As students use strategies, they become more and more aware of their reasoning process as they make sense out of print; skills seldom involve this kind of self-awareness. Finally, the strategies readers use change with the purpose for reading and the genre, while skills are not adaptable.

I read before entering kindergarten and recall the feeling I had that what I completed in school had little to do with how I unraveled confusing parts or figured out the meanings of tough words. Many years later, while I was coaching a fifth-grade teacher, a boy in the teacher's class taught me the importance of activating strategies with real books. In reading class James did well on all skill sheets that asked him to select the main idea. The passages were short and either the first or last sentence contained the main idea. "Sometimes," he told me, "I don't read all the words because I know the pattern."

One day I observed James reading a chapter in a book about the first woman pharaoh, Hatshepsut. As he read, James grimaced, sighed, shuffled his feet, and stared at the ceiling. I kneeled next to his desk and asked, "Is everything okay?"

"Nope," came the terse reply.

"Can you tell me what's wrong?"

"Sure," he said. "This book isn't like those sheets I fill out in reading. There's facts and more facts. I can't decide what's important. They left out the story, and I can't keep the facts in my head."

James's frustration was logical. His books did not have the controlled structure of a work-book sheet. James had never learned to adapt a strategy to longer texts with different writing styles; all along he had been practicing a skill rather than learning a strategy, and the skill only took him so far. With strategic practice, James would have been exposed to adapting the strategy to different kinds of texts (Pearson et al., 1992). One way to help the Jameses in our classrooms develop flexible reading strategies is to have them practice with a variety of real books and other reading materials.

PLACING READING STRATEGIES IN A THREE-PART READING MODEL

In a strategic-reading curriculum, it's beneficial to isolate a strategy so students can comprehend and practice it. However, strategies, once understood, work together, and good readers naturally integrate the strategies needed to explore the meanings in a text without consciously thinking of them.

To develop students' reading potential, invite them to apply and adapt strategies before, during, and after reading. In the chart on the next page, I've selected strategies that middle school students need control over in order to become good readers.

Teach these strategies in mini-lessons and use what you're constantly learning about students to decide which ones to emphasize. For example, at the start of the year, you discover that students can make logical predictions but have difficulty locating specific support from the text. Quickly review predicting and emphasize finding supportive story details. As you interact with students during mini-lessons, strategic-reading groups, book discussions, one-on-one conferences, and read their journal responses, you will be able to provide students with the strategic-reading mini-lessons that respond to their needs. Such systematic observation is tough work, but it's the only sure way that teachers can support students who are growing and changing as readers throughout the year.

Writing about reading encourages thinking and deepens understanding of the text.

THREE-PART READING MODEL

Some Strategies to Use Before Reading

These activate past knowledge and experiences.

- ✦ Brainstorm/Categorize
- ✦ Predict/Support
- ✦ Skim/Preview
- ✦ Pose Questions
- ✦ Fast-Write
- ✦ Preteach Vocabulary
- ✦ What Do I Know? What's New?
- ✦ Visualize/Recall other Sensory Experiences

Some Strategies to Use During Reading

These enable students to make personal connections, visualize, identify parts that confuse, monitor understanding, and recall information.

- ✦ Make Personal Connections
- ✦ Use Prior Knowledge
- ✦ Predict/Support/ Adjust or Confirm
- ✦ Pose Questions
- ✦ Identify Confusing Parts
- ✦ Visualize
- ✦ Self-monitor for Understanding
- ✦ Summarize
- ✦ Synthesize
- ✦ Reread
- ✦ Use Context Clues
- ✦ Infer

Some Strategies to Use After Reading

These enlarge past knowledge, deepen understanding and engagement with text, and can create connections to other texts.

- ✦ Skim
- ✦ Reread
- ✦ Question
- ✦ Visualize
- ✦ Evaluate and Adjust Predictions
- ✦ Reflect Through: Talking, Writing, Drawing
- ✦ Infer: Compare/Contrast, Cause/Effect; Conclude; Theme
- ✦ Note-taking
- ✦ Summarize
- ✦ Synthesize

PLACING READING STRATEGIES IN A MEANING-CENTERED AND STUDENT-CENTERED CONTEXT

A primary goal of a strategic reading program is to develop students' understanding of and use of strategies so they can broaden their prior knowledge, improve comprehension, and enjoy their reading experiences. As the chart on page 62 outlines, a strategy curriculum that emphasizes comprehension of texts supports readers before, during, and after reading. Therefore, the purpose of reading becomes making meaning, a process that clarifies prior knowledge and enables readers to construct new understandings. To accomplish this, students have to be actively involved in understanding, using, and self-evaluating the effectiveness of reading strategies (Vacca and Vacca, 2000; Dowhower,1999; Graves and Graves, 1994; Robb, 1994, 1995; Ogle, 1988/1999; Paris, Lipson, Wixon, 1983). This comprehension framework is the backbone of *Teaching Reading in Middle School*. As you read on, you'll explore strategy lessons and teaching vignettes all aimed at helping students become independent readers who can access strategies to solve problems they encounter in a variety of texts and materials.

Supporting strategic readers starts with building background knowledge as students prepare to read literature, study a content area topic, or textbook chapter. At this point, the teacher has three key goals:

1. Take the time to assess students' prior knowledge. Determine whether students know enough about a topic to comprehend and recall as they read.

2. Reserve time to enlarge students' background knowledge if they know little about a topic before starting the study (see pages 117–119). Investing time here can make a difference in students' learning.

3. Explicitly focus students' attention on the strategies to be practiced (Dowhower, 1999). Name the strategy, make it visible to students, and clearly explain how it can benefit them. Here's what I say to raise students' awareness of *synthesizing* before they read a history textbook:

   When you read the chapter on the Middle Ages, you'll be selecting important details from sections, then using these details to decide on the main idea. Educators call this strategy synthesizing *because it asks you to select data and then categorize it under a general heading called the main idea. Readers can use synthesizing to help monitor recall and understanding because as you synthesize, you choose details and use them to think of the big ideas in a chapter. If you can verbalize the big ideas, then you know you are comprehending and building new understandings.*

   What I've done is name the strategy for students, explain its purpose, and share why it's important to their reading. As students practice the strategy, I invite them to think aloud and explain how it supports their reading and thinking.

It's important to teach students how to set purposes for reading chunks of a textbook or several chapters of a novel. Setting clear purposes while reading deepens comprehension because students have strong reasons for reading (Ogle, 1986; Dowhower, 1999). Helping students self-monitor—determine what they do and do not understand as they read silently—empowers them to know when to access a fix-it strategy, such as reread, and moves learners toward independence.

During and after reading, when teachers invite students to discuss content and meanings of a text as well as the strategies that supported comprehension, students can grow as strategic readers. Such talk enlarges meaning-making and builds, within each student, an awareness of how specific strategies support comprehension. (Alvermann, 2000; Dowhower, 1999). Practice and self-awareness can help students transfer, to their independent reading, the understandings gained while teachers guide them through a strategic-reading curriculum (Pearson et al).

The strategy lessons in this book focus on the types of texts students encounter in a middle school reading program, and many can be used in content area subjects. To enlarge your repertoire of content area strategies, dip into the suggested titles in the Resource Box below.

RESOURCES FOR CONTENT-AREA READING STRATEGIES

Most textbooks that middle school students learn from in math, science, and social studies are challenging because they contain an abundance of new vocabulary and information. The titles that follow offer reading strategies specifically designed for content-area textbooks.

+ *Content Reading and Literacy: Suceeding in Today's Diverse Classrooms* by Donna E. Alvermann and Stephen F. Phelps, Allyn and Bacon, 1998.

+ *Reading and Learning in Content Areas,* second edition, by Randall J. Ryder and Michael F. Graves, Merrill, 1998.

+ *Content Area Reading: Literacy and Learning Across the Curriculum,* sixth edition, by Richard T. Vacca and Jo Anne L. Vacca, Longman, 2000.

SOME STRATEGIES THAT CAN MOVE MIDDLE SCHOOL READERS FORWARD

In contrast to a reading skills program that outlines a sequence of specific skills to be taught at each grade level, a strategy curriculum recognizes that readers of all ages use the same strategies but with differing levels of expertise and sophistication (Pearson et al., 1992; Fountas and Pinnell, 1998). As reading instructors in the middle grades, it's our job to discover each student's knowledge of and level of expertise with the key strategies that follow (see page 66 and pages 115–182), and through mini-lessons, small strategic-reading group instruction, and individual conferences, improve the way students apply strategies to their reading.

First, identify the strategies that readers in your class are using before, during, and after reading. Reteach strategies that are familiar and strive to deepen students' knowledge of how these can support them. Offer many opportunities for students to use these in pairs or small groups with your support.

Next, introduce and have students practice the key strategies listed on page 66—one at a time. Move to a new strategy once students demonstrate that they comprehend and apply the strategy they are practicing (see box, right). Some students will be ready to move on after two or three guided-practice sessions. Others will need additional practice when you work with pairs, a small group, or a one-on-one conference. See Chapter 9 for more on how students and I make these decisions so you can construct a clearer picture of the process.

The list on the following page will help you to identify some key reading strategies that proficient readers use.

How Do I Know That Students Can Use a Strategy?

+ Circulate and watch students during guided practice.

+ Observe partners practicing a strategy.

+ Note how students apply a strategy during strategic reading groups.

+ Discuss a strategy during one-on-one meetings with students.

+ Read students' journal entries and self-evaluations.

KEY READING STRATEGIES

STRATEGY	READERS GAIN CONTROL OVER:
Select Books	Choosing readable books that can support growth in fluency, word knowledge, and comprehension.
Make Personal Connections	Relating their experiences and knowledge to information read in the text.
Visualize	Comprehension when they create mental pictures of information they understand.
Predict/Support	Engaging with the text, setting purposes, and finding evidence that supports predictions.
Confirm/Adjust	Confirming or adjusting predictions while they read and collect more data.
Identify Confusing Parts	Knowing what they don't understand while reading. Pinpointing parts that don't make sense is the step that precedes applying a helpful strategy.
Pause, then Retell or Summarize	Coping with the information in books by evaluating whether they recall details.
Self-Question	Setting purposes and creating interest while they read by posing questions, then reading to explore answers.
Self-Monitor	Knowing what is and is not understood. Seeking help when they can not solve a problem independently.
Understand Text Structures (Genres)	Accessing what they already know about text structures to support the meaning-making process.
Synthesize	Summarizing information from large sections of a text. In their own words, as they read, students create a topic sentence for small sections of text and list the important details.
Determine What's Important	Selecting the important information in a chapter or section. Knowing what's relevant and what's irrelevant is crucial to comprehension and reading for a purpose.

DEMONSTRATE HOW STRATEGIES WORK WITH MINI-LESSONS AND THINK-ALOUDS

Whether you have a 45- or 90-minute workshop, the mini-lesson, a practice developed by educators Nancie Atwell (1987) and Lucy Calkins (1986), and the think–aloud, described by Susan Lytle (1982), are the ideal teaching techniques for showing students how a strategy works. Learning and questioning occur as students observe the teacher write on large chart paper and listen to her share the questions, doubts, and wonderings that cross her mind as she processes print and applies strategies. Originally, Atwell and Calkins conceived of mini-lessons that lasted five to ten minutes; they have revised their thinking, stating that some mini-lessons can run 15 to 20 minutes. Many of the mini-lessons, which I call Strategy Lessons, in Chapters 5, 6, and 7, will last 15 to 25 minutes, especially when you reserve time for students' questions and exchange of ideas.

Teachers and skilled students can present mini-lessons to the entire class or small groups, and the number presented will vary because mini–lessons respond to students' needs. Mini-lessons can occur at the start of or any time during a workshop.

THREE KINDS OF MINI-LESSONS

1 **Planned Mini-Lessons:** You'll prepare and think through these reading strategy lessons before presenting them.

2 **Impromptu Mini-Lessons:** As you coach pairs and groups of students, watch them during guided practice, and briefly confer with them during independent-reading time, you'll observe a need and respond to it by presenting an unrehearsed mini-lesson. For example, as pairs or groups skim a text to find support for questions they've raised, I notice several students rereading large sections of the book. That's my cue to gather them together, present a demonstration, and support them as they try to apply the skimming strategy.

3 **Review Mini-Lessons:** Throughout the year, you will revisit strategies by first reviewing mini-lesson charts and then coaching pairs or groups who require additional support.

Mini-Lessons I Repeat Annually

In addition to the sample mini-lessons in this book you'll also find ideas for mini-lessons in the reading strategy list on page 66, and the student strategy checklist on page 102. The topics that follow are ones I repeat year after year:

+ Finding specific details to support a position.

+ Comparing and contrasting two characters.

+ Exploring mood through language.

+ Selecting themes from books.

+ Knowing what's important and what's irrelevant.

+ Writing interpretive, story-specific questions.

+ Deciding whether or not to keep reading a book.

+ The form and structure of journal entries.

+ Connecting books to other books, your life, community, the world.

FINDING TOPICS FOR MINI-LESSONS

While you manage the reading-writing workshop, you'll constantly be collecting topics for mini-lessons. Reading students' response journal entries is an especially rich source of topics. Often I have so many ideas that I feel overloaded and overwhelmed, not knowing where to begin. To organize these ideas I write lists, sift through and prioritize items, and make decisions. Here are some strategies I use:

1. Immediately integrate into workshop a strategy you've discovered all or most of the class needs—such as summarizing key ideas—and temporarily set aside your original lesson plan.

2. Reteach the mini-lesson in one large or several small groups until students can use the reading strategy.

3. Group small numbers of students who require support on a strategy, such as selecting important details from a passage. Make time during workshop to meet with them and guide their reading.

4. Continue working on mini-lessons that support the reading goals of your curriculum *after you've addressed the needs students revealed to you.*

Tips for Presenting Strategy Mini-Lessons

Start a 15- to 25-minute session with a think-aloud. Tell students how your mind solves a reading problem such as a confusing passage, or applies a reading strategy such as read/pause/summarize (see pages 143–144). As you model and write on the chart, continue sharing all your thoughts and feelings, worries and frustrations. It's comforting for students to realize that adults experience the same doubts and anxieties while reading and problem-solving.

I encourage students to jot down questions they have as they watch and listen. These questions fuel the follow-up discussions, which are the power behind mini-lessons. Questions students raise and the insights they share provide you with vital information about their level of understanding and/or confusion. Here's a sampling of comments and questions a group of struggling seventh graders asked in our follow-up discussion after I demonstrated the predict-and-support strategy using the title, cover, and first chapter of Betsy Byar's *The Pinballs* (HarperTrophy, 1977).

✦ It's hard to find good examples from the story at this point. I guess it's easy to be off target when you just start the book.

[My response: Exactly, for the author can move the story in many different directions. However, toward the end of the book, it will be easier to predict the story's outcome.]

✦ Do you always predict when you read?

[My response: Absolutely! That's what helps make the reading enjoyable.]

✦ Is it okay to put your own ideas in when you haven't read much?

[My response: Yes, as long as you also include story examples.]

Cyrena

Strategy Lesson : Ask Questions

Notes: Quest. Before, During, After

Personal Con.

Want to know more

Questions :

Is it like predicting?
What if I have no personal connections?
Why think about quest. book doesn't anser?

Notes and questions taken by seventh graders during strategy lessons.

Strat. Lesson:

Notes   Reading Rate

— fast means 1st done
— slow – remem. more

Questions
How did I know when to slow down?
How can I get faster and finish books?

After a mini-lesson and follow-up discussion, introduce guided practice while the mini-lesson suggestions and peer comments are fresh in students' minds. If you're short on time, initiate guided practice during the next workshop.

INTEGRATING THINK-ALOUDS INTO STRATEGY MINI-LESSONS

When you think aloud during a mini-lesson or your daily read-alouds and model how you apply a reading strategy or how you solve a problem in the text, you are offering students a strategy that can enhance their comprehension and self-monitoring abilities (Alvermann, 1984; Baumann, Jones, and Seifert-Kessel, 1993).

To think aloud, readers pause periodically, think about what they remember and understand, integrating the name of the reading strategies they used. Naming the strategy can be a challenge for students, but can become part of their thinking through practice and as teachers explicitly identify the strategies they invite students to practice before, during, and after reading. In the study conducted by Baumann et al., the group of children taught how to think aloud included more fix-it strategies in their monologues than the group exposed to the Directed Reading-Thinking Activity (Stauffer, 1976).

Instructing Students in Think-Alouds

I agree with Baumann et al. that it is necessary to provide a series of lessons to students so they understand what to do during a think-aloud and why the strategy can support their comprehension. Here's how I help middle school students recognize the purpose and importance of thinking aloud:

1. Explain that thinking aloud means that you say what is going on in your mind as you read and try to understand what you are reading.

2. Add the self-monitoring component of the think-aloud by inviting students to ask questions such as: Does this passage make sense? Can I restate it in my own words? Can I say what part or parts were hard? Post these self-monitoring questions on chart paper so students can refer to them as they read and think aloud.

3. Demonstrate how you think aloud to solve problems readers encounter with different

materials. Here are some questions that identify problems readers meet and can help you plan think-alouds.

- ✦ How do I pronounce that word?
- ✦ What does that word mean?
- ✦ How do I figure out that analogy?
- ✦ Why don't I remember what I've read?
- ✦ Why can't I get into this story?
- ✦ How can I figure out the main ideas?
- ✦ Exactly how do I skim pages?
- ✦ How can I figure out implied meanings?

4. Present your demonstration. Prior to thinking aloud, I placed the passage and the diagram on gasoline motors on an overhead transparancy and read the passage to the students. Here's a think-aloud I presented on "Why don't I remember what I've read?"

   Yesterday, an eighth-grade girl asked me to help her with the section on gasoline motors in the science textbook. Before we met, I decided to read this section because I know little about motors. I reread three times and was still not able to say what I read in my own words. Then I studied the diagram and tried to imagine how the motor would work. I reread the text and kept looking at the diagram so I could visualize the steps. Rereading the words was not enough for me, but having the words and the picture really made a difference. Then I asked my husband to show me the gasoline motor in our car, and that really helped.

5. Ask students to note any questions or observations that bombard their minds or alternate ways of thinking aloud. Here are some student comments and questions:

   - ✦ What helped you the most?
   - ✦ You didn't have enough background knowledge.
   - ✦ It seems impossible to picture something you know little about.
   - ✦ I would have looked at the real motor first and had someone explain how it worked.
   - ✦ Did you help that student?

6. Have pairs of students practice thinking aloud to each other using a book, story, magazine, or newspaper article. Invite partners to comment and question one another. Circulate and make sure you listen to all pairs over two to three days.

7. Reserve some time for you and students to continue practicing thinking aloud with the strategies you introduce: predict/support/confirm/adjust, raising questions, and so forth.

Record Your Mini-Lessons

I record all of my mini-lessons on large chart paper, printing with a heavy, felt-tipped marker. Charts can be easily displayed on a classroom wall or on bulletin boards, readily available for students to reread and use as a resource. Date each chart, and at the top, print the name of the mini-lesson.

Visible charts are personal reminders for me—they jog my memory, ensuring that I review their contents when groups or the entire class need the information.

Move students from speaking out loud to using their in-the-head voices. Explain that you are always thinking aloud while you read to check what you do and don't understand, but your think-alouds are with your inner voice. Support in-the-head think alouds by asking students to use INSERT, an Interactive Notation System for Effective Reading and Thinking, developed by Vaughan and Estes, 1986. As students read, they can use a pencil to place the notations in the margin of their text (see box).

INSERT Notations

I agree = ✓

I disagree = X

That's new = +

I don't understand = ??

WOW! That's terrific! = !

GUIDED PRACTICE IN READING WORKSHOP

Guided practice is a short session of 10 to 20 minutes that occurs during workshop time, often following a strategy mini-lesson. Shortly after the demonstration and follow-up student discussion, move into your guided-practice session. Isolating key reading strategies and practicing them on the heels of teacher modeling gives students a deeper understanding of how a strategy can support reading.

During the first session, the entire class practices a strategy as you, the expert, circulate and actively support students. Observe students to determine how they independently apply the mini-lesson's suggestions.

Circulate and coach students with questions that scaffold the strategy (see pages 222-224). Let students know what strategies you observe them applying. Make what they're doing visible by offering comments that showcase the strategy they're using:

- That's a great connection to your family. Books give those kinds of insights and make me read on to find others.
- Those questions are terrific. Good readers always pose questions.
- You used the plot and dialogue to make that prediction. Using the prior knowledge from the story helps you make predictions.
- Your summary shows me that you can select key details. That's an important strategy to use when reading textbooks.

STRATEGY IN ACTION
Fifth Grade Guided Practice: Making Personal Connections

I'm always searching for interesting, well-written short texts to use during guided practice. Short, accessible texts are ideal because students can practice a strategy and think about how that strategy supports reading in one 15- to 25-minute session. In my file cabinet, I store short pieces that range in readability from grade three on up. *Storyworks* and *Scope,* both Scholastic magazines, are great resources. Basal readers and/or anthologies are helpful because the selections are leveled by grade. I also dip into collections of folk and fairy tales and short stories. Often students work in their free-choice reading books, which are at their independent-reading levels.

Materials: *Stone Fox* by John Reynolds Gardiner, HarperTrophy, 1999

Background Information: This guided-practice lesson was one of many with a group of six fifth graders who told me and their teacher during "getting-to-know-you-conferences" that it never occurred to them to think about how stories connect to their lives. During daily read-alouds of *Words By Heart* by Ouida Sebestyen (Dell), Ms. Woods, the teacher, thought aloud, modeling how she made personal connections while reading.

Great Short Texts

Here's a selection of magazines that will help you find many well-written short texts to use in guided practice.

Boys' Life, 1325 Walnut Hill Lane, P.O. Box 152079, Irving, TX 75015-2079.

Calliope, Cobblestone Publishing, Inc., 30 Grove St., Peterborough, NH 03458.

Cobblestone, Cobblestone Publishing, Inc., 30 Grove St., Peterborough, NH 03458.

Storyworks and **Scope,** Scholastic, 2931 E. McCarty St., P.O. Box 3710, Jefferson City, MO 65102-3710.

National Geographic World, P.O. Box 2330, Washington, DC 20013-2330.

Time for Kids, P.O. Box 30609, Tampa, FL 33630-0609.

Students have read the first three chapters silently. During guided practice the six students work in pairs, rereading chapter one silently and placing a sticky-note over pictures and text that prompted personal connections. The teacher circulates among the pairs, prompting when the dialogue stops, or encouraging students to continue probing an idea.

The transcription that follows is of the exchanges between Monisha and David, with teacher prompts, after rereading Chapter 1.

Monisha: The picture of Willy and Searchlight [opposite the title page] reminds me of my brother and our dog. My brother always plays with our dog, Lucky. He says Lucky is his best pal.

David: We don't have a dog. But I remember when my mom had the flu. [long pause]

Teacher: How was that like Willy and Grandfather?

David: She couldn't move. She just stayed in bed for three days. My dad was sad. My grandma came to help us.

Monisha: Little Willy didn't have a mom like us. I think he felt awful. He had to do everything alone.

David: He had Searchlight. [long pause]

Teacher: How did having Searchlight help?

Monisha: Searchlight is little Willy's friend.

Teacher: How do you know that?

Monisha: I just know.

David: Searchlight barks real loud when little Willy says he'll make Grandfather want to live. It's like they can talk together. Do Lucky and your brother do that?

Teacher: Good question, David.

Monisha: Yeah. I guess my brother thinks Lucky is his friend.

David: Willy runs to get Doc Smith. I would get our neighbor if I was alone and someone got sick.

Monisha: Looks like Searchlight is worried in this picture [page 8]. His paws are up on the bed and he's looking at Grandfather.

David: I was worried when my mom was sick. She slept a lot and she hardly ate. But no doctor came to our house.

Monisha: Yeah. That's different. You go to the office. Willy was lucky.

Prompt with a question when the conversation stops or you want to encourage students to support their thinking with story details. Always offer positive feedback such as "good question" or "good use of actions to infer motivation."

Continue guided practice for developing a strategy until students show you that they have begun to apply the strategy on their own. Reading is boring for students who don't make personal connections and visualize characters, events, and setting. Near the end of the school year, as part of students' self-evaluation process (see Chapter 11), I ask students to complete these statements:

I used to…

Now I…

"I used to hate reading. It was just words on a page," wrote Monisha. "I didn't read most of the stuff we had to, but now I like some books better. I'm starting to see more pictures in my head. I have fun thinking about how the story is like my life. Or different." Clearly, Monisha's responses show a new awareness of how books can connect to her life.

Not all reactions were as upbeat as Monisha's. Carl's response reveals his inability to express some of the changes that his written and oral work reveal: "I used to think reading was boring. Now I still think it's boring." Such comments are discouraging and upset me. The only consolation is to recognize that one school year is not enough to turn around years of failure—especially when you're working with 25 to 35 students. Keep reaching out to the Carls in your classroom, telling them what they do well, and offering an alternative to their negative, internal voices.

Kid-watching Brings a Range of Responses

Watching a student for a few minutes during guided practice provides me with information about the level of a student's understanding—and his willingness to try suggestions. There are times when a student refuses to try a strategy. First, I ask "Why?" to determine if it is possible to negotiate. Sometimes I can penetrate students' negative feelings and reactions. Other times, I wait a day, especially when I sense anger. I always try to see the student alone, to probe further, hoping to hear something that will open a door, such as, "If I can read the stuff, maybe I'll try," or "It never helped before, why is this different?"

STRATEGY IN ACTION
Sixth-Grade Guided Practice: Skimming a Science Textbook

In a sixth-grade science class, I use a think–aloud to open a demonstration on skimming a textbook to locate answers to questions:

First I'll read the three questions so I get a sense of what information I need to recall and remember. The first questions asks, How do viruses cause infection? There was a diagram that showed this, so I'll skim and look for it. Here it is on page 85. Now I'll reread the captions and study the drawings. I close the book and tell myself what I remember. The virus attaches itself to a cell and enters the cell. If the virus takes over the cell's metabolism, new viruses grow. *Now I'll check my thoughts against the textbook. I left out one point*—the virus spreads to other cells after it takes one cell over. *Now I can write this down in my own words.*

When I invite students to raise questions, they ask several. I've included three queries and my responses.

Question: Why did you read all the questions first?
Response: To get an idea of the assignment and to start my mind thinking about where in the text I might find answers.

Question: Why didn't you just reread it and stop when you came to an answer?
Response: That wastes time. All I need is to locate the part that answers the questions and reread it.

Question: Why not write what you remember? That takes the least time.
Response: Because, with one reading, I won't remember every important detail. Skimming, rereading, and writing helps the information go into my long-term memory.

For guided practice, I ask students to work on the next two questions while the science teacher and I circulate around the room and observe students. I note that José uses the glossary instead of skimming; I ask him to try what I've modeled to get a more complete answer. Cecily is having difficulty answering the question, When can viruses reproduce? I show her how to skim for the word *reproduce* and she spots it before I do.

Remember, until students are near independence with a strategy, guided practice is often teacher-guided practice—that is, you circulate among students and coach them, so they have opportunities to clarify and deepen their understanding of how a strategy works before giving it a go on their own. The purpose of practice sessions is for students to understand a strategy so well that they can apply it to their independent reading

If time permits, I end the practice session with a debriefing (see pages 255–259), during which students discuss their reactions to practicing the strategy. Or, if we're out of time, I have students debrief next workshop. My observations and students' debriefings help me decide whether the entire class or a group needs additional practice.

Students who don't require extra practice can work on a project or read. Once students have a feel for a strategy and how it can improve their reading, students apply the strategy to their free-choice books (see page 263 for details on how to monitor this).

Students who cannot independently apply a strategy, and students who "don't get it" after the mini-lesson and guided practice, will benefit from work in a small group where you "guide" their use of the strategy. You can also schedule one-on-one conferences with students who require additional support in internalizing a repertoire of strategies that work (for more on this, see Chapter 9).

The Headless Haunt and Other African-American Ghost Stories, collected and retold by James Haskins, illustrated by Ben Otero, HarperCollins, 1994.

Mama Makes Up Her Mind and Other Dangers of Southern Living by Baily White, Vintage Books, 1993.

A Piece of the Wind: And Other Stories to Tell, edited by Ruthilde Kronberg and Patricia C. McKissack, HarperCollins, 1990.

The Rainbow People by Laurence Yep, HarperTrophy, 1989.

Short and Shivery, retold by Robert D. San Souci, illustrated by Katherine Coville, Bantam, Doubleday, Dell, 1987.

Stories To Tell a Cat by Alvin Schwartz, illustrated by Catherine Huerta, HarperCollins, 1992.

Sleeping at the Starlight Motel and Other Adventures on the Way Back Home by Baily White, Vintage Books, 1995.

Trickster Tales: Forty Folk Stories From Around the World, retold by Josepha Sherman, August House, 1996.

Budgeting Time for Guided Practice

Teachers always ask me, "But how many practice sessions should I devote to each strategy?" The number of sessions and the length of each one will vary with the strategy and the mix of students in your class. It might take five or six sessions for students to adequately practice selecting the main points for summarizing a novel in a paragraph. Practicing writing open-ended, story-specific questions, or finding words in a chapter that express mood, might take much less time. As I move most of the class to working in pairs or independently, I'll spend several additional sessions supporting one or two groups.

Based on your observations of and students' feedback from practice sessions, you can decide whether or not you should repeat the mini-lesson for the class or a small group or have a competent student repeat it with a group. The diagram at right provides a pictorial view of this process.

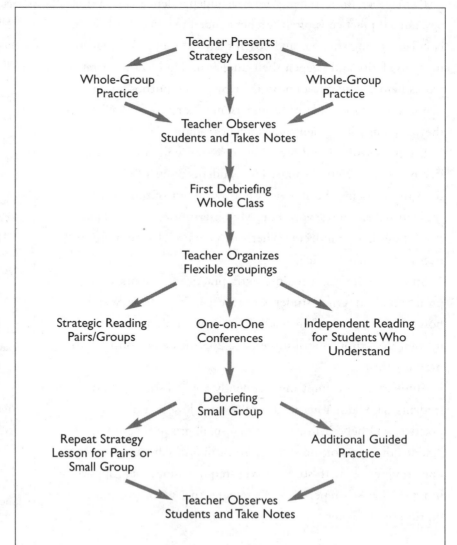

PLACING READING STRATEGIES IN THE CONTEXT OF A SCHOOL YEAR

It is impossible to frame a strategy curriculum that outlines what to teach first, second, third, etc., and how long to remain on each strategy. Because the experience with strategies differs from student to student, grade to grade, and changes as the year progresses, *I must determine the needs of my students at the start of each new school year and continue assessing their needs all year.* Suggestions for this ongoing evaluation and assessment are in Chapters 9 and 11.

In Chapter 1, I pointed out how Pearson and his researchers showed that emergent and proficient learners use combinations of reading strategies as they make meaning from texts. Therefore, committing to a scope and sequence of skills that are to be taught in a specific order at each grade level is to go against the process readers use to make sense of print. Marie Clay (1979), and Irene Fountas and Gay Su Pinnell (1996), also support this belief.

In my opinion, teachers who organize reading and test-taking strategies in units of study remain stymied in the "scope and sequence" mode. Units of study in basal anthologies are still organized around strategies presented in a specific order. If a strategic curriculum responds to the needs of an entire class or group of students, then a prescribed order for presenting strategies won't work. Why? Sometimes teachers will spend time on a strategy students already understand and not have enough time to practice one students aren't applying. Or teachers following an outline that sequentially orders strategies might introduce selecting important information from a chapter when students have had little experience with setting purposes for reading.

The strategic curriculum is an integral part of reading workshop. Here learning about, practicing, and independently applying valuable reading and test-taking strategies occur all year long with authentic texts that represent the purposes for which people read in the community and the workplace. Yet I understand the desire for specific suggestions and guidance among beginning teachers and experienced teachers trying workshop for the first time. What follows are some guidelines to support teachers' decision-making as they solve the puzzle of placing a strategy curriculum in the context of their year.

Some Starting Points for Strategy Demonstration

If you absolutely don't know where to begin, start with Pearson's seven and my two additional suggestions (see pages 14–17). However, as you invite students to respond to the mini-lesson by asking questions and sharing how they adapt a strategy, you will start collecting data that informs you about students' knowledge of a strategy (see Chapter 4). Here are some general guidelines:

◆ Introduce a strategy to the entire class in a mini-lesson, which is a great review for students who understand it. Moreover, proficient readers might discover something new as they observe and listen.

◆ Repeat the mini-lesson for groups of students who need several opportunities to understand the process, while the rest of the class completes independent reading and/or journal entries.

◆ Offer students guided practice with a strategy until you observe that they understand it. Circulate and watch as students practice and jot down notes on sticky-notes. For example, I've completed a mini-lesson on rereading with the entire eighth grade. I've asked students to read a page from their independent-reading books once and list what they remember, then draw a line under the first list. Read a second time and add details under the line. As I walk from group to group, I jot down these notes:

Josiah, 11/8	LaShaundra: 11/8
• long list, 1st read	• 3 things, 1st read
• added 4 ideas, 2nd read	• added 1 item, 2nd read
• uses strat well, focuses	• confer to find out why

After I complete my notes, I speak to LaShaundra, who is a good reader, and ask, "Why do you think you recalled only four things?"

LaShaundra shrugs, then says, "I guess it's [the book's] too hard."

"But we selected that book together," I reply. "It seemed just right. Could it be something else?" I probe.

"Well, I hate having to write what I remember. It's hard for me."

"Can you tell me exactly what is hard?"

"Concentrating. I keep thinking of math. I know I'm failing."

"Have your talked to the teacher?" I ask.

"No." [pause]

"Would you like me to ask him to speak to you?"

LaShaundra wants to think about my suggestion. She explains that she knows she should be able to open this conversation with her teacher. But because she failed a quiz and a test, she's embarrassed. My job, however, is to help LaShaundra compartmentalize her math worries so she can focus on reading. A strategy that focuses her on the task is breaking the page into smaller chunks: read several lines, pause, retell. If LaShaundra can't retell, she rereads and continues this way until she can remember many details.

KNOWING WHEN STUDENTS HAVE INTERNALIZED A STRATEGY

Complex strategies such as synthesizing or predict/support/confirm/adjust can take six to eight weeks of mini-lessons and guided practice until all or most students can apply the strategy. This process varies with grade levels and whether or not students have had instruction and coaching in applying the strategy. If there are only two to five out of 30 students who still struggle with a strategy, move the class forward and try to reserve time to work one-on-one with the two to five for 10 minutes each workshop. Sometimes it's effective to stop practicing and allow time for the strategy to settle, much like the basement of a building needs time to settle. After a break of two to four weeks, returning a student to a strategy often, not always, results in deeper understanding. Remember, with a strategy curriculum students revisit the same strategies throughout the year, refining their understandings and raising their level of expertise with each review.

Often you'll work for several weeks on a key strategy, such as activating and using prior knowledge, while working on some fix-it strategies, such as rereading and using context clues to figure out unfamiliar words.

For many middle school students, selecting information that answers a question from many details in a text is a difficult task. If

Guidelines for Strategic Reading

1. Assess students' prior knowledge

2. Select a strategy

3. Demonstrate and discuss the strategy

4. Offer guided practice

5. Invite self-evaluation

6. Encourage independence

7. Evaluate, then respond to students' needs

most students appear to struggle with practicing a strategy, shelve it temporarily and return to it later in the year.

In a mini-lesson, I introduce the strategy and have students practice. If most struggle, I tell them: *This is a tough strategy. You've begun to understand how to use it, but I think we'll take a break from practicing. From my teaching experience, I've noticed that when we return to this strategy, it will be easier for you because your subconscious minds are working hard to understand it.*

Deciding which strategies your students need is a challenging task for beginning teachers who are also figuring out how to manage a classroom, complete required lesson plans, fill out administrative forms, cope with recess, hall, and lunch duties, and teach reading and writing effectively.

As you gain experience and can attend more to assessing students' needs, you'll be able to make informed decisions about which strategies to demonstrate early in the year. For me, the most energizing aspect of teaching is knowing that every year will be different because I teach a new group of students. Our job is to problem-solve, to study the data on each student and make informed decisions for individuals, groups, and the entire class—a challenging, daunting, and exciting task!

STRATEGIES CAN SAVE OUR STRUGGLING READERS

"It's hopeless. I'll never learn how to read," Tony, an eighth grader said. "I don't care," he added, averting his eyes. "I've done worksheets and hate them. You got something new?" Tony is what I call a *fragile learner;* he's failed so often that he views himself as hopeless. Today too many Tonys get lost in our middle and high schools. Recently students like him caught the attention of the International Reading Association.

At a 1997 meeting of the International Reading Association, the Board of Directors created a commission on adolescent literacy co-chaired by Richard Vacca and Donna Alvermann. The board's action and excerpts from the commission's resolution were published in the autumn 1999 issue of *Reading Today,* and brought national attention to a tragedy that middle and high school teachers have long recognized: that many adolescents struggle with reading or can't read at all.

The board's position paper put forth a set of principles for teachers and their struggling students that sounded like a bill of rights. The principle that especially struck me highlighted the unique personality of this age group, and stressed that for struggling readers to experience success, teachers must respect these complex young adults, accept their individuality, discover what each student needs to move forward, and develop the reading strategies that lead to success and involvement.

The struggling and reluctant readers I teach are all fragile learners. Their self-esteem has been repeatedly pierced with negative experiences and feedback. At school they watch others complete work at high levels and achieve success, reinforcing their negative feelings. "Tapes" in their minds that reinforce their weaknesses cannot be removed easily. However, students can learn to replace these "I can't do anything right" thoughts when positive experiences, borne of progress and improvement, outnumber the negatives. The fear and anger experienced by middle school students who struggle with reading is obvious in Mark's story.

Mark was one of 24 sixth-grade students who worked with me in an extra reading class that met three times a week from 7:30 to 8:30 a.m. at Johnson Williams Middle School in Clarke County, Virginia. When I studied his folder, I noticed his grades were solid B's in reading and writing. His fifth-grade teacher had written, "Mark always complains that reading is hard and boring, but he does well in spite of his complaints." That was the only clue that something might be amiss.

Polite and charming, Mark always greeted me at the door and engaged me in talk about the weather or my evening. During our third class, I paired students and invited them to complete a written conversation about their reading interests, strengths, and needs. In a written conversation, two people "talk" to one another on paper; they can ask each other questions and respond to their partner's written comments.

That evening, curled in a comfortable chair, I read 12 written conversations. Even today Mark's words are painful for me to reflect on.

Mark: I hate reading. I hate school. I hate coming.

Maria: Why?

Mark: I can't read the books in most classes. I'm dumb.

Maria: How can you do the work?

Mark: I listen and remember. And I try to get in good with the teacher. Like never make waves or talk out of turn.

Maria: Does anyone know?

Mark: Only you.

At that point I, too, knew Mark's secret. The next day we met during lunch, and I told him I had read the conversation. "Will I fail now?" he asked.

"Of course not," I replied. "But I would like you to work with the reading specialist so we can learn more about your reading." After our fourth meeting, Mark agreed.

The evaluation results revealed that Mark was right; he was reading three years below grade level. In middle school, with different teachers for each subject and large reading and note-taking assignments, it was more difficult to use charm and listening skills to get by.

That year, in addition to the extra reading class, and instead of exploratory courses in foreign language, art, and music, Mark worked with me one-on-one for three 30-minute sessions a week. For the first time he read a book from beginning to end, *Stone Fox* by John R. Gardiner. On his own, Mark drew illustrations for the book, and showed them to me during a reading lesson. What a wonderful talent he had! In seventh and eighth grade, the school fit art into his schedule. Studying a subject he adored and was tops at, combined with two more years of one-on-one reading instruction, developed Mark's confidence. No longer a "hopeless case," Mark graduated eighth-grade reading on a seventh-grade level, and knowing that with hard work, he would continue to progress.

SUPPORT READERS BY SCAFFOLDING

Outside of education, the word scaffold conjures an image of a wooden platform that supports workers while they construct or repair a building. This image is apt when thinking about scaffolding instruction in reading, for when teachers scaffold, they are providing a supportive framework for students' to stand on and steady themselves on as they build their reading comprehension abilities. As you will see in this book, scaffolding of students' use of reading strategies occurs before, during, and after reading.

Mini-lessons are a powerful kind of scaffolding, in that they give all students the opportunity to observe an expert share how a strategy works and supports his reading process. During such scaffolding, a teacher can model building background knowledge before reading, demonstrating ways to monitor recall and comprehension while reading, or showing students how to skim for information after reading.

Readers who struggle and readers who "don't get it" require one-on-one scaffolding. I sit side-by-side and show students how I pause, then retell to check my recall or how I look for key words from questions when skimming for details. I think aloud (pages 70-72), sharing my frustrations, to help students accept their concerned inner voices.

Some students require scaffolding for many weeks; others move forward at a faster rate. When they're ready, move students to independence by gradually turning more of the process over to them.

WAYS TO SUPPORT
STRUGGLING READERS

The suggestions for supporting struggling adolescent readers, listed below and embedded throughout this book, contain many of the key principles suggested by the IRA.

Be positive. Focus on what students *can* do. Accept students where they are and find ways to help them move forward.

Set reasonable and doable goals with students. Continue to revise these as students improve throughout the year.

Give students reading materials *they can read independently*. When students do the reading, they will improve.

Get students actively involved in their learning by using strategies that ask students to "do" instead of passively listening.

Help students learn a strategy or information a different way if the method you've introduced isn't working.

Sit side-by-side and explain an idea to a student who isn't getting it. Closing the gap between students and the explanation can improve students' understandings.

Give students additional time to process new information, to complete class work and tests.

Invite students to retell information to a partner or in small groups. Talk helps learners remember and clarify their ideas.

Make sure students understand directions. You might have to sit close by some students and repeat directions, for struggling students often shut down when they think they can't complete an activity.

Help struggling students see their improvement. Invite students to reflect on their progress and verbalize it to you or write it down.

Students who require the support of an expert in addition to a nurturing classroom teacher should have access to a reading specialist.

All students, from struggling to proficient, will benefit from observing how in-the-head reading strategies enable you and their peers to cope with challenging texts and vocabulary.

Pause and Reflect on:
Implementing a Strategic Reading Curriculum

As you prepare your strategic-reading program, here are some guidelines to consider:

1 Offer students a wide range of materials so they can learn how to adapt strategies to the problems posed by each text.

2 Have students read at their independent and instructional levels, so they can continue to develop expertise with using strategies to comprehend.

3 Take the time to learn the strengths of each student, and recognize that the surest way to success in reading is to accept a student where she is and gently help her improve.

4 Construct a workshop environment that allows middle schoolers to negotiate choices, interact with you and peer experts, discuss books, evaluate their progress, and set achievable goals.

Chapter 4
Discover What Students Know About Reading

"You'll never know anything about me if you don't try to find out."
—Eighth Grader

I t's September. Twenty-eight students enter the same seventh-grade reading-writing work-shop. Twenty-eight individuals at different reading levels with varied literary tastes, ranging from X-Men comics to Tolkien's *The Hobbit*. Twenty-eight boys and girls with a wide range of instructional and emotional needs.

In "getting-to-know-you-conferences," students talk to me about their reading lives (see pages 103–105). I jot down key phrases on sticky-notes, refraining from interjecting comments that could make students feel judged. Often students reveal information that can help me organize beginning-of-the-year groups, decide whether I need to administer an Informal Reading Inventory (for IRI, see pages 248–254), or meet with particular students for a series of brief one-on-one conferences.

There's seventh grader Karla, who defiantly states: "I haven't read a whole book since second grade, and I don't intend to change things this year." She takes out an emery board and smooths her nails. Fifth grader Chantell tells me, with a dramatic shrug of her shoulders, "Reading? I can take it or leave it. I read the books, but I don't like to do it."

I meet with her classmate Jacob, immediately noticing a stack of Arthur C. Clarke books on his desk. When I ask him about these, he explains: "This is the second time I'm reading these. I'm also reading Tolkien's *Lord of the Rings.* I only read science fiction and fantasy. I don't like required reading because most [books] are boring."

With each of these meetings, a teacher has the potential to open the door and develop trust with a student—or shut it with a comment that passes judgment on his reading attitude. Be an active listener and honor students' feelings and attitudes. One negative comment will not change an attitude that has been developing over many years. Show that you care, you understand, and that you recognize the fact that the student needs time and support to change. Only with mutual trust and respect and an ever-deepening knowledge of students' reading strengths, needs, and interests can teachers help their students progress.

FOUR KINDS OF MIDDLE SCHOOL READERS

During those first weeks of school, instead of plunging headlong into your curriculum, set aside time each day to try some of the getting-to-know-you ideas in this chapter. Not only will you gain insights into students' attitudes toward reading, but you'll also start identifying the four kinds of readers that populate middle school classrooms.

Struggling Readers

These students read below grade level. Since textbooks in science, mathematics, and social studies are on grade level, struggling readers daily experience difficulty reading and collecting information. Because they have not developed personal reading lives and avoid books, struggling readers often have limited vocabularies as well as problems with decoding or pro-

Providing blocks of time for independent reading allows students to get into their books.

nouncing multisyllable words. They may be disfluent, reading word-to-word rather than in meaningful chunks. They lack strategies that engage them with texts and enable them to solve problems that print presents—strategies such as making personal connections, visualizing, self-monitoring, predicting, and adjusting predictions. For these students, reading is a boring, painful chore.

It's crucial to develop strategies that enable them to cope with unfamiliar words. Building their prior knowledge so they have countless experiences to bring to their reading is equally as important (see Chapters 5, 6, and 7).

Reluctant Readers

These are students who read at or above grade level, but read only when they must complete school assignments. Rarely do they choose to read during free time at school or at home. Since these readers possess solid strategies and skills, but don't enjoy books, I consider them reluctant readers. From the countless reading interviews I've conducted with middle schoolers, I've learned that these students have never imagined themselves talking, living, dressing, and thinking like a character, or picturing an event or setting they read about. The exhilarating feeling of, *I can't put this book down for anything!* or the longing one sometimes feels after finishing a great book, of missing the characters as though they were dear houseguests who left, is one they haven't experienced. Helping these students learn to link their lives and experiences to stories can create the *personal connections* to books that these readers lack.

Grade-Level Readers

A classroom of students who read on grade level is every teacher's dream, because they can read content-area textbooks and recall the important information. They apply problem-solving strategies such as using context clues to figure out an unfamiliar word, reread confusing passages, raise questions and search for answers, predict and confirm, visualize, and make personal connections. Sometimes they choose reading during free time at school, but don't often read at home.

Many could become proficient readers if they read more, thereby enlarging their vocabulary and overall knowledge base. The broader a student's knowledge base, the better equipped she is to read and enjoy a wide range of topics.

However, these students often have interests that take them away from reading—important interests such as ballet, training for a sport, painting, playing a musical instrument, in-line skating. Some will continue to pursue their interests passionately and place reading and academics in a secondary slot. Others will improve their vocabulary and ability to connect reading to other books and life experiences. And these improvements will propel them forward. They may well become avid readers as adults because the in-the-head strategies are there.

Proficient Readers

These students read above grade level and possess and use a large repertoire of reading strategies. Their reading is fluent because they read with expression and capture the different voices of characters. They keep a stack of books in their cubbies so they always have one to read during workshop. They talk to friends about favorite parts in a story. They read for long periods of time at home and at school. Books nurture them and reading is a necessity. Their heightened ability to imagine, connect, and visualize enables these students to journey into the past, experience other cultures, travel into the future, and live inside the hearts and minds of different characters.

Though proficient readers can read any text well, they need to be taught the complex strategies that enable them to appreciate the nuances of mood, tone, and theme in books.

They need to be guided to make deeper text-to-text connections, so they can relate the elements and themes of one book to other books, to their community, and their world. The issue these students struggle with in middle school is coping with being labeled a "nerd" and being excluded from social activities in and out of school. (Proficient readers fortunate enough to have athletic talent can escape this stereotyping.)

FIND "THE" BOOK FOR EACH READER

It's free-choice time in my eighth-grade reading-writing workshop. Two groups discuss books, three students are at the computer, working on final drafts of their memoirs, the rest read alone or in pairs. As I circulate casually to see if anyone needs my help, I listen to snippets of conversations, which don't always focus on reading and writing. Today I jot down the remarks of Julie and Alex:

Julie: As soon as I did extra work in reading and Ms. Robb asked me to read my poems, they dropped me like I was poison. I'm out of the in-group. If I want in, I'll have to stop acting nerdy.

Alex: Were you invited to Jessica's party this weekend? I haven't been invited to anything since third grade. My grades are lousy and that doesn't even help.

Lapses into social talk are daily occurrences in the lives of middle school adolescents, who believe socializing is one of the most important aspects of their lives. I don't squelch these conversations as long as they're brief and students complete their work. Listening to students chat maintains my connection to their world and my awareness of the ever-shifting cliques. After all, learning for middle school students is a social event and talk clarifies students' comprehension of texts (Hynds, 1997).

In the middle grades, avid readers take their passion for books underground and rarely show enthusiasm for schoolwork, for that's not "cool." My job is to reach them, not change them. Their academically aloof behavior is normal as they desperately explore ways to bid farewell to childhood and move toward adulthood.

The personal data you glean, as well as the information you collect about each student's reading and interests, will help you find *the book* that might transform a student into a reader. This information will also help you group for instruction and plan interventions that can sharpen students' in-the-head strategies and develop the motivation to read. Your students probably won't advertise their pleasure in reading, and that's okay, as long as they're progressing.

Organizing Those First Weeks to Learn About Students

I use the first three weeks of school to collect information about students' reading lives. But I also want students to get to know about *my* reading life and interests, and so I model each activity and write about myself. I also share samples of students' work from past years, being careful to white out their names. The more models you provide students with, the easier it is for them to write, because you have shown them clearly what you're looking for. However, there will always be a core of students who reveal little about themselves; they challenge us to work diligently to help them verbalize what they cannot do in order to support their reading and learning.

I store all the information I collect about each student's reading in a literacy folder. Here are some of the data-gathering methods I recommend for use with your students:

1. Review their standardized test scores and Informal Reading Inventory Reports and prepare two tentative lists: one of students reading below grade level, the other of students reading at or above grade level. As I gather more and more information these lists change, because standardized testing is only one measure of reading development.

2. Invite students to reflect on and write about their reading strengths and needs in a "What's Easy? What's Hard?" exercise.

3. Have students write "all-about-me" letters. These give me background about friends, family, interests, atti-

Name *Krista Lynn Sulser* ___ Date *January 20, 2000*

WHAT'S EASY and WHY?

What I think is easy about reading is getting addicted to it. Once I start reading, I don't want to ever stop until I finish the book although I usually have to stop.

WHAT's HARD and WHY?

What I think is hard about reading is some of the words that you don't understand. If you don't understand the words most people just put the book down and search for another one.

tudes toward reading, and favorite books, and give me insight into students' writing strengths and areas that require additional support.

4. Ask students to complete a "Reading Strategy Checklist" (see page 102) and learn about the strategies students use before, during, and after reading.

5. Create a schedule for "getting-to-know-you" conferences. This activity comes last because the information you've collected will help you plan a meaningful first conference.

6. Listen to each student read orally from a 150- to 200-word passage at their independent and instructional levels. Mark their errors or miscues (see pages 248–254). Assess struggling and reluctant readers first so you can plan appropriate interventions and provide support early in the year. The results will give you a good sense of how a student uses reading strategies to solve problems the text presents. Along with other data, this information can help you decide whether a student has internalized a strategy or whether he needs additional support.

Set aside 10 to 20 minutes of many workshop periods and allow students to complete steps 2, 3, and 4 in class. If you balance the time spent on instruction with data-collecting activities, you'll learn about students and move forward with your curriculum.

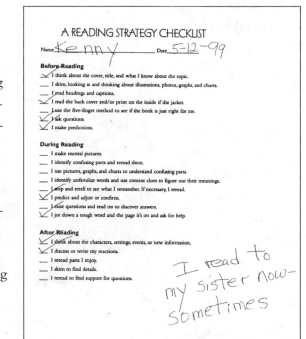

Above: In September, Kenny's checklist was empty, his mood angry. Below: By May, with one-on-one work, Kenny had made great strides in applying strategies.

Keep a
Literacy Folder

Before school opens I label file folders with each student's name and I store them in a cabinet. It's helpful to have important information in one accessible place, including all the information I collect during the first three weeks of school. Throughout the year I add dated observational notes, records of reading conferences, error analyses of oral reading, and key journal entries. Every other week I review the folders of struggling readers—other students every four to six weeks.

I refer to these folders to plan student and parent conferences, to group students with common needs, to help students select appropriate books, and to monitor their progress in reading.

Tune in to Students' Reading Lives with These Three Experiences

By inviting students to reflect on their reading lives, you can gain important information early in the year that will help you pair or group students for strategic reading and inform your decision on which strategies to emphasize. What follows are three experiences that I offer students during the first six weeks of school: "What's Easy? What's Hard?," "All-About-Me Letters," "Strategy Checklist."

PLAN ON
2 or 3
30-minute
sessions

What's Easy? What's Hard? This activity poses two questions: *What's easy about reading and why?; what's hard about reading and why?* Before asking students to respond, I model, with a think-aloud, how I go about answering these questions. First I write the prompts on large chart paper, then I share these thoughts: *I'll jot down some notes under each question so I do my thinking before writing. Maybe one idea will generate another. It's tough to admit that reading can be hard. But I know that at times I struggle.*

Invite students to write about their reading lives.

ROBB'S NOTES FOR
WHAT'S EASY? WHAT'S HARD? EXERCISE

What's Easy and Why? Notes:

mysteries, magazines, action stories, adventure, predicting, questioning, rereading, making pictures and personal connections

Magazine articles and short action stories are easy because I can finish them quickly and relate to them. Mystery is what I read for pleasure, and I love predicting and thinking about clues. I always ask questions and read on to see if I can find answers. Searching for answers keeps me interested in turning each page. When I have enough knowledge to make personal connections and mental pictures, then I really enjoy reading because I can relate to the characters and the information.

What's Hard and Why? Notes:

tough vocabulary, when I have no background knowledge, technical articles about computers and other machines, concentrating on boring factual books, reading and recalling when rushing to finish

When I have no knowledge of a topic, such as installing a computer, I can't keep the information in my head. I'm reading words, without constructing meaning. When a page has many unfamiliar words, and I can't figure out their meaning, that makes reading tough. Boring books that just state fact after fact, or ones on topics I dislike, are difficult to read. My mind wanders to other things, and I can't recall any details. I also have trouble reading when I can't relate to the characters, because they're terribly violent or not sympathetic in some way. Sometimes I have to read a lot for school or a class, and when I rush, it's harder to remember what I've read. This happens because I'm nervous about time and don't concentrate well.

I invite students to comment on or ask questions about what I've written. Students express relief and delight with the fact that I bump into difficult reading situations. A seventh grader summed up students' reactions, saying, "All the things that are hard for you [Mrs. Robb] are hard for me. And when we talked about it in class, I saw that most of the time it wasn't my fault. It was that the stuff [texts] was too hard or boring or something I never heard of."

It's important for students to see how others in their grade have responded to these questions. After sharing several from the past year, without naming those students, I invite my class to think of ideas, jot down notes, and write a paragraph.

I prefer using these two open-ended questions over a fill-in-the-blanks format because they nudge students to reflect, then write. Some will say, "I don't know," or "I have nothing to say." That's fine. But make sure you tell them to write those words on paper, so you can tease out why in a conference with them.

Eighth grader reflects on "what's easy?" and "what's hard?" about standardized tests.

> Standardized Testers
> Laura Hunter   January 27, 1999
>
> ① What's easy about standardized tests and why?
>
> The easiest thing about these tests is that you always have multiple choice. (except for the SAT grid-ins) If you are unsure about what your doing you have a few options to get you on the right track.
>
> ② What's hard about them, and why?
>
> The hard parts of these tests are, they are very long and you get tired, and sometime you have a short amount of time to do a lot of questions. The hardest thing is that they are standardized. Sometimes there is material you haven't covered yet, because this is what the test makers think people your age should know.

Teaching Reading in Middle School

Here are some responses to these questions:

What's Easy and Why?

✦ Books I choose for reading. I pick what's interesting to me. *Grade 6*

✦ Sports magazines because there's lots of pictures. *Grade 8*

✦ Vocabulary work in science. The words are bold and easy to find. *Grade 7*

✦ Talking about a book I liked with my group. I remember more after I talk and hear what others think. *Grade 8*

✦ Making pictures in my head. It's easy for me to see places and I always decide how I think characters look and talk. *Grade 5*

What's Hard and Why?

✦ Saying long words. I don't like to look at them so I skip them. *Grade 6*

✦ Looking up answers in my history book when I don't understand [the assigned reading]. *Grade 8*

✦ Finding support for predictions. It's dumb looking back. *Grade 5*

✦ Skimming. I don't know what to do so I turn pages and fake it. *Grade 8*

✦ Understanding hard stuff. I don't get it. *Grade 7*

When a student writes, "I don't know," I arrange a mini-conference to probe further. Questions such as, "What's your least favorite subject? Why?" and "How do you feel when you have to read in school?" can help students verbalize their thoughts. If not, I let it go and wait, hoping that once the student trusts me, he or she will share his or her attitudes toward reading.

Those who candidly respond, as you can see from the student samples, provide insights into reading behaviors that offer a starting point for scaffolding instruction early in the year.

2 All-About-Me Letters When middle school students write letters introducing themselves to me, I can learn about their reading likes and dislikes, as well as their interests and friends—information I will use to plan reading instruction. I'm not looking for deep, personal revelations—that's an inappropriate expectation at the start of the year. Moreover, this age-group values privacy and is far more open with peers than with adults. However, inviting them to write about school, favorite subjects, and hobbies takes the spotlight off the personal and students often reveal useful information.

Students complete "all-about-me" letters in class. This takes three or four 40-minute sessions. They enjoy the opportunity to be candid about school, reading, hobbies, family, and friendships without being graded. One sixth grader told me during our first conference,

"I can't believe you didn't freak when I wrote I hate reading and didn't intend to read anything in this class. I exaggerated a little, but I wanted to see how you would *really* react." If you accept what students write without passing judgment, then you've taken the first step toward developing trust—and you'll learn a great deal about them.

Brainstorm Before Writing

Before writing, students and I generate a list of questions that can spark ideas to include in letters. I model how I take notes for each question, then frame my notes into a letter that I print on chart paper. Not only do students observe how I go about composing, but they also learn about me. Brainstorming notes before writing is a strategy I require and want students to adopt and use across the curriculum. Thinking and taking notes prior to composing usually results in richer details and frees students to attend to organizing their ideas and expressing them clearly.

If students say, "I have nothing to write," I ask them to put that on paper. Having nothing

---

STUDENT-CREATED QUESTIONS AND PROMPTS FOR ALL-ABOUT-ME LETTERS

Note that I select some questions and have students choose some.

Directions: Using details, answer and explain questions 5, 6, and 7. Choose three or more additional questions that you want to write about. Before writing the letter, brainstorm notes for each question. Turn your notes in with the letter.

1. What do you do in your spare time?
2. Do you have hobbies that you continually work on?
3. Do you have a favorite family member? friend? Why do you like these people?
4. If you have a job, tell me about it.
5. Do you have favorite books? Name one and explain why you enjoyed it.
6. What are your favorite subjects? Why do you like these?
7. What subjects do you dislike? Why?
8. What sports do you enjoy watching? playing? Why?
9. What was the best thing that happened to you last year? the worst?
10. Explain how your best teachers enabled you to learn from them.

---

to write raises a red flag that tells me, "Meet with this student as quickly as possible."

I've included a fifth- and eighth-grade letter here, as well as some excerpts on the next page.

There's a greater chance that students will write candidly when they know that these letters will be read *only by you*.

You can learn about students from All-About-Me letters.

Dear Mrs. Robb and Mrs. Book,

There are 4 in my family—me and my brother and mom and our dog. My brother likes school but I don't. School is good because I get to see my friends and we talk!

My best subject is math. I like solving problems. I like writing poems but not long stories. I'm ok at reading but I rather play or listen to music. Sometimes I can predict and it makes it more interesting. I like Ramona books and Nancy Drew books.

Your student,
Anna

Dear Mrs. Robb and Mrs. Hobbs,

I enjoy being around people with a happy, upbeat attitude so I can be myself and have fun. My brother, Nate and my best friend Alanna are my favorite.

My favorite things to do in life are acting and running. When I'm acting I can let go of all my problems and just become someone else. I love running so much, cross country or sprinting I just can't resist. I think I enjoy it so much because its as close as I can get to flying.

My least favorite part of school is math I have a very hard time with it. I also have an incredibly hard time paying attention and sitting still. I have to be tapping a finger or foot or something. Paying attention is such a struggle. I have to constantly remind myself "Hold still", "Pay attention," and ask "What did she/he say?" So I need people to be patient with me.

I hate homework so much I think that we are at school for 5½ hours and should not have to take extra work home. We need time to just have fun and be kids while we still can without worrying

about homework. It has been hard my entire life to get homework done and I think that our homework is any should be reading or optional free writing.

I enjoy writing stories and poems because I can express my feelings about anything my fears, hopes, or just something I saw. I need to work on sticking to one project at a time though.

I read whenever I get a chance, but the book definitely has to get my attention. I like horror, fantasy, and action. I don't really have a favorite author or book because I always find one I like better.

This year I would like to become a faster reader because I have so many books and never enough time to read them.

Sincerely,
Phoebe

Excerpts From All-About-Me Letters

"The subject I hate is reading. Reading is boring and it takes too much time. I can read OK but I hate it. I never [have] read a book I wanted to finish. When I come home, I turn on the TV and watch until late. I eat supper by the TV I like TV cause theirs action and things happen fast. Not like books. I don't play outside and I don't talk to anyone much after school."

—Charlie, Grade 7

My Follow-up: In a conference with Charlie, I book-talked several titles and told him to try the one he thought he might enjoy the most. If after Chapter 3, the book did not appeal to him, he could choose from the two remaining titles. The books I gave Charlie were: *The Not So Jolly Roger* and *Tut, Tut* both by Jon Scieszka. (In history, Charlie had just completed a study of ancient Egypt.) These books are short and packed with action. Charlie read both and then completed the rest of the "Time Warp Trio" books.

"I spend most of my free time building model airplanes and rockets. My favorite thing to do is to set off a rocket in our back yard. My dad helps me build them. I like to read about airplanes and rockets, and I look through *Popular Science* Magazine. It's too hard for me, so my dad reads some to me. I do my work for school, and I like math the best. Reading books makes me sleepy unless they're about planes and rockets."

—Sam, Grade 6

My Follow-up: Building on Sam's interest in math and science, I gave him Seymour Simon's *The Paper Airplane Book* and asked him to browse through several of Simon's "Einstein Anderson" titles. *The Paper Airplane Book* became one of Sam's all-time favorites. The others did not appeal to him. What I then offered Sam were books that would help him construct an electric circuit, backyard rockets, etc. Sam enjoyed reading to learn how to construct things, and I hoped this interest would eventually lead him to read other kinds of books.

> "Reading can make me feel sick sometimes because if I read for a long period of time I will get sick I don't like to read unless it's a scary book. I read any place it is quite and not noisy."   —*Sandy, Grade 5*

Follow-up: Reading one year below grade level, Sandy struggled with required school reading. Sandy's teacher offered her some copies of R.L. Stine's *Goosebumps* since she loved "scary things." During independent reading, Sandy's teacher suggested she wear the earphones from their listening center so she could concentrate.

Such letters make me chuckle, for young adolescents revel in shocking adults by being overly candid. Yet, each student has provided me with material I can discuss at our first conference. As with their responses to the What's Easy? What's Hard? exercise, when students write nothing, I open the conference by casually asking, "Can you tell me why you haven't written anything?"

"I have no hobbies" or "It's a boring assignment" are typical responses I've received. I offer help, but students don't always let me into their learning lives. Over time, once the student trusts me, I might be able to coach and support.

PLAN ON

giving
the checklist
3 times
a year

3 **Reading Strategy Checklist** Reserve time to discuss the term *strategies* to ensure that students understand the items on the checklist (see next page). In a think-aloud, I explain the term this way:

A strategy is a tool stored in your memory and experience that can help you figure out the meaning of a tough word or select important information from a book. For example, if a word or sentence confuses me, I'll reread the sentence to see if that helps. If I'm still confused, I'll look for clues in the sentence or paragraph that might help. Having many reading strategies I can use means I have more tools, more choices to understand confusing passages.

Explain that you will use this checklist to help students improve their reading. I suggest that you have students complete the checklist three times: during the second or third week, halfway through the year, and at the close of the year. It's a simple way for students to monitor their reading growth.

A READING-STRATEGY CHECKLIST

Name _____ Date _____

Before Reading

____ I think about the cover, title, and what I know about the topic.

____ I skim, looking at and thinking about illustrations, photos, graphs, and charts.

____ I read headings and captions.

____ I read the back cover and/or print on the inside if the jacket.

____ I use the five-finger method to see if the book is just right for me.

____ I ask questions.

____ I make predictions.

During Reading

____ I make mental pictures.

____ I identify confusing parts and reread them.

____ I use pictures, graphs, and charts to understand confusing parts.

____ I identify unfamiliar words and use context clues to figure out their meanings.

____ I stop and retell to see what I remember. If necessary, I reread.

____ I predict and adjust or confirm.

____ I raise questions and read on to discover answers.

____ I jot down a tough word and the page it's on and ask for help.

After Reading

____ I think about the characters, settings, events, or new information.

____ I discuss or write my reactions.

____ I reread parts I enjoy.

____ I skim to find details.

____ I reread to find support for questions.

WHY I ASK STUDENTS TO COMPLETE THE CHECKLIST THREE TIMES

At the start of the year, asking students to complete the checklist provides insights into the type of reading instruction they've had. I want to know whether or not students have been exposed to a strategy curriculum. If students have had experiences with a strategy curriculum, I want to know how much they recall. The first checklist is a baseline against which students can measure their progress as we work to develop and fine-tune in-the-head reading strategies.

A Conferring Tip

Holding "getting-to-know-you" conferences early in the year means my students have not thoroughly practiced how to use literacy centers. While I confer with a student, the rest of the class completes a journal entry or reads independently—something students can work on without interrupting me for help. When conferring, it's important to give your attention to the student meeting with you.

Information in letters, completed Reading Strategy Checklists, and "What's Easy? What's Hard?" write-ups provide me with issues to discuss during the first reading conference: an 8- to 12-minute "getting-to-know-you" conference.

PLANNING FIRST READING CONFERENCES

PLAN ON

5 weeks in Sept. & Oct. to complete an 8- to 12-minute conference with each student

Planning can prevent "getting-to-know-you" conferences from derailing. I create two lists of students' names. Students who tell me they hate reading, don't know what's easy or hard for them, and those who write, "I have nothing to say" land on my "See ASAP" list. The rest of the class comprises my second list, and I confer

Read Between the Lines

Below are some statements typical of struggling and reluctant middle school readers. Actually, these students are begging for support, but often couch their feelings in tough language. Their academic self-esteem is low, so they put down reading and adopt an, I-don't-give-a-hoot attitude.

◆ Reading is dumb.

◆ Reading is useless.

◆ All books are boring.

◆ You can't make me read.

◆ I'm dropping out in 2 years. Why bother?

◆ Why do you care? I don't.

It's important not to get riled by these responses; these kids need your help. Try to move them beyond anger by listening and offering support.

with these students next. By the end of five weeks, I've usually touched base with everyone.

Teacher's Conference-Planning Checklist

Hold conferences in a quiet place away from the rest of the class. Students need to feel safe in order to risk talking about their reading lives.

1. Explain that you will be taking notes during the conference so you can recall important ideas and figure out how to help each student. I always invite students to read my notes so they don't feel I'm writing "bad things."

2. Think of some openers—you'll find these in students' responses you've collected. Here are some I've used that you can easily adapt:

   ◆ Can you tell me why you wrote nothing about yourself?

   ◆ I read that you enjoy all sports. Do you belong to a team?

   ◆ I see that Tolkien is your favorite author. What about his stories appeals to you?

   ◆ You wrote that all reading is hard. Can you tell me some specific things that make it hard?

   ◆ You told me that you've read *Charlotte's Web* three times, and loved it better each time. Do you have a favorite part you could tell me about?

   ◆ You write that you hate reading. Can you tell me what about reading makes you hate it?

   ◆ You wrote that you can never find a book that interests you. Can you tell me some things you'd like to learn about or the kinds of movies you really enjoy?

   ◆ Is there anything you'd like to tell me that you haven't written about?

3. Listen carefully. Don't give in to the urge to fill in pauses with talk.

4. Ask the student to discuss something from his or her "all-about-me" letter or the "What's Easy? What's Hard?" responses.

104

5. Review the strategy checklist sheet by asking students to comment on what they know. Raise questions at this time.

6. Negotiate reasonable goals with students and jot these on a sticky-note or a sheet of paper and file in their literacy folders. At this point in the year, goals might be to work on one fix-it strategy such as rereading, to help a student find some books that match personal interests, or to introduce a new genre.

7. Add some strategies you hope to reteach and some goals you'd like to negotiate in the future.

STRATEGY IN ACTION
Fifth-Grade Getting-to-Know-You Conference

The snippets of conversation that follow illustrate the valuable information that is possible to collect from these brief encounters. I can complete conferences with grade-level and profi-cient readers quickly. It's important to meet with these students, because they crave positive feedback as much as struggling students do. I share or pose questions with some of the notes taken before I confer with students.

Here are the notes I've taken before Jerrell and I meet:

- Science and history books are hard.
- Predicts while reading.
- Reads on fourth grade level.
- Can't remember what he reads.
- Likes basketball and soccer.

Robb: I will be jotting down some things you say so I can figure out ways to help you improve. When we're done, we can read these notes together. [Jerrell nods his consent.] You really enjoy basketball and soccer. Do you play after school?

Jerrell: Yeah.

Robb: Do you play for a team?

Jerrell: I'm on a soccer team. I shoot baskets with friends.

Robb: When does your team practice?

Jerrell: Thursdays. After school. It's better than homework.

Robb: [Jerrell has given me the opportunity to move to another topic.] Is homework hard in science and history?

Jerrell: Yeah. I don't read the books. I look up vocabulary in the glossary. My sister helps me find the answers.

Robb: What makes the reading hard?

Jerrell: I can't read lots of words. It [the text] doesn't make sense. [Shrugs shoulders.] Why bother. But I like *Goosebumps*. They're cool. Almost as good as the movies.

Robb: So you like mystery and action.

Jerrell: Yeah. My friends and I trade *Goosebumps*. I'd read more if I could read those all the time.

Robb: Do you remember what happens in the *Goosebumps* books?

Jerrell: Yeah. Sometimes, I even reread a book. Then I really know it. [I make a note of this rereading strategy.]

Robb: On your strategy checklist I notice that you predict when you read. It's a terrific strategy. How does it help you?

Jerrell: In *Goosebumps* I like to guess what will happen after every chapter. It makes it [the reading] fun.

Robb: I agree. Predicting keeps me interested in a book. I'm glad you use it. You also told me that you reread *Goosebumps* books and that helps you remember the story even more.

Jerrell: Well, yeah. But only the scary parts.

Robb: Rereading is a strategy that can really help you remember, Jerrell. So you have two strategies—predicting and rereading—that can help you.

Jerrell: I guess.

Robb: Is there anything else you'd like to tell me about your reading?

Jerrell: Yeah. [pause] Can you find a history book I can read?

Robb: I can try. But it would also help if we worked on strategies for saying unfamiliar words and figuring out their meanings. Would you like to do that?

Jerrell: I guess.

Robb: Good decision. This year the whole class will be doing vocabulary study all year.

Robb's Conference Notes: After the conference, I record key points that Jerrell and I discussed. These I store in Jerrell's literacy folder (see page 94).

✦ **Not keen on doing homework.**

- **Rereads.**
- **Likes action and mystery.**
- **Good question about history book.**

Goal: Provide him with vocabulary in context strategies. Group with other students who need same strategy.

Post-Conference Notes: After reviewing my conference notes and other data I've collected, I create a plan that outlines what I hope to accomplish and store the plan in student's literacy folder.

- Strategies to Introduce: Paired reading and retelling; paired questioning; personal connections; visualization
- Strengthen predicting to include story details. Use strategy prior to reading.
- Help him find other mystery and action books—tap into what he likes.
- Would he like sports books?
- Have Jerrell read aloud in the history textbook to analyze reading.
- If time, try to offer some homework tips such as setting time limits per subject, focusing the entire time, taking a break between subjects, and doing hard subjects first.

During the first weeks of school I gather information on each child and use the data to plan mini-lessons I'll present the first few months of school. This list is flexible, for if students show me that we need to work on something else, such as synthesizing infor-

Possible Mini-Lessons for Fall 1999

- Choosing a free reading book - practice 5 finger method
- Reading — retell small chunks
- Adjust to kind of text - rate of reading
- Adjust predictions
- Vocab. in context - teach clues author's leave

10/14 - Switch to skimming - sci. teacher says students need practice - start with sci. textbook

Taking Observational Notes: Resources

Barrentine, Shelby J., ed. (1999) *Reading Assessment: Principles and Practices for Elementary Teachers* (IRA).

Goodman, Kenneth, Goodman, Yetta, and Hood, Wendy (eds). (1989) *The Whole Language Evaluation Book* (Heinemann).

Power, Brenda. (1996) *Taking Note: Improving Your Observational Note Power* (Stenhouse).

Robb, Laura. (1994) *Whole Language, Whole Learners: Creating a Literature Centered Classroom,* hardback edition (Morrow).

mation, then I switch gears and respond to their needs.

I also reserve time to explain the reasoning for grouping for reading instruction to the entire class. Here's what I say:

> During workshop, I will meet with pairs, small groups, and individuals to help you improve as readers. Throughout the year, groups and partners will change because as you gain control over a reading strategy, I will place you in a new group to work on a different strategy. This occurs because each one of you will improve at a different rate, and I want to respond to those changes so you can constantly move forward in reading.

It's comforting for students to know that reading groups are flexible and will change as their reading abilities and interests change. The goal of dynamic grouping is to constantly meet the needs of struggling, reluctant, and proficient readers based on teacher observations, brief conferences, and what students write and say.

LEARN ABOUT YOUR STUDENTS BY WATCHING THEM

All year long you'll collect assessment information about students by observing them as they read silently, work with others, complete journal entries, and confer with you. Yetta Goodman called this observation process "kid-watching" (1985) and declared that by watching students, teachers can develop a stronger theory of how each child reads and learns. Regie Routman adds a caveat (1990) when she asserts that good observation is a key element in evaluation, and a teacher's ability to observe and interpret what she sees is only as good as her theoretical knowledge base. Therefore, to be expert observers, we must be expert learners.

The teachers I coach groan when I invite them to jot down

observational notes. Planning literacy centers, strategic-reading groups, partner work, and mini-lessons, assessing students' use of strategies, selecting books for instruction, coping with behavior problems, scheduling and conducting brief conferences, completing administrative forms, and recess and bus duties can overwhelm. If you're a novice at taking observational notes, start small and reserve five to ten minutes twice a week to observe one student at a time. Once you gain comfort and confidence, do more.

Some Guidelines for Taking Observational Notes:

1. Use sticky-notes. Place the student's name, the date, and the situation at the top of the note.

2. Carry sticky-notes and a pencil all the time.

3. Tell students what you are doing so they don't feel that you are writing "bad things" about them.

4. Start by observing one student in one situation during workshop. When you're comfortable, try two, then three students. Jot down notes on each student during different learning situations.

5. Note what you see and hear when you talk to students, listen as students discuss books with each other, observe students working, and read students' written work.

6. Use shorthand as you write what you see. Don't editorialize (see margin box at right).

7. Share observations with students. Letting them know what you've observed, and discussing it with them, can help students and you negotiate productive and reasonable goals. Resist an accusatory tone. Encourage the students to solve the problem (see next page).

8. Store notes in students' literacy folders. Reread these and conference notes and continuously update your literacy plans for students.

Sample Observational Notes

**Maria—10/14/98
(Grade 7)
Independent Reading**
- fidgets—starts reading, puts book down
- gets up, looks at class library
- tries to talk to Jenna
- starts to read after about 10 minutes

**Tony—2/15/99
(Grade 6)
Book Discussion**
- forgot book
- interrupts
- said: "You took my idea."
- taps pencil on desk
- no other participation

FIVE-MINUTE OBSERVATIONAL NOTE CONFERENCE WITH TONY, GRADE 6

I met with Tony during independent reading.

Robb: How do you think book discussion went today?

Tony: I don't know. [long pause, giving Tony plenty of time to talk]

Robb: Let me read what I observed. [I read notes aloud.] Can you help me understand these behaviors?

Tony: Yeah, well, I didn't read the chapters and didn't tell the group. I did this yesterday, and I guess I didn't want them to get mad.

Robb: Who would they be mad at?

Tony: Me—and the rule that says if you don't read the stuff you read in class you can't be in the group.

Robb: I'd like to see you make up the reading and come prepared on Thursday. If you're unprepared then, I'll call home and you'll have to read the pages after school. I prefer that you solve this work issue without me calling home. What do you think?

Tony: I'll do it.

Robb: Good. Your group needs your input.

Always end conferences with students on an upbeat note. My goal is for students to leave feeling that I respect them and care about their work and progress. Even a brief meeting, when it ends on a positive note can inspire students to work hard to reach a goal.

During lunch I added this to the sticky-note dated 2/15:
Tony commits to making up reading and coming prepared Thursday. Check on this.
Then I put the sticky-note in Tony's literacy folder.

Prompts That Support Observational Notes

The prompts that follow can help you become skilled at observing your students. These are starting points—be as specific as you can in your notes. For example: *Questions show mini-lesson did not connect—silent in small-group discussion; watched closely.* Always note all behaviors you see. These prompts are suggestions that can help you become a first-rate observer. Use them to focus on what students do and do not say, how they interact, and what they do:

During/After Mini-Lessons the Student:

+ Listens to demonstration.
+ Watches chart carefully.
+ Asks questions.
+ Shares strategies and process.
+ Remains silent in follow-up discussion.
+ Questions/statements show confusion.

During Sustained Silent Reading (Independent Reading) the Student:

+ Settles into reading quickly.
+ Fidgets, moves around for a long time.
+ Frequently talks to others.
+ Concentrates on book.
+ Occasionally pauses to share a section.
+ Changes book several times.

During Student-led Book Discussions the Student:

+ Comes prepared with book, pencil, journal.
+ Reads assigned pages.
+ Listens while others speak.
+ Participates in discussion.
+ Takes notes when appropriate.
+ Values others' ideas.
+ Supports points with story.
+ Reads examples from text to prove points.
+ Shares in group decision-making.

During Short Conferences the Student:

- ✦ Talks about issues.
- ✦ Can explain confusions.
- ✦ Participates in goal-setting.
- ✦ Can apply strategies to reading.

When Strategic-Reading Group Meets the Student:

- ✦ Comes prepared with book, pencil, journal.
- ✦ Reads assigned pages.
- ✦ Shows an understanding of strategy and how it helps reading.
- ✦ Talks about how strategy works.
- ✦ Asks probing questions.
- ✦ Shares process.
- ✦ Uses text to show an understanding of strategy.
- ✦ Thinks aloud and shows monitoring and comprehension.

During Paired Reading the Student:

- ✦ Listens carefully.
- ✦ Follows text as partner reads.
- ✦ Retells sections in great detail.
- ✦ Supports partner.
- ✦ Skims, rereads to improve retellings.

When Writing in Journals the Student:

- ✦ Heads page correctly.
- ✦ Follows journal entry guidelines.
- ✦ Returns to book to collect specific details.
- ✦ Stays on task.
- ✦ Volunteers to share entry with group/class.

The Student's Journal Entries:

- ✦ Follow guidelines.
- ✦ Offer support from text.

◆ Use story details.

◆ Show understanding of character/setting/plot/theme.

◆ Make inferences from text.

While I can show you the kinds of data to collect and evaluate as you group students for instruction, I cannot give you a recipe for success. As you read students' records, interact with them, collect data from conferences and writing, and confer with last year's teachers, you will be able to identify students' needs and know where to place them. The key point here is to base your decisions on what you learn about students, and knowing that these decisions will change as students improve.

Throughout the year, watch your students as they work in pairs, groups, or alone, and then reflect on what you've observed. This will inform your teaching decisions. Think about and complete the checklist that follows. It will provide insights into your observation style. By watching the students in your classroom, you'll come to understand how they process print.

Student Observation Style Checklist

_____ I circulate around the room and rarely sit at my desk.

_____ I pause and chat briefly with each student to learn about his or her reading and thinking.

_____ I observe, for five to ten minutes each day, one or two students and jot down objective notes about what I see.

_____ I read students' written responses to literature to learn more about their recall and comprehension.

Pause and Reflect on:
How Do You Interact with Students?

As you interact with students, be a good listener, set a nurturing tone, negotiate realistic reading goals, tap into students' interests, and share your past and present reading life and attitudes toward learning. When my son, Evan, taught sixth-grade reading-writing workshop, he shared his own personal struggle to learn to read with students. "I'd tell my students that I struggled to read until high school, and watch their eyes widen," he told me. "Then I'd get specific, and tell them I reversed words and found it tough to pull out important ideas and recall details. This confession helped many because it broke down barriers and allowed them to honestly look at their deficits and strong points and know that there was hope."

What you and I say to students about homework, participation, maintaining a response journal, and the books they read, reverberates and replays in their minds for a long time—in some cases, a lifetime. Pinpoint what students do well, and tell them about it. After all, it is only possible to nudge students forward by building on these strong points.

🌿 Chapter 5

Strategy Lessons That Prepare Students to Read

"How could I understand anything about Vietnam?
I couldn't even find it on a map." —Sixth Grader

Adapt the Mini-Lesson

In Chapters 5, 6, and 7 you'll find students' comments for each mini-lesson. I've included comments from grades five through eight to help you see how students from different grades respond to the lessons. These mini-lessons are appropriate for all middle school students and introduce strategies that take several weeks for students to comprehend and learn to apply to their own work.

The first-period bell rings and 25 seventh graders chat as they file into reading-writing workshop. Of the 15 girls and 10 boys in this class, six read two years below grade level and four read three years below. It is a challenging class for Karen, for with only two years of teaching experience, she often wonders how she can meet the needs of this diverse group.

Today I'm watching Karen present a mini-lesson that will prepare students to read *Lyddie* by Katherine Paterson. Karen and the history teacher have selected this book to tie into his unit on the Industrial Revolution. They know that *Lyddie* will be too difficult for the 10 students reading below grade level. Karen plans to read aloud to this group as well as have them listen to the book on tape.

Students sit in five heterogeneous groups. Karen presents a five-minute overview of the book to pique students' interest and weave in some background about the nineteenth-century mill towns. Then she invites groups to discuss, for six or seven minutes, everything they think they know about mill towns: working conditions, who could work, how workers were treated, where they stayed. We both circulated as students talked; we asked questions to spark additional talk; we listened and jotted down notes on a clipboard.

Next, Karen asked students to stop talking and write, in their journals, everything they recalled. The discussions I heard lacked substance and details, so I wasn't surprised that many wrote, "I don't know anything," or only one or two phrases.

Karen then made an excellent decision, one based on her knowing the relationship between students' prior knowledge and their depth of comprehension, and on her observations of students. She decided that before rushing students into reading *Lyddie,* she'd show them filmstrips about the mills and read short selections about the girls who worked there. I suggested that Karen read *The Bobbin Girl,* a picture book by Emily Arnold McCully (Dial); picture books are powerful texts for providing background information quickly.

"You know," Karen told me over lunch, "I thought the reading about schema theory we did for our study group was something I'd never use. This morning it all came together in my head, and I knew what I had to do to help my students comprehend and connect to the story." How right Karen was, for theory, based in research, informs teachers' decision-making and plays a key role in their ability to select appropriate interventions.

THE IMPORTANCE OF ACTIVATING PRIOR KNOWLEDGE

While reading, readers constantly construct meaning by using past experiences and knowledge to fill in implied information. Good readers find this process so natural that they are unaware that they are filling in data that has never been mentioned in the book (Gillet and Temple, 1990). For example, in a passage about a birthday party, a young boy is sad because he attends without a present, yet the word *present* is never used. Only readers who have prior knowledge of birthday parties will identify the implied reason for the child's unhappiness.

For teachers, one of the most important tasks is to provide rich and frequent opportunities for students to access prior knowledge and *enlarge* that knowledge (Pearson et al., 1992). Taking the time to engage students in strategy lessons that prepare them to read a text can develop a strong base of prior knowledge that deepens students' comprehension of books and other texts, which in turn helps them to construct new understandings.

If you're tempted to gain time to cover more curriculum by abandoning getting-ready-to-read mini-lessons, don't give in. Researchers have shown that plunging students into a book or a study without activating, assessing, and enlarging their prior knowledge causes many students to have difficulty reading the material, which results in diminished learning (Pearson et al., 1992).

What the Research Says on Prior Knowledge

"Research in the late 1970s and early 1980s consistently revealed a strong reciprocal relationship between prior knowledge and reading comprehension. The more one already knows, the more one comprehends; and the more one comprehends, the more one learns new knowledge to enable comprehension of an even greater and broader array of topics and texts."
—Linda G. Fielding and P. David Pearson, (1994) "Reading Comprehension: What Works" *Educational Leadership,* Feb., vol. 51, no. 5

FOUR KEY
PREREADING STRATEGIES

With the four prereading strategy lessons that follow, beginning on page 119, you can teach students different ways to access what they already know about a topic and form a bridge between themselves and a book. Introduce and work on one or two strategies until students demonstrate they can use them without your support. Here are some considerations to keep in mind as you launch the lessons:

✦ **Having the class share information and personal connections is a vital part of each mini-lesson.** Through sharing, everyone has the opportunity to enlarge their prior knowledge, strengthen their personal connections, bring more information to a text, and ultimately, improve comprehension of a text.

✦ **Students need to see you activating prior knowledge—relating your life to a book's settings, or its characters' problems, decisions, and conflicts.** Think aloud as you predict, brainstorm, and question to prepare to read one of your books. Recreate a natural reading experience. For example, you pull out a paperback novel you've brought to read during a long flight. Think aloud how you recall what your friend said when she recommended it, how the setting entices you because you spent a summer in that region as a child, how you predict it will make the flight go faster because it's both a love story and a mystery, that the photo on the cover reminds you of your sister's friend—all the associations that dance through your head as you read the back cover, quotes from other writers, plot synopsis, and so on. Continue to model this process while students are practicing it. Emphasize how the strategy helps you commit to a book before you even read it, and helps you further bond to the book as you read it.

✦ **When you're introducing a genre, perhaps historical fiction or fantasy, or starting a new topic, such as the Middle Ages, determine how much students know before you invite them to read.** Listen to their discussions, collect their ideas on chart paper, or read their written responses. Like Karen, you'll be able to determine the amount of prior knowledge students have and decide whether you can move forward or need to set aside time to increase students' knowledge base.

✦ **Get students up to speed.** If they know little about a genre, then read aloud picture books and discuss the elements of that genre. If students know little about a topic, build their background knowledge by viewing a filmstrip together, studying pictures in books and magazines.

✦ **Have students return to their initial ideas later.** The key to making these prereading strategies meaningful is to have students return to the original chart during and after the study. Teachers who don't encourage students to return to their early thinking reinforce students' view that activating prior knowledge is more busywork. When students revisit predictions to confirm and/or adjust them, add new understandings to their brainstorming or categories, and adjust early ideas, they get the powerful message that activating prior knowledge is useful and important, and enables students to observe how much they have learned.

STRATEGY LESSON
Predict and Support

ADAPT
for grades
5 and up

Introduction

Predicting involves readers in books because they feel compelled to read on and confirm their hunches. Prediction especially engages readers with fiction and develops a purpose for reading.

In fact, making predictions is a natural part of our lives. We predict which horse or runner will win a race or which ice skater will become the next champion. And we use snippets of information we've gathered from the newspaper, magazines, television, and radio to made these predictions.

When my children were teenagers, my husband and I delighted in predicting, over dinner, how many telephone calls they'd receive that night. Our prior experiences with incoming phone calls enabled us

In Chapters 5, 6, and 7 I've included suggestions for each mini-lesson that will enable you to plan and implement successful demonstrations. Here's the format for 15- to 25-minute lessons:

✦ Strategy Name
✦ Introduction to the Strategy
✦ Purpose
✦ Materials
✦ Guidelines
✦ Suggestions for Guided Practice

ARE THERE DEGREES OF PREDICTION?

While all proficient readers make predictions, some readers seem to predict more explicitly than others—it's a bigger part of their reading experience. Their minds actively guess whether two characters will remain in love, or whether one will win a contest, or what the author intends for the novel's outcome. Like dogged detectives, they spend time—even if it's mere seconds in their reading process—trying to figure out the mystery of plot. Another reader may allow himself to be swept up in the plot—"get lost in the book"—and not make any conscious predictions, though unconsciously premonitions may flicker through his head as he reads.

Whether prediction is a big or small part of your own reading process, you'll want to model the strategy so that it's a deliberate act; students will internalize it to suit their reading style.

to predict accurately. On long trips in the car, my husband spends a good part of the drive predicting our arrival time, making adjustments for an extra bathroom or food stop. Help students see that predicting is part of their lives by stimulating a discussion of prediction and their experiences as well as what information they use to make these predictions.

During the process of predicting, a reader compares what he already learned from a completed book to what he thinks he is going to read. At the same time readers continuously connect their prior knowledge to the text. Gillet and Temple (1990) point out that predictions are the connecting links between prior knowledge and new information in the book. It's the interaction of these processes that coalesce—much like sparks firing before the bright flame ignites—and give readers new understandings from the text.

Materials
picture books, chapter books, or a short story; chart paper; marker pens

On The First Day, Here's What I Do
1. Prepare the chart: write "Predictions" on the left-hand side and "Support" on the right-hand side.

Teaching Reading in Middle School

2. Think aloud and show students why it's important to predict and support before reading. Here is what I might say:

> When I read, I make predictions or guesses about what I think will happen or what a character might do. Making predictions keeps me interested in the story. I'm always trying to figure out what the author will do. In the beginning, it's hard to predict because I don't have many clues. Close to the end, I'm better at figuring out what will happen. By then I have many examples from the story. I never worry if I'm off base or off target with my predictions. I can always adjust them as I continue reading. Sometimes I have to reread parts or skim pages to find evidence to support my predictions. Rereading helps me get all the details.

3. I invite fifth graders to study the front and back covers and the title of *The Story of Ruby Bridges* by Robert Coles before thinking aloud.

4. I read the first two pages of this picture book (or you can use a chapter book) and explain how I predict and support. I want them to see how carefully I look at the cover and how much detail I include as support. For *The Story of Ruby Bridges*, I say: *The girl on the cover is African American—the only African American person shown. In the background are angry, shouting people. A banner says, "Keep this a WHITE School." On the back cover, Ruby is alone in school. I predict that this book is about integrating white schools in the South, because the story says they live in New Orleans. It also says they're religious. Maybe that's why Ruby can do such a tough thing alone.*

5. I ask students to comment and raise questions. One fifth grader observed, "You made predictions using all the information you read." Another said, "You had very specific details."

6. Often students will beg to hear the rest of the story and you can continue reading, pausing two or three times to ask for predictions and support from the text.

A Whole-Group Follow-up Guided Practice

1. I involve students in the predict-and-support strategy with a picture book or novel. I use *The Well* by Mildred Taylor (Dial) and read pages 9 and 10 aloud.

2. I tell students that I'll take two different predictions. (When you're clear about guidelines, students accept that everyone won't have a turn.)

3. Here's a fifth grader's prediction: "Last year, my teacher read *Roll of Thunder, Hear My Cry* aloud. It's by Mildred Taylor and about the same Logan family, so there's bound to be trouble. I predict there'll be big trouble because in the part you read, the white Simmses need the black Logans' well water. The title tells me that the story has to be about the well. The

Use insights like Michael's, page 123, as the basis for subsequent mini-lessons and discussions that explore an idea further. Michael's comment about fairy tales and folktales can spur a series of lessons on genres and story structures. Continually looking at how authors organize their stories aids comprehension and positively influences students' writing.

cover shows two whites looking angry and hollering at the Logan boys—maybe they're saying what you read—that the Simmses were jealous the Logans had the well and they had to go to blacks for water."

4. I repeat this activity with other picture books, until most students understand the strategy.

Guided Practice with a Partner

1. Organize students into pairs.
2. Have each pair select a picture book, study the title and cover, and read the first two pages. If students use chapter books, have them read the first two pages of the first chapter if it's long or an entire first short chapter.
3. Ask partners to take turns predicting and supporting.
4. During the final moments of guided practice, have several students share their predictions and support, so the class can observe how others used the strategy.
5. Repeat this experience on subsequent days until students show they can use specific details for support.

Predict with a Partner Before Free-Choice Reading

Encourage students to use the predict-and-support strategy before reading their free-choice, independent-reading books. Students can share their predictions and support with a partner before reading. Partners can help one another make sure their support is specific. An added benefit: Students become familiar with titles classmates are reading.

Vary this activity by occasionally asking students to first head a journal page with the date, title, and author. Then, in addition to students supporting their predictions with the title, front cover, and first pages of the text, encourage them to inform their predictions with prior knowledge of literary genres and connections to other books. Model this for kids. For example, when I predict that in Hans Christian Andersen's "The Traveling Companion," good will overcome evil because that happens in other fairy tales, Michael, a sixth grader, adds, "And the main character will have tasks to do because that happens in every fairy and folk tale I've read."

STRATEGY LESSON
Brainstorm and Categorize

ADAPT
for grades
5 and up

Introduction

A strategy that works well with fiction and nonfiction, brainstorming is a free flow of thoughts about a topic [*survival*], a key word [*revolution*], or a concept [*What is justice?*]. When categorizing, students organize brainstormed items into general headings or categories which Estes and Vaughan (1986) call *concepts*. Categorizing allows students to see their prior knowledge in an

---

TIPS FOR PAIRING STUDENTS

When pairing students, I avoid bringing together kids with great differences in reading abilities. I'll pair two proficient readers, a proficient with a grade-level reader, a reluctant but good reader with a grade-level or proficient reader. I support my weakest readers as they select independent-reading books from our classroom or school library. Usually I'm helping five to ten students in a class of 26. Students who read

below level and can benefit from helping one another, I organize into pairs.

It's frustrating for proficient readers and struggling readers to work together as partners. The self-esteem and confidence of the struggling reader can plummet if he's paired with an outstanding reader who is impatient to move forward quickly.

What Seventh Graders Know About Bats

upside down

caves

nocturnal

blood suckers

guano

fertilizer

eat insects

vampire bat

sonar

Bat Man

Transylvania

brown bat

attack humans

mammals

carry young

Dracula

furry

wings

beady eyes

organized framework and then use the framework to add new understandings after they've completed reading their books.

I tell students that my weekly shopping list is an example of brainstorming. And when my husband accompanies me, I categorize the list into meat, fish, dairy, canned goods, and cookies and crackers, giving him sections to complete. The categorizing prevents him from running back and forth looking for items that were listed randomly.

In combination, brainstorming and categorizing before reading gives students content, ideas, and vocabulary to look for while they read, which fosters comprehension and enhances motivation.

While reading, students categorize information they've learned about characters, settings, and conflicts. Eighth grader Jake explained to his group that while reading *Beowulf* (retold by Robert Nye), it helped him categorize characters who were like Beowulf and those who were foils or the opposite. Said Jake, "Organizing this gave me a chance to visualize the forces of good and evil and to understand why the story of Sigemund and Fitela is there."

Materials

chart paper; marker pens; a topic or theme [such as bats, the Holocaust, peer pressure, decimals, or friendship]

Guidelines

1. Organize students into groups of four or five.
2. Have each student head the journal with name, date, and topic.
3. Give students four or five minutes to talk about the topic. I have seventh graders discuss what they think they know about bats.
4. Ask students to take two or three minutes to jot down everything they recalled and any new ideas that have popped into their minds. Explain that they can write in phrases.
5. Collect, on chart paper, all of the students' ideas. (See box at left for seventh-grade list.)

6. Model how you reread ideas to create categories. I suggest a category to students: "Physical Appearance."

7. Write "Physical Appearance" on the blackboard and place *furry, wings,* and *beady eyes* under the heading.

8. Invite groups to create headings and place these in their journals. Ask groups to help one another organize data under headings.

9. Point out that some items will fall under more than one heading. That's acceptable, as long as students can defend their decisions.

10. Collect one heading and data from each group. Print on chart paper.
    Seventh graders created these headings: *Legends, Uses, Habitat, Behavior.*

Suggestions for Guided Practice

1. Next time students prepare to study a topic such as fractions, the Industrial Revolution, or plant and animal cells, have pairs or groups of students work together to establish categories and organize brainstormed ideas under the headings.

2. When you work with strategic-reading groups, invite students to categorize characters by positive or negative personality traits or to categorize the symbols of good and evil in a book.

Refining Information and Ideas

During and after our study of bats, I invited students to return to their brainstorming lists and categories to remove inaccurate information and add new data. This process benefits learners on a few levels: it can give them an appreciation of how much they knew at the outset; it motivates them by helping them to see how far they've come in clarifying initial ideas; it reinforces the notion that facts and ideas are not fixed, that information and hunches about a topic can be reordered, reconsidered, restated to reflect new information gathered and understandings reached. The act of adjusting and adding encourages recall and thinking. It also helps struggling readers by modeling how learners sort and select data as they refine their knowledge.

It is not necessary to categorize all brainstormed information. I love to categorize brainstorming for in-depth studies of topics and to show students how it helps them organize information they've read.

KEEPING A LITERATURE-RESPONSE JOURNAL

Literature-response journals are the story of students' thinking. In them, students record and revisit predictions and reflect, test, and change their first ideas as they read and discuss a book.

I view journal entries as first-draft writing where students can explore new ideas and use prior knowledge and the information in a book to construct new understandings about people, friendships, family relationships, or an historical period (Robb, 1994). Therefore, I look for ideas and don't focus on spelling and punctuation. The student who writes little or nothing sends just as powerful a message as the child who floods a journal with notes and writing. Privately, I show a student her journal and ask, "Can you tell me why you didn't respond?" Here are some answers students have given—answers that provide insights into the kind of support each one needs:

✦ You can't read my writing.

✦ My spelling's so bad.

✦ I don't know how to predict.

✦ I don't understand the stuff.

✦ No one ever reads this stuff anyway.

In a small notebook, I keep a log of the journal entries I ask students to complete. During the year, I ask them to return to a specific entry and compare it with the one we've just completed, or I'll have them reread an entry written in October and explain how it connects to a poem we've read in January. So students can readily locate material or return to and enlarge an entry, I have them head each entry with name, date, and a title. The title might be a topic or the title of a book, poem, or article. I tell students that placing their name on each page helps me when I'm reading journals because I don't have to constantly flip to the cover to see the writer's name.

CLUSTERING: A VARIATION OF BRAINSTORMING

Like brainstorming, clustering is a free-association activity, during which you branch out from a central word or phrase that represents a topic or concept to be studied. Gabriele Rico (1983) developed this strategy for prewriting, but it works well for prereading fiction and nonfiction.

Students write a word or phrase in the center of a page and circle the word. Then they write and circle their ideas so that they radiate outward from the central word, clustering connected ideas.

After several minutes, the teacher collects students' ideas and creates a collaborative cluster on chart paper. In the process, the teacher discusses the clustering ideas and vocabulary, and can clarify them for students. After reading, foster the connection of prior knowledge to new learning by having students review their collaborative cluster, adjust ideas, and add new information.

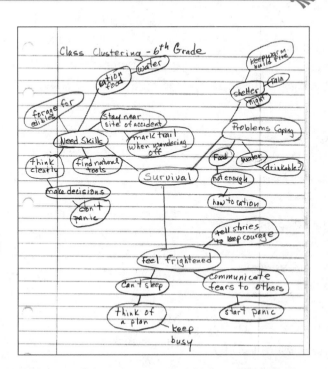

STRATEGY LESSON
Pose Questions

ADAPT
for grades
5 and up

Introduction

I tell my students that raising questions occurs all day long as well as prior to and while reading a book, newspaper, or magazine. When students don't quite get my directions, they ask a question or if a word in a text puzzles a student, she'll ask, "What does *reincarnate* mean?"

Sample Student Questions

The questions that follow were posed by guided groups as they read and compared Gary Paulsen's *Hatchet* and *The River* (Dell Yearling), James Marshall's *Walkabout* (Sundance), and Will Hobbs's *Down River* (Bantam Books).

+ Why do some people survive?

+ How are survivors changed?

+ Are there survival skills? What are they?

+ Does a will to live play a part in surviving?

+ How do circumstances affect survival?

+ Is being alone more dangerous than having someone along?

+ What are some key suggestions for survival in any situation?

+ What do people think and feel when they are in a life-death situation?

+ Does age affect people's ability to survive?

If I'm following a stock in the newspaper, I might wonder when the best time to purchase this stock might be. Information in the newspaper might not be adequate, so I'll consult with my stockbroker or a friend whose hobby is investing in the market. All books raise questions in readers' minds. Many questions raised before and during the reading will be answered by the text. However, reading often raises questions that the text doesn't answer, sending readers to the library or to an expert in search of additional information.

The questions that students pose before reading provide specific purposes for reading and can engage students with a text. Students easily generate questions after they've brainstormed or clustered what they know about a topic or a concept or listened to part of a story.

Like predicting, posing questions can deeply involve students in their reading as they link prior and new knowledge to search for answers.

Materials

a topic such as survival or space; students' journals; chart paper; marker pens

Guidelines

1. Organize students into small groups.

2. Have students head their journals with name, date, and topic. Sixth graders write "Survival."

3. Ask groups to generate questions and record them in their journals. Allow 10 to 12 minutes for this activity. For content topics such as space or the American Revolution, have students browse through library books or textbooks, reading pictures, captions, graphs, charts, boldface headings, and words. Set aside 15 to 20 minutes for browsing.

4. Collect questions from groups and write them on chart paper. (See margin for questions seventh graders posed about survival.)

5. Use these questions for group discussions while students read

and after they complete their book. Seventh graders pose story-specific questions as they read and continue adding these to their first list (see box below).

Suggestions for Guided Practice

1. Have pairs generate questions prior to reading, using fiction and nonfiction picture books and magazine articles.

2. Have the whole class work in pairs and write open-ended discussion questions for a story, book, or poem you are reading aloud or have completed. An open-ended question has more than one valid answer (see box below).

3. Have partners who are reading the same book create discussion questions.

4. Enlist the support of the science and history teachers. Ask these

---

WRITING STORY-SPECIFIC AND OPEN-ENDED QUESTIONS

To write story-specific questions, students must have thorough knowledge of the text. Help students understand that there are two kinds of questions: a factual question that has only one answer (How many sisters did Jesse Aarons have? from *Bridge to Terabithia* by Katherine Paterson), and an open-ended, interpretive question that has many possible answers (Why does Jesse bring Maybelle to Terabithia?).

Teach students to pose open-ended questions by asking themselves: Can I respond to this question with more than one answer? Next, set a standard for valid interpretations of the questions by asking for two or three pieces of evidence from the text as support. Research shows that students who are taught to generate questions after reading outperform those who receive no training (Pearson et al., 1992).

Verbs That Lead to Open-Ended Questions

Make students aware of verbs that are often used to introduce interpretive questions. Start small, and invite them to use three or four verbs. Slowly introduce others, allowing time for practice. Always permit students to use other verbs, as long as their questions meet the standard of having more than one answer.

compare	design
contrast	classify
evaluate	examine
connect	analyze
show	relate
ask why	

colleagues to let students compose chapter review and discussion questions.

5. Whether students are working as a whole class, in strategic reading groups, or in pairs, come together as a class to share.

Standardized Test Link: Preview Questions

Have students read the questions they must answer *before* reading the passage on a comprehension test. Beginning with the questions has two benefits: 1) Students' minds begin to search for past experiences that might connect them to the text; 2) Knowing the questions enables students to read for the important purpose of searching for places in the text that answer the questions.

STRATEGY LESSON
Fast-Write

ADAPT for grades 5 and up

Introduction

Many middle school students I teach enjoy activating prior knowledge with a fast-write because it seems safer than verbally generating ideas in front of peers. Fast-writes, which work well as "cognitive warm-ups" for reading fiction, nonfiction, and literary genres, become springboards for discussions, offering an opportunity to expand prior knowledge and clarify information.

Materials

a topic such as *journeys* or *insects*, or a genre such as *biography* or *science fiction;* chart paper; marker pen; students' journals

Guidelines

1. Explain how you fast-write. I tell students that I write about a topic for a few minutes. I don't stop writing, even if I'm stuck and no ideas come. I write, "I'm stuck," or "Nothing to write," or I rewrite the last word over and over until a new thought surfaces.

2. Complete a fast-write on chart paper so students can observe the process. Model how you "get stuck" and rewrite a phrase until a new idea springs into your mind.

3. Encourage students to ask questions.

Suggestions for Guided Practice

1. Invite students to complete a fast-write.

2. Have students read their fast-writes to group members or invite several students to volunteer to share theirs with the class.

3. Continue practicing until students demonstrate they can use fast-writes.

STRATEGY IN ACTION
Eighth Graders Use Fast-Writes

Eighth graders are reading *Ulysses,* retold by Bernard Elvsin, (Bantam) as part of a 12-week study of myths and legends. One of my primary goals is to have students explore Ulysses's long and adventurous journey to Ithaca, his home-land, as an inner journey of self-awareness as well as an outward adventure. To lay the foundation for this goal, I ask students to think about the term *journey* and view it as an inward and outward experience. Then, I invite each student to fast-write for eight minutes. The fast-writes that follow illustrate the repetition of a word or phrase that keeps students focused on the task and ideas flowing.

> English
>
> Phoebe   March 1, 1999
>
> A journey is a chance to discover new things about yourself. You have a chance to reflect on past relationships, past actions, and words you've said. Journeys can be be be be a time for self-reflecting, soul searching. They can also be a time to plan for the future. One on a journey can acquire new skills, and discover new ideas. After after after a journey the traveler goes home a changed person, with new ideas and skills, and a new sense of how to approach relationships after learning from past experiences.

> Reilly   Odyssey
>
> They can teach you what your strengths and weaknesses are. How far you would go to struggle for your life- they can take you to your limits and beyond. They can give you a better outlook on life-make you appreciate the slightest grain of dirt, land, or water. They make you feel invincible, nothing can stop you from reaching your journey's end. If you give up, then you have not learned anything. Think... Think... Think... You smile in the face of danger, then beat it. You will fight for anything you believe in, with all of your heart.

Fast-writes quickly reclaim students' memories, feelings, and experiences.

Pause and Reflect on:
Preparing Students to Read

Review the amount of time you reserve for preparing students to get-ready-to-read. With increased prior knowledge about a topic, students will better comprehend your modeling and explanations of how to apply strategies to their reading (Pearson et al., 1992).

When students brainstorm and exchange ideas before reading a book or studying a topic, they can better comprehend difficult texts and construct new understandings by linking what they already know to the information in the book. In addition, preparing students to read develops a curiosity about the book or topic and can motivate them to learn.

🍃 Chapter 6

Modeling
During-Reading Strategies

"Independent reading is fun when you can share favorite parts."
—Seventh Grader

Carlos, a sixth grader, met me in my office. It was October and our third meeting. During the first two, Carlos and I chatted, for my goal was to learn about his interests and feelings about school. Basketball was Carlos's passion. He played hoops after school with his buddies. For Christmas he wanted a basketball hoop attached to the garage, so he could play with neighbors in his driveway. Now he was ready to talk about school. "In second grade I started having trouble with reading," he confided. "Nothing made sense. I couldn't remember much. My grades got worse every year. This year I'll probably fail." Carlos spoke these words with indifference.

Carlos's teacher had expressed concern about his reading. "He reads words," she told me, "but his retellings are sketchy even though his reading group reads at Carlos's independent level. He seems bored and uninterested." The reading inventory given at the end of fifth grade revealed that, instructionally, Carlos was reading two years below grade level; his independent level was mid-third grade.

During that third meeting, I asked Carlos to read. I also invited him to try to tell me what was going on in his mind. What I discovered was that Carlos's mind wandered off to thoughts about basketball, a science quiz that he wasn't prepared for, a girl he met on the bus. He pronounced the words, but he was not constructing meaning. Several meetings later, I also discovered that Carlos could decode any word, and he even named several strategies his teachers had talked about: questioning, predicting, rereading. However, Carlos was unable to tell me how he might figure out the meaning of unfamiliar words, summarize sections in his own words, and maintain his interest in a book.

Older struggling readers, like Carlos, are often not aware that they lack strategies to comprehend texts or are the victims of reading interference such as letting one's mind wander (Garner, 1992). Many know the names of strategies and can even define them. However, a huge gulf exists between *knowing about* something and *using it*. *Using a strategy* means that readers can independently adapt and apply a strategy to various materials and reading purposes because they have practiced thinking about how they apply strategies to comprehend texts. To bridge this gulf, students need to practice during workshop when you can respond to queries and guide students. Insufficient practice can prevent students from reaching a point where they can access a strategy and apply it to their reading.

METACOGNITION: THINKING ABOUT IN-THE-HEAD READING STRATEGIES

Every time you and I think about rereading a confusing passage, or which diagrams to revisit to clarify our understanding of a topic, we are using metacognition. As we think about our reading process, we are searching for strategies to solve problems in our comprehension.

Good readers use metacognition to self-monitor their reading. Metacognition enables good readers to identify what they understand and what confuses them. Once readers pinpoint a confusing word, they think about which strategies to employ to figure out the word.

While students read, they self-monitor and try to make sense of the text. Researchers use two words, *clunk* and *click*, to describe readers' metacognitive process. When the answer is "no" to the question, "Do I understand this?" readers experience a *clunk* that informs them there's a need for strategic action. Understanding is often described as the *click of comprehension,* telling readers that it's okay to continue (Estes and Vaughan, 1986; Garner, 1992).

All readers, whether proficient or struggling, young or mature, experience clunks as they bump into reading stumbling blocks such as figuring out how to pronounce a word or understanding what a new word means. Fix-it strategies to use during reading should be easy and quick to apply so the reader does not disconnect from the text.

How to Encourage Self-Monitoring

Having time to practice strategies, having the vocabulary to think metacognitively, and modeling by teachers and peers all contribute to developing strong, self-monitoring readers.

Time: Developing metacognition, or the ability to self-monitor the clicks and clunks that occur during reading, takes a long time. The process starts with beginning readers (Fountas and Pinnell, 1996) and should continue until students demonstrate that they can self-monitor and access fix-it strategies (see pages 137–151). At every grade level, students should study and practice metacognitive strategies to develop more expertise. It's important for teachers to recognize that most students won't learn to self-monitor in one year. This is a slow process in which readers stockpile their experiences and observations of others as they learn to think about which strategy will help them solve a particular problem.

Vocabulary: In order for students to think, talk, and write about their reading process, they need the words that describe this process. I use and explain terms such as *metacognition,* *self-monitoring,* and *in-the-head strategies.* By naming each strategy, students can engage in meaningful conversation about their process with themselves, peers, and me.

Modeling: When adapting and presenting the four mini-lessons in this chapter, make sure you tell students that when you read, you use these same strategies. After you demonstrate and students are practicing a strategy with their books, bring in examples from material you're reading and show how you cope with the problems that follow.

1. **"Tough" word:** Select a word you didn't understand from your free-reading book, a magazine article, or a text you're using in a graduate class. Write the word and passage on the chalkboard or chart paper and think aloud, explaining how you figured out its meaning.

2. **Confusing passage:** Print, on chart paper or the chalkboard, a passage that befuddled you. Think aloud, showing students how you were able to recognize that the selection was confusing. Then, carefully explain what you did to comprehend the passage: reread it, study a diagram, reread several paragraphs that came before this passage, connect the material to another book or experience.

3. **Pause to Recall and Reflect While Reading:** Tell students that you stop to monitor how much you recall after reading several pages or a chapter. Explain how stopping for a short time enables you to savor a terrific or challenging part and retell, to yourself, what has happened. Think aloud and explain that pausing helps you know whether or not you are retaining information. And that if you are, then you continue to read. If not, you reread, slowly.

4. **Questions the Book Doesn't Answer:** Bring in a book or article that raised many questions in your mind. Explain that posing questions kept you interested in the book, gave you a purpose for reading on—to discover answers. Also point out that there were questions the book didn't answer. Share some and explain how you went about searching for answers. I am careful to tell students that I don't always have time to look for answers. What I want them to understand is that they will probably have more questions than a book or article can ever answer. Such questioning is a byproduct of a reader's curiosity and use of prior knowledge to understand new information.

Set aside time for students to share how they self-monitor and know when to employ strategies. This debriefing process is an important element of self-awareness (see pages 255-259).

STRATEGY LESSON
Using Context Clues to Figure Out Tough Words

ADAPT
for grades
5 and up

Introduction

Developing expertise with this strategy leads to independence in reading and improved comprehension, for students learn to explore the clues authors embed in texts that enable them to clarify the meaning of new words and phrases. Show students how to discover a word's meaning by exploring clues in the sentence, in sentences that come before or after the unknown word, and in illustrations, diagrams, photographs, and charts.

Materials

overhead transparency and projector or chart paper; sample sentences from a textbook, fiction, or nonfiction

Guidelines

1. On the transparency or chart paper, print three or four difficult sentences and/or passages that you've taken from students' reading. (See sample sentence at right.)

2. Uncover samples one at a time. I read the selection from Seymour Simon's *The Brain.* First, I read the sentence with the word *dominant.* Then, I back up and read the sentence that came before the one I just read.

3. Think aloud, showing students how you use the clues to determine a word's meaning. Here's what I told students for the passage from *The Brain:*
   "I couldn't find the meaning of dominant *from the sentence, so I reversed and read the sentence starting with* If. *In that sentence it uses similar examples, but with the right hand. It explains that with right-handed people, the left hemisphere of the brain is in control. So* dominant *must mean in control for the right hemisphere."*

Sample Sentence

If you usually kick with your right foot and point with your right hand, then your left hemisphere is in control. But if you usually use your left foot and left hand, your right hemisphere is **dominant.** (unpaged)

—from *The Brain: Our Nervous System,* by Seymour Simon (Morrow)

4. Continue the process with the second sample.

5. Have students study the third sample. In their journals, students can jot down the context clues they used.

6. Call for volunteers to share the clues they uncovered.

Suggestions for Guided Practice

1. Repeat the demonstration several times during a couple of guided practice sessions with the entire class.

2. Have partners work together, using their independent-reading books, and help one another use context clues to figure out unfamiliar words.

3. Work one-on-one with students who need additional practice using their instructional and independent-reading books.

4. Invite students who have internalized the strategy to work independently.

Robb's Examples for Sixth-Grade Mini-Lesson

Following are three excerpts from readings that I use to model how context clues can help readers clarify a word's meaning.

I put the excerpts on an overhead transparency and read the first example to the entire class. Next, I think aloud, explaining how I used clues to figure out a word's meaning. Here is how I approached number 1:

"You watch." He grips the bars hard, and his eyes drill into me. "You watch for a chance to strike against the murdering, thieving lobsterbacks. Be **vigilant**, and your chance will come."

—*The Keeping Room* by Anna Myers, page 76 (Walker)

My think aloud: *The sentence with* vigilant *doesn't give me good clues, so I better reread the sentences that came before. [I reread these aloud.] Two* *times the author repeats the phrase* you watch *and he says I should watch for the chance to strike against the lobsterback. And* chance *is repeated in the sentence with* vigilant. *So* vigilant *must mean to watch very carefully—to be alert for the right moment.*

2 Snow melted into mud. The white mountain next to the driveway **dwindled** to a hill.

—*Blue Sky, Butterfly* by Jean Van Leeuwen, page 48 (Puffin)

3 The seafood is different from what we ate at home. Captain Sibsey **loathes** the lobsters and says, "Such crawly things are unfit for human **consumption**."

—*Stranded at Plimouth Plantation, 1626* by Gary Bowen, page 8 (HarperCollins)

Each time I think aloud to show how I use context clues, I ask students to comment and raise questions. Then I pair students and ask them to use clues to figure out the meanings of tough words. Students share their thinking, which provides everyone with many opportunities to observe the process. Students' sharing also helps me decide when to move them to independent practice.

When Context Clues Aren't Enough

Using context clues to figure out unfamiliar words is a key vocabulary-building strategy students should practice, internalize, and apply (Ryder and Graves, 1998; Vacca and Vacca, 2000; Graves and Graves, 2000). Students who make use of context clues are able to quickly and efficiently determine the meaning of a tough word; instead of interrupting meaning-making, their reading continues smoothly, without pausing to use the dictionary or to ask a peer or an adult.

However, there will be times when readers will confront passages where there are few to no context clues, making discovering words' meanings a frustrating task. Moreover, for struggling readers, even when context clues are strong, using them is a difficult and slow process because the strategy is unpracticed and not part of their problem-solving repertoire. These students need a great deal of scaffolding and practice before they can independently access and successfully apply a reading strategy. Scaffolding, a framework of support that teachers offer students before, during, and after reading, supports students in their quest to comprehend deeply (Graves and Graves, 1994). As students demonstrate that they understand and can apply a strategy, the teacher gradually diminishes the amount of scaffolding.

If using context clues is not working for some students, then try scaffolding their reading with these word-building strategies:

Strategy 1
Preteach Vocabulary: Prepare Students for the Tough Words Before They Encounter Them.

1. Present a sentence that has an unfamiliar word but is rich in context clues. Make sure your sentence has a similar meaning to the way the word is used in the text.

2. Create a collaborative word web by inviting students to tell you what they know about the word (Vacca and Vacca, 2000). Record students' ideas on large chart paper. Return to the word web after students have read the material and invite them to add any new understandings they gained from reading and discussing.

Strategy 2
Strengthen Students' Word Knowledge.

1. Teach students the meanings of prefixes, suffixes, and roots. In a think-aloud, show how you use your knowledge of word parts to figure out the meaning of a tough word. For *incredible* I say:

    The prefix *in-* means *not, in,* or *into;* the root *cred* means *to believe.* In this case
    I think the prefix means *not* and *incredible* means *not believable.* After I stop
    reading, I can check the dictionary to verify my hunch.

2. Invite students to jot down tough words on a sticky-notes or in their journal, noting the title of the book and the page of the word that stumped them. In pairs or groups, have students use the dictionary. To ensure that students search for the dictionary meaning that matches the word's meaning in the text, showcase your process. Here's what I say for a new word in *The Way of the Earth: Native America and the Environment* by John Bierhorst, Morrow, 1994:

    Page and Sentence: *But the reticent Taos were never required to give a public explanation* (page 103).
    I'll read all the definitions and then try to figure out which one fits the sentence. I don't think its silent because I don't think the author means that the

Taos people are silent. Maybe it means reserved or not very communicative. Either one of those could work in the sentence.

Work with pairs and think aloud several times or until you feel they can think aloud for one another.

Teachers often ask: Why can't I just let students look up words in the dictionary? It's difficult for students to use a dictionary to determine the meaning of an unfamiliar word; they tend to focus on the shortest or the first meaning. By modeling, show students how you are using clues in the sentence along with the dictionary definitions. Your modeling and thinking aloud provides students with insights into how you access strategies to determine the meaning of tough words (Baumann, Jones, Seifert-Kessell, 1993).

STRATEGY IN ACTION
Struggling Sixth-Grade Readers Practice Using Context Clues

Book: *Hiroshima, A Novella* by Laurence Yep (Scholastic)

In a guided-practice session, three sixth graders and I sit at a table and practice using context clues to figure out words that stump them. All three have developed the habit of reading on—even if they don't comprehend a passage—or taking wild guesses when confronted with an unfamiliar word. Finishing the task is their goal—having them understand what they've read and pinpoint confusing parts is my goal.

Before the three students joined me at the table, I had asked them to read pages 4 to 13 of *Hiroshima*, and write on sticky-notes words they couldn't figure out on their own: *shrine* on page 5; *scans* on page 6; *interrupted* on page 9; *devastated* on page 11. The following is an excerpt that reveals the careful guidance and affirmation these students require.

Robb: Who would like to point out a tough word?

Tony: I had trouble with one on page 11. I figured out how to say *devastated* because it has *stated* in it. I looked for a word I knew.

Robb: I like the way you told us what you did and the strategy that you used.

Tony: But I don't know what it means.

Jenna: Read the sentence.

Robb: Good suggestion. Tony might find clues there.

Tony: [reads] "American planes have dropped bombs and started fires that have devastated large areas." I know fires burn stuff, but I'm not sure of *devastated*.

Robb: Read the sentence that came before and tell me what you learn from it.

Tony: That their [Japanese] buildings are made of wood and paper.

Delia: What would happen to the buildings if a bomb hit?

Tony: They'd catch on fire and burn to the ground real fast.

Robb: Can you link what you've just said to *devastated?*

Tony: Does it mean that the buildings were all burned and there was nothing left?

Robb: I liked the way you connected what you know about fire and wood and paper to thinking through the meaning. Can anyone find a synonym or similar word for *devastated* that we could substitute in the sentence?

Tony: [excited] I think I got it. Is it *destroyed?*

Delia: Put it in the sentence and see if it makes sense.

As you practice with students, ask questions that lead them to clues in the book, help them connect the clues to what they already know about the word, and then invite them to explain the word's meaning. To provide additional reinforcement, ask students to reread a challenging chapter so they meet the words again and have the opportunity to experience the benefits of their new word knowledge.

After several sessions with you, invite students to work in pairs, so they can help one another; students use passages you've selected. Once pairs are comfortable with the strategy, move students to practice it with their independent reading books. You can monitor students' successful strategy use by questioning them about a strategy during a conference, and by inviting them to debrief and self-evaluate (see Chapter 11).

Teaching Reading in Middle School

STRATEGY LESSON
Read/Pause/Retell/Read On or Reread

ADAPT
for grades
5 and up

Introduction

During a conference, an eighth grader told me, "I've read this chapter, and I don't remember one thing that's in it." All of us have had similar experiences with a page or two from a difficult text. Good readers, however, self-monitor as they read, pausing many times to restate information in their own words and evaluate whether they comprehend and remember. This is an important strategy to practice with middle school students who have to recall details from challenging textbooks in science and social studies. If a passage confuses, students can access a fix-it strategy and reread, skim, etc.

When students choose books they can and want to read, they can connect to the story.

Materials

a transparency and overhead projector; a difficult passage from a textbook, fiction, or nonfiction

Guidelines

1. Print the passage on the blank transparency and place on the overhead projector. Here's the passage I share from Seymour Simon's *Comets, Meteors, and Asteroids* (Morrow):

   There are hundreds of comets, but we cannot usually see them. That's because a comet in the outer regions of the Solar System is only a few miles wide and too small to be seen from distant Earth. Far out in space, a comet looks like a large, dirty snowball. It has an icy core, or nucleus, covered by a layer of black dust. The nucleus is mainly water and gases, all frozen and mixed together with bits of rock and metal.

2. Read the passage to students. Think aloud, expressing your feelings about this passage. I tell students: "There was a lot of information in this section."

Standardized Test Link: Rereading

Rereading is an effective strategy for comprehending a complex, information-loaded and/or confusing passage. On the reading comprehension section of standardized tests, students will be asked to read about unfamiliar topics. Rereading two or even three times is a worthwhile investment, for it can often unlock the meaning and free students to answer questions well.

3. Recap everything you recall from the first reading without looking at the passage. Here's my recap:

> *There are lots of comets. They are too small to see from Earth. A comet is like a dirty snowball. Black dust is around the frozen nucleus.*

Now I compare what I've said with the passage in the book, telling students: *I could only remember four details and I missed many important facts. I better reread this and see if I recall more.*

4. Reread the passage to students out loud, then silently.

5. Retell again, without looking at the text:

> *There are hundreds of comets, but we can't see these from Earth. Comets are only a few miles wide and are found in the outer regions of the Solar System. A comet is like a dirty snowball. Black dust is around the frozen nucleus that is made of water and gases mixed with bits of rocks.*

Think aloud and point out how much more you remembered by rereading. Emphasize that by rereading an information-packed or difficult-to-comprehend passage, it's possible to recall many details and gain a deeper understanding of the text.

6. Tell students that sometimes you have to reread a tough passage three times before you can recall many details.

7. Explain that if you can recall the key information, then simply continue to read.

Suggestions for Guided Practice

1. Invite pairs of students to practice this strategy for eight to ten minutes after your demonstration. Use students' free-choice reading book or a science or social studies textbook.

2. Continue having pairs practice until they can verbalize the benefits of the strategy and share how they apply it to their reading.

STRATEGY LESSON
Partner Reading and Retellings

ADAPT
for grades
5 and up

Introduction

Because middle school students are social, they enjoy practicing strategies with a partner. Partner reading and retelling allows students to interact as they take turns and practice recalling details from a passage in their own words or listen to a classmate.

When you pair students, make sure that each can support the other. Avoid having a struggling and proficient reader work together. If students who struggle work in books at their independent level, they can support one another. I always move back and forth between pairs of struggling readers, making myself available to support them. This is a great strategy for pairs to practice the mini-lesson on pages 143–144.

Materials

fiction, nonfiction, or textbooks at students' independent reading levels

Guidelines

1. Model this lesson in front of the entire class.
2. Model the process by asking a proficient reader to be the listener. I take the role of reteller.
3. Select a book. We use *Bat 6* by Virginia Euwer Wolff (Scholastic).
4. Mark off two or three sections to be read separately. Sections can be one paragraph, a half or whole page. We divide the reading into two sections: page 12 to the end of paragraph one on page 13, and the rest of page 13.

Two students get ready to do a partner retelling.

Moving Forward with Retellings

Once students' retellings have rich plot and character details and are in sequence, have them read and retell larger sections until they recall an entire chapter from a book at their independent-reading level. If students have difficulty sequencing, make this the focus of a mini-lesson. The time needed for students to accomplish excellent retellings differs. Proficient and grade-level readers will internalize the strategy quickly. In a one-on-one conference, meet with struggling readers to monitor their progress and offer suggestions for moving forward.

5. Read together, silently, one agreed-upon section, in the same book. If one of the pair finishes the selection before his partner, then he rereads until his partner has finished.

6. Place a marker in the book and put it aside.

7. Start the retelling. I recall and say everything that I remember from page 12 to the end of the first paragraph on page 13 to my partner. I purposely omit information and include one incorrect fact:

   School had started. The narrator sees a girl with shoes that were for boys that she thinks the girl bought at a secondhand store. The girl's dress looked like it didn't come from a store. It looked like someone worked hard to make it.

8. Have the listener do the following: a) Correct any incorrect ideas; b) add any omitted ideas. The listener does not criticize or pass judgment on the retelling. He simply corrects, if necessary, and adds what he recalls. The fifth grader said:

   "It was the first day of school. The shoes were probably from a rummage sale at the Gospel Church. They belonged to a boy who moved away because his dad went to jail. The shoes were like new."

9. Refer to the text now to check what has been said.

10. Alternate roles of listener and reteller during the reading of two or three pages.

11. Demonstrate until students understand how to use this strategy.

12. Ask the class to raise questions about what they observed. Fifth graders asked: How hard did you have to concentrate to remember? Did you feel bad when you were corrected? Was it hard to find the places in the story that you needed to reread?

Suggestions for Guided Practice

1. Reserve 10-minute chunks of time for students to practice together. Then have students continue reading on their own.

2. Repeat the mini-lesson for groups or pairs, using a new passage.

3. Continue practicing until students can work independently.

STRATEGY LESSON
Predict and Support

ADAPT
for grades
5 and up

Introduction

Similar to the prereading prediction strategy students have been learning, practicing the predict-and-support strategy during reading helps learners to make *logical* predictions. In this lesson, you guide students to see that the predictions are based on using prior knowledge gained from completed portions of the story.

While reading, students use the predict-and-support strategy, continuously setting and adjusting predictions as they complete more and more of the text. With this strategy students are actively involved with the text as they constantly set purposes for reading on.

As you listen to students' ideas and read their journals, look for logical predictions that relate to what has happened in the text. Explain that as readers know more and more of the story, it's easier to predict the outcome.

If students jot down their predictions and support in journals, wait until they've completed the entire text before asking them to make adjustments to the predictions and the support. Stopping the natural flow of reading and predicting can cause students to lose interest.

Materials

fictional texts: a short story, fairy tale, chapter book, or picture book; chart paper; marker pens

For this lesson I use a fairy tale from Pakistan called "The King Who Wanted to See Paradise" from *A World of Fairy Tales,* collected by Andrew Lang and illustrated by Henry Justice Ford (Dial, 1994).

Note: *With such a short text, it's tempting to read ahead, which would ruin the predict/support mini-lesson. Therefore, I cut the story into three parts and give students one section at a time.*

Guidelines

1. Explain and write on the chart how the predict-and-support strategy assists comprehension and recall. Tell students that this is a key strategy and share several purposes from the introduction.

2. Choose a short story, picture book, or fairy tale to model the predict/support process. With these, I can complete the predict/support demonstration in about 30 minutes.

3. Print the title [i.e., "The King Who Wanted to See Paradise"] and author on the chart. On

continued on page 150

The King Who Wanted to See Paradise

A Fairy Tale from Pakistan

Once upon a time there was a king who, one day out hunting, came upon a fakir, or holy man, in a lonely place in the mountains. The fakir was seated on a little old bedstead, reading the Koran, with his patched cloak thrown over his shoulders.

The king asked him what he was reading; and he said he was reading about Paradise, and praying that he might be worthy to enter there. Then they began to talk, and by and by the king asked the fakir if he could show him a glimpse of Paradise, for he found it very difficult to believe in what he could not see. The fakir replied that he was asking a very difficult, and perhaps a very dangerous, thing; but that he would pray for him, and perhaps he might be able to do it; only he warned the king both against the dangers of his disbelief, and against the curiosity which prompted him to ask this thing. However, the king was not to be turned from his purpose, and he promised the fakir always to provide him with food, if he in return would pray for him. To this the fakir agreed, and so they parted.

Time went on, and the king always sent the old fakir his food according to his promise; but whenever he sent to ask him when he was going to show him Paradise, the fakir always replied, "Not yet, not yet!" **[Stop #1]**

After a year or two had passed by, the king heard one day that the fakir was very ill—indeed, he was believed to be dying. Instantly he hurried off himself, and found that it was really true, and that the fakir was even then breathing his last. There and then the king begged him to remember his promise, and to show him a glimpse of Paradise. The fakir replied that if the king would come to his funeral, and when the grave was filled in, and everyone else was gone away, he would come and lay his hand upon the grave, he would keep his word, and show him a glimpse of Paradise. At the same time he implored the king not to do this thing, but to be content to see Paradise when Allah called him there. Still the king's curiosity was so aroused that he would not give way.

Accordingly, after the fakir was dead, and had been buried, the king stayed behind when all the rest went away; and then when he was quite alone, he stepped forward, and laid his hand upon the grave—instantly the ground opened, and the astonished king, peeping in, saw a flight of rough steps, and at the bottom of them the fakir sitting, just as he used to sit, on his rickety bedstead, reading the Koran!

At first the king was so surprised and frightened that he could only stare; but the fakir beckoned to him to come down, so mustering up his courage, he boldly stepped down into the grave.

The fakir rose, and making a sign to the king to follow, walked a few paces along a dark passage. Then he stopped, turned solemnly to his companion, and with a movement of his hand, drew aside a heavy curtain, and revealed—what? No one knows what was shown there to the king, nor did he ever tell anyone; but when the fakir at length dropped the curtain, and the king turned to leave the place, he had had his glimpse of Paradise! Trembling in every limb, he staggered back along the passage, and stumbled up the steps out of the tomb into the fresh air again. **[Stop #2]**

The dawn was breaking. It seemed odd to the king that he had been so long in the grave. It appeared but a few minutes ago that he had descended, passed along a few steps to the place where he had peeped beyond the veil, and returned again after perhaps five minutes of that wonderful view! And what was it he had seen? He racked his brains to remember, but he could not call to mind a single thing! How curious everything looked, too! Why, his own city, which by now he was entering, seemed changed and strange to him! The sun was already up when he turned into the palace gate and entered the public durbar hall. It was full; and there upon the throne sat another king! The poor king, all bewildered, sat down and stared about him. Presently a chamberlain came across and asked him why he sat unbidden in the king's presence. "But I am the king!" he cried.

"What king?" said the chamberlain.

"The true king of this Country," he said indignantly.

Then the chamberlain went away, and spoke to the king who sat on the throne, and the old king heard words like "mad," "age," and "pity." Then the king on the throne called him to come forward, and as he went, he caught sight of himself reflected in the polished steel shields of the bodyguards, and started back in horror! He was old, decrepit, dirty, and ragged! His long white beard and locks were unkempt, and straggled all over his chest and shoulders. Only one sign of royalty remained to him, and that was the signet ring upon his right hand. He dragged it off with shaking fingers and held it up to the king.

"Tell me who I am," he cried. "There is my signet, I who once sat where you sit—even yesterday!" **[Stop #3]**

The king looked at him compassionately, and examined the signet with curiosity. Then he commanded, and they brought out dusty records and archives of the kingdom, and old coins of previous reigns, and compared them faithfully. At last the king turned to the old man, and said: "Old man, this ring belonged to a king who reigned seven hundred years ago, but he is said to have disappeared, no one knows where. Where did you get the ring?"

Then the old man struck his breast, and cried out with a loud lamentation; for he understood that he, who was not content to wait patiently to see the Paradise of the faithful, had been judged already. And he turned and left the hall without a word, and went into the jungle, where he lived for twenty-five years a life of prayer and meditation, until at last the Angel of Death came to him, and mercifully released him, purged and purified through his punishment.

the left side write "Predict" and on the right side, "Support."

4. Leave space between each prediction and its support so you have room to make adjustments using a different-colored marker pen.

5. Read the title and invite students to predict and support at each of three stopping points. Explain that you will take two different predictions. Here's what seventh graders offered:

Predictions After Stop #1

- The fakir delays because he knows something terrible can happen.

- The fakir has no intention of keeping his promise to the king so he keeps on delaying the time to see Paradise.

Support

- He warns that the king's curiosity is dangerous.

- The fakir tells the king this is difficult and dangerous and he prays for the king. Maybe the fakir prays the king will stop asking.

Predictions After Stop #2

- He saw things that human words can't explain.

- The king will be punished, maybe with death, because he saw what no man should see when alive.

Support

- The king came back trembling and he staggered.

- He trembled and staggered because he is so ill and weak from what he saw.

Predictions After Stop #3

- Time stopped when the king looked at Paradise.

- If he lives, his life will be changed. No one will want to be with him because he's different from men.

Support

- The king saw what no one who is alive should see.

- The king is old and dirty and falling apart. It's like he's lived his life, he's old, but not in his kingdom.

6. Confirm and adjust the predictions the next day (see pages 155-156 to learn how students confirmed and adjusted).

Suggestions for Guided Practice

1. Complete one or two additional whole-class predict-and-support practices using short texts.

2. Continue with small groups or pairs who require extra practice developing logical predictions and using the text as support.

3. Have students who understand the strategy work independently, recording their predictions and support in journals. Fold a journal page in half lengthwise, and write "Prediction" on the left-hand side and "Support" on the right-hand side.

One eighth grader's predict/support/adjust journal entries.

Jaime Lockhart
California Blue, David Klass

Predict: Support:
I think his father   His dad is already in
might die which will   bad condition and
make John want to get   because John's relationship
out of the house more   with his dad isn't close
to go run, to get his   anyway, that would be
father out of his mind.   more of a clue telling
I think he might hear   you that John's dad
his dad's spirit in the   will die. Also, if his
woods while he's running   dad dies he is going
                               to feel something,
                               which is why I
Adjustments: think it will make
His father didn't die   John want to run more.
and his father didn't   I mean, since he already
make him train   runs, he'll just run
more than usual for   more, which leads into
his track meet.   him practicing a lot so
                               he can get first in his
                               track meet.

Jaime Lockhart
California Blue, David Klass

Predict: I think he'll   Support:
go to the town meeting   I think he'll go to
and find out some   the town meeting
good news. I also think   because he's been
that his father and   talking about it and
mother will be gone   it's important. I
longer than they   also think his parents
planned. So, when the   will be gone longer
people, I think, will   than planned because
try to cut down the   when his mom called,
mill, he'll have to do   she didn't have good news.
it on his own.   Furthermore, I think
                               their going to cut down
                               the mill because of the
Adjustments: butterfly and because it
He didn't get good news   was an open option
at the meeting, in fact he   earlier. I think he'll try
got beat up because of   to stop them because
the meeting. Also, his   the forest is like his
parents weren't gone as   home. He's in there a
long as I had predicted.   lot of the time.
They returned, his parents,
when John last expected
it.

Pause and Reflect on:
Self-Monitoring

"Until this year I thought I was the only one who didn't understand parts," Myra told me during a reading conference. Relieved that there were other students in her class who struggled to comprehend parts of a book, Myra began to focus on what she did well. Each time we conferred, she recognized that there were many more clicks of comprehension than clunks of confusion. However, her buildup of anxiety and low grades convinced Myra that she was "a failure" at reading and "would never catch up."

As you offer students many opportunities to practice self-monitoring, also provide them with models that illustrate how you and peer experts access fix-it strategies to repair confusing parts of text. Help students see their successes and build self-esteem and confidence. Always keep in mind that it takes a long time for struggling readers to develop metacognitive strategies and move from knowing the names of repair strategies to accessing and using them as they read.

The handwritten notes on the whiteboard read:

April 28, 1999

Mini-Lesson: Explore Themes

Theme: an unstated topic embedded in the story.

To find: reflect on characters' decisions, changes in characters, events, conflicts, problems, interac[tions]

T[o] state a T[heme use ge]neral language— "family, friends, people" instead of naming specific characters or places.

Chapter 7
Modeling
Post-Reading Strategies

"You're dumb if you have to look back. Smart kids get it after the first reading" ——Eighth Grader

More than any other activity, seventh grader Samantha loves to read. In her cubby, she keeps a stack of books, "So if I finish one, I always have another one waiting," she explains. Instead of playing outside at lunch recesses, Samantha reads. She reads on the bus to and from school. At home, her mother told me, "Sam reads during all her spare time. We can't get her nose out of a book."

During a reading conference, Samantha and I reviewed her log of completed books. That week she had entered 12 titles. When I selected one, Samantha could not remember what the book was about. "But I know I liked it," she said, a bit of defensiveness in her voice. I invited Samantha to choose a book and tell me about the main character. Samantha chose M.E. Kerr's *Deliver Us From Evie* and said: "It's about a gay girl and her problems. It was okay. That's all I remember."

Samantha's reading pattern reminded me of a goat gobbling up bag after bag of goodies. Samantha gobbled books, reading one after the other, never pausing to mull over a book or savor her favorite parts. Becoming involved with characters' decisions, conflicts, and experiences, then using this involvement to think about her own life, was not happening, because Samantha recalled few details. Samantha read without reflecting, and the story and characters rarely moved from her short- to long-term memory.

Reflecting on a book after completing it invites readers to re-experience favorite parts, to think about a story's meanings, and to relate its themes to their lives. The five strategy lessons in this chapter encourage reflection and lead readers deeper into a book, allowing them to probe and clarify ideas. When readers become better acquainted with the characters, plot, and details of a story, they can use events in the text to explore implied meanings and make connections to other books as well as to community and world issues.

STRATEGY LESSON
Confirm and Adjust

ADAPT
for grades
5 and up

Introduction

"I don't mind adjusting, but I hate going back and finding different support," Rico muttered to his group. Many students mirror Rico's reaction to the adjustment part of the prediction strategy, because it requires students to first evaluate early predictions, then skim/reread the text to confirm or adjust these. "When I'm finished," Rico continued, "I'm done. Why look back and think about what I wrote?" As he shrugged his shoulders, Rico added, "Why look for more work? I was right at the end."

Like Rico, many middle school students don't understand how rereading and analyzing predictions, confirming ideas, or making necessary adjustments improves comprehension and recall of details. This strategy lesson teaches students to analyze ideas they generated by comparing these to the text after reading and evaluating the way they used their knowledge of the story. Jenna explained the importance of the confirm-and-adjust strategy to Rico's group this way: "Looking back, I want to see if the predictions and adjustments I made in my mind were logical. When I adjust one [prediction] to the story, I'm thinking more about what really happened, not what I thought might happen."

Good readers constantly predict and adjust while reading. The purpose of asking students to practice this strategy is to raise their awareness of how the strategy creates strong purposes for reading. Practicing also moves students closer to the end goal: where adjusting predictions becomes a natural part of their reading process.

Materials
a completed fictional text: short story, novel, picture book, myth, legend

Guidelines
1. Think aloud and show students how you evaluate and adjust the first set of predictions. I reread the predictions students made after the first stop for "The King Who Wanted to See Paradise" (see page 150).
   Both predictions were logical because you used the fakir's warnings and delays to make each one. Now I'll skim the story to boost my memory of specific details to make and support an adjustment. I think the fakir knew what would happen to the king if he saw Paradise because the fakir was a holy man, in touch with Allah. Before the fakir died, he continued to warn the king against seeing Paradise because the fakir must have known the dangers. Instead of saying that the fakir "never intended" to show the king Paradise, I think it more accurate to say the holy man hoped he could convince the king to retract the request. However, the king kept his promise by always giving food to the fakir, and the fakir on his deathbed felt obliged to keep his promise to the king.

2. Model how you confirm and/or adjust the predictions students made after the second stop. Return to the text to collect specific evidence.

3. Ask students to confirm and/or adjust the third prediction. Here's what a seventh grader said:
   Both predictions are logical and happened. Time was different in Paradise because the king walked

into Paradise a young man and left old and decrepit. It makes me think about the difference between time on earth as compared to time after death. I think the second prediction that said the king left because he was different needs adjusting. The king was punishing himself by living alone and praying and meditating and asking forgiveness for doing something that living men should never do. I think the story is saying that the king should have spent his time enjoying being king and helping his people and not wanting to see Paradise before it was meant to be.

★ This think-aloud reveals another benefit of adjusting predictions: the thinking can lead students to a deeper understanding of the story's theme and draw them into contemplating concepts such as time on earth and after death. See next page for the prediction log, and monitor how students apply this strategy independently.

Suggestions for Guided Practice

1. Continue to demonstrate the predict/support/confirm/adjust strategy until students can make logical predictions based on the text, find specific evidence to support predictions, evaluate and analyze predictions, then adjust and/or confirm them.
2. Have students read short folk tales or stories and adjust or confirm their predictions.
3. Work one-on-one or with small groups who need your coaching to apply the strategy.

STRATEGY LESSON
Involving the Senses

ADAPT
for grades
5 and up

Introduction

The senses play a crucial part in comprehending and enjoying texts. A character's food, such as the chestnuts and groats Aaron eats in Paul Fleishman's *Half-a-Moon-Inn* conjures taste, the sounds of cooking, a visual image of thick wheat kernels, the sensation of peeling hot chestnuts, and chewing the meaty, sweet white nut-meats.

Developing students' ability to involve their senses as they read makes the text relevant to their lives. It helps move readers deeper into the story as they blend scenes from their lives with scenes in the book. When a fifth grader wrote, "When I see, smell, feel, taste, and hear, I understand what's happening, I can explain it, and it's like I'm living the story." This student clearly expressed the relationship of sensory involvement in a text to comprehension and enjoyment.

A perfume can remind me of a teacher I had in elementary school. The smell of pot roast

Teaching Reading in Middle School

USING A PREDICTION LOG

Once students understand and can independently use the predict/support/confirm/ adjust strategy, invite them to apply the strategy to independent reading, recording their work in their prediction logs. This is an easy way for you to monitor students' use of the strategy. Students bring these logs to one-on-one meetings with me, and I help them evaluate their work and practice skimming to improve support and adjustments. Partners and/or small groups share and discuss their prediction logs.

Preparing The Log

Before reading, have students prepare two or three small sheets of paper.

1. At the top of each sheet, write your name and the title and author of the book.

2. Under name, title, and author write "Prediction." Halfway down the paper write "Support." On the back write "Adjustments and New Support."

3. At the end of the first chapter of a novel, at the end of a chapter in the middle of the book, and at the end of the next to last chapter, place one of the sheets of paper.

4. For a short story, use two prediction sheets.

> I Hadn't Meant to Tell You This by J. Woodson
> Chapter 2   David Thomas
>
> Prediction: My prediction is when Candice told her sister she was not going to tell anybody what had happened to her, she is going to say something and it will be all over school.
> Support: On p.5 she said "I am not going to tell anybody not even my best friend."

Guidelines for Completing the Prediction Log

1. Study the cover illustrations and read the first chapter. On the paper, write a prediction and provide specific support.

2. Stop when you come to the second and third prediction papers, predict what will happen next and offer detailed support from the story.

3. Reread all of your predictions when you have completed the book. If your prediction was on target, place a check next to it.

4. Make necessary adjustments on the back of each piece of paper.

5. Staple the sheets and turn these in to your teacher.

always returns me to my grandmother's kitchen, when I helped her fill an old cast-iron pot with onions, garlic, tomatoes, peppers, and beef. Sensory experiences stored in our memory become a part of our prior knowledge, and we use these memories as we read, watch a movie, or travel.

In fiction, our senses enable us to see and experience the spaces characters inhabit, to hear the tone and timbre of characters' conversations, to connect to their innermost feelings, and to inhabit the psyches of our favorites. Our senses enable us to understand new vocabulary in fiction and nonfiction. If I'm reading about snakes, I can feel the reptile's skin because I have held a black snake; I can hear the menacing rattling sound of a rattler because as a child, I heard that sound when our family spent summers in a cabin in the Catskill Mountains; I can see the tongue flicking in and out of the snake's mouth as it slithers through the grass. With my prior knowledge, I can comprehend new information about snakes—information that's not part of my life experience, but that I can imagine and understand from the rich sensory descriptions in the text.

The ability to visualize is similar to the ability to write. We write and picture what we know and understand. However, in this era of ready-made visual images on television and computer screens, students don't have to visualize—make their own mental pictures—as much as when people listened to radio or storytellers. Developing students' sensory involvement with text is important because it is this involvement that enables them to fully enter a character's life, and assists them as they work to understand new words and information.

Materials
pictures books, passages from teacher read-alouds, passages from students' independent reading books

Guidelines

1. Invite students to visualize settings or characters as you read aloud passages from picture books or novels.
2. Have students draw what they envision. An eighth grader, T. Johnson, drew this illustration of Beowulf's face, based on a description on pages 12–13 of the retelling by Robert Nye.
3. Ask students to create oral and/or written texts about other sensory experiences.

A seventh grader describes her experience with touch after I read "Reach out and touch the blue whale's skin. It's springy and smooth like a hard-boiled egg, and it's as slippery as wet soap." [From *Big Blue Whale* by Nicola Davies.] Here's what she said: *I thought of the feel of moist hard-boiled eggs I peel at Easter and the feel of wet glass I collect—glass smoothed by the ocean. Then I imagined the slippery feeling of slime that I think is just like a wet bar of soap. I've never touched a whale's skin, but I think I know how it feels.*

4. Find rich descriptions of new words and ask students to use context clues and their senses to comprehend the word. On an overhead transparency, I print these sentences from Seymour Simon's *The Brain*.

   Deep inside and between the two cerebral hemispheres are the thalamus and the hypothalamus. Thalamus *means "inner room" in Latin. It is kind of a relay station between your spinal cord and your cerebrum. The thalamus is the place that first receives messages signaling such sensations as pain, pressure, and temperature from sensory neurons.* (unpaged)

   I model sensory involvement by thinking aloud: The phrase "inner room" helps me see that the thalamus is deep inside the brain and we can't see it from the outside because there are no windows to help.

5. Invite students to react to other parts of the passage. A sixth grader says: " 'Relay station' makes me think of relay races I'm in when the baton passes from racer to racer. The thalamus is the relay station that passes messages, not batons, between the brain and spinal cord."
   Another student says: "When it [the text] said the thalamus first receives pain and temperature, I see a place in our brain that takes in uncomfortable feelings and then translates them—like you translate a secret code—into something I can feel."

6. Continue practicing with groups, pairs, or individuals who need to work on involving their senses with texts.

Suggestions for Guided Practice:

1. Ask students to find short passages in their free-reading books that appeal to the senses.
2. Have a few students share their findings over several workshop sessions.
3. Invite others to respond to the passage a student reads by explaining how the text affected one, two, or all of their senses.
4. Let students choose a poem to illustrate and discuss how the text affected what they chose to draw.

STRATEGY LESSON
Skimming for Information

ADAPT
for grades
5 and up

Introduction

Skimming is a strategy adult readers use constantly. To find facts about a political candidate's views on public education, I'll skim a newspaper article. I'll skim the dialogue in a chapter I've just read to find the expression I loved and want to tell a friend about. When I plan to bake a lemon meringue pie, I skip the index and skim the chapter on pies so I can scan other dessert possibilities, to see if there's another pie I'd rather bake. Part of the skimming process is *learning how to select information that relates to your purposes and set aside data you don't presently need.*

Many middle school students avoid returning to texts to answer questions or adjust predictions. They believe, as Kara explained, "You're dumb if you have to look back. Smart kids get it after the first reading." I believe students feel this way because they lack skimming strategies. Instead of reinspecting small sections of text, they reread several chapters, which becomes laborious and frustrating—overkill to anyone, young or adult. Teaching students how to skim will provide them with a strategy they will use in all their subjects. It will also enable students to select those ideas that support the purposes of skimming.

Materials

a chapter in a textbook, nonfiction, or a novel students have completed

Story

"Seventh Grade" from *Baseball in April* by Gary Soto

Questions Students Posed after Completing the Story

I recorded questions on chart paper, and students used them to discuss the story.

1. Why does Victor pretend to know French?

2. How do you know Victor and Michael are growing up?

3. Why is Victor embarrassed?

4. Why doesn't Mr. Bueller get angry at Victor?

5. Why does Victor think that Teresa is a "great girl" at the end?

Guidelines

1. Explain that you can use information in a question to help you skim a narrative text. Look for names of *people, places,* or, as in question one for Gary Soto's "Seventh Grade", the *name of a language.*

2. Have students reinspect the text as you think aloud. For the first question, I say: "I think that's at the beginning of the story. I'll open to page 65 and look for the word *French*. It's in the first paragraph. I quick-read and discover that Victor took French as an elective because he might travel to France one day. He also wants to be in the same class as Teresa, a girl he likes."

3. For the second question, I explain: "I know Victor met Michael before the first day started. I'll turn to page 66 and look for Michael's name. I fast-read and remember that Michael read in *GQ* that if a man scowls, he can attract girls. Michael tells Victor that Belinda Reyes looked at him when he scowled. Both boys want to attract girls; that's a sign of growing up."

4. Have students practice skimming for the rest of the questions. Encourage them to explain the skimming strategies they used.

On Another Day: Skim a Novel

1. Model how you skim a novel. Read the chapter titles to get an idea of where you might locate information.

2. Recall whether the information was in the beginning, middle, or end of the book or a chapter. A chapter title might provide a clue.

3. Skim through a chapter or section, looking for a key word in the question that can help you locate support. Think aloud to show how you would locate information about what one character said to another. Model how you skip over descriptive passages and dialogue that involves other characters.

On Another Day: Skim Nonfiction

1. Set a purpose for skimming a nonfiction text:
   + Preview to discover new vocabulary or information you know and new information.
   + Raise questions about the content.
   + Search for specific data.
   + Discover details that answer a question.

2. Model how you skim a nonfiction text. Read the chapter titles and bold-faced headings and words within a chapter to locate a specific section.

3. Read the captions under photographs, charts, and diagrams to assist your search for answers to questions. Think aloud about how each element does or does not guide you to find what you're looking for.

4. Select key words in a question to help you find information. A group of sixth graders had to reread their science textbooks to answer this question: *How do heterogeneous and homogeneous mixtures differ?* They searched for pages and captions that had the words *heterogeneous* and *homogeneous,* skimmed them and gathered details that explained these terms, and offered examples of each one.

ORAL PRESENTATION:
BOOK-TALKING WITH STORY SYMBOLS

With this kind of book talk, you invite students to think deeply about an independent-reading book, then select details that resonate for them, and are symbols of what they consider the book's deepest meanings. You can use fiction, historical fiction, folk or fairy tale, myth or legend, or biography. The first time I introduced the activity, eighth graders groaned and said, "This is too hard. I'll have to reread parts because I don't remember all the details. I can't do it." Yet, I believed that these eighth graders could present book talks that utilized their ability to select important information, because students were reading books at their comfort or independent levels, and we had practiced selecting information from novels, nonfiction, and textbooks. After I presented the think-aloud that follows, and told students they had one week to plan their book talk, most felt that the task was within their reach.

Robb's Think-Aloud Using *Beowulf*, retold by Robert Nye
My first symbol is Beowulf and his mind. I chose Beowulf's mind because it is a symbol of good and the ability to plan a way to defeat evil without using weapons. Beowulf destroys the Firedrake by sending the queen bee into one of its jaws. When the bees follow their queen, they enter the mouth and stomach of the Firedrake and sting him until the dragon dies. Beowulf's mind connects to a main point of this book, which is that goodness and man's mind can overcome evil.

Suggestions for Guided Practice

1. After the class reads a short folk tale, myth, article, or story, have students skim the text to revise their getting-ready-to-read activity.

2. Have students create discussion questions for the reading they completed in step one, select key words from these questions, and skim to find details.

3. Use a science or history textbook chapter and ask students to skim for explanations of key vocabulary or for details that answer a question.

4. Practice with a variety of texts: fiction, nonfiction, math, science, and history textbooks.

Guidelines for Planning a Symbolic Book Talk

You may have notes on a 4-by-6-inch index card or a half-sheet of notebook paper.

✦ State the title and author of your book.

✦ Give a two- or three-sentence summary of your book.

✦ Select three symbols that are important to the book's purpose and theme.

✦ You can draw these, cut out symbols from magazines or newspapers, or bring in small items such as a drum, boots, or a stuffed animal.

✦ Name the symbol and explain why you chose it.

✦ Show how the symbol is significant to the story. Does it reveal information about the character? a conflict? an event? the setting?

✦ Show how the symbol relates to the theme of the book.

✦ Keep your book talk to three or four minutes.

Twenty-four students presented book talks during two workshops. For Avi's *The Fighting Ground* (Lippincott), an eighth grader discussed a small drum, a picture of a musket, and the word *dreams*. A black leather boot, a piece of barbed wire, and a drawing of tears were the focus of a book talk on Jane Yolen's *The Devil's Arithmetic* (Puffin). Students enjoyed these presentations and experienced success. The fact that several asked, "Can we do this for our next contract?" signaled that students understood and could use the selecting process. More importantly, the process had struck a chord: thinking symbolically is in concert with middle schooler's intense desire to make sense of their lives and the world.

STRATEGY LESSON
Making Connections

ADAPT
for grades
5 and up

Introduction

"It was cool the way my group figured out how *No Promises in the Wind* (by Irene Hunt) related to our lives. I mean, like, we never lived through a Depression, but we all argue with our parents and are scared when we make big mistakes." This eighth grader expresses the power books have to stir students to reflect on their own lives. The more personal connections students make, the more involved they become with the story.

In *Mosaic of Thought* (Keene and Zimmerman, 1997), the authors point out that as readers link stories to their lives, other books, and the larger world, they use what they know to construct new and meaningful understandings. Connecting to books can deepen our understanding of personal values, family relationships, and universal problems, hopes, and dreams.

For this lesson, start by making a connection between life today and the story, then invite students to give specific examples from their daily experiences.

As you help students make these connections, they will discover the riches that outstanding books hold.

Materials

a novel students have just completed; or a folk tale, myth, or story you've read aloud, if you want to work with the entire class

Book

"The Children of Lidice" from *Witnesses to War: Eight True-Life Stories of Nazi Persecution* by Michael Leapman (Viking)

Grade: Eighth

Summary of the Text for Teachers

In 1941 Reinhard Heydrich, a fanatical Nazi leader became governor of Czechoslovakia. Angry Czechs shot Heydrich as his car neared Prague. As a result, Hitler was determined to punish the Czech people. German soldiers forced the men, women, and children out of Lidice and burned the town to the ground. All the men were shot, and the women and children were taken to separate concentration camps. This chapter tells the story of three children who survived the Lidice massacre and are alive today. In 1946, survivors returned to Lidice after it was rebuilt.

PART I: Connections to Daily Living

1. First, I explain to my eighth graders how this true account stressed the importance of family and home to these people. Then, I forge connections to my life and tell students: "No one in my family told me how ill my grandmother was until it was too late; her death was a shock. The journey from Virginia to New York City took seven hours, and she died before I arrived. I still feel the loss and shudder when I ask myself if my grandmother wondered why I didn't come to the hospital."

2. Next, I ask students, "How do you feel about losing a person or pet that you dearly love?" One student bravely told this story: "My parents, a brother, and sister were killed in a car accident when I was in fifth grade. My aunt and uncle are raising me. Chance massacred my family, and I had to face it just like Emilie in the story. Emilie lost her mother when she was little and her aunt and uncle raised her. Then the Nazis killed them, and she lost everything. I still have some family." *(Although most students will not have such a dramatic connection, they will discover passages and events that relate to their lives.)*

3. To extend the connecting strategy, I first recap these key points for students: "This book illustrates how returning to a place you lost, or one you associate with dreadful memories, can be horrifying. Once Germany had been defeated, several Czech children who survived the war returned to Lidice. They experienced shock when they realized that there were no houses and no people. Despite this anguish, they began to rebuild their lives."

4. Next, I ask: "Can you connect the loss of homes, friends, and family people coped with in World War II to experiences you've lived through or read about?"

   "A fire destroyed my grandma's house," a student shared. "I felt scared and shaky when I returned to the rubble and knew why she cried and cried. We all cried with her."

   Others point to the destruction earthquakes and floods cause to towns, cities, and homes. They explain that television newscasts show everything: the people crying, the broken furniture, the feelings of despair, and, finally, determination to rebuild and start over—just like the Czech children who survived the war.

PART II: Connections to Community and World Issues [Complete on Another Day]

1. Read the last three sentences of the story:

Prompts That Spark Connections

Post these prompts on chart paper so students can refer to them when discussing books or reading independently.

+ Do you have feelings and thoughts similar to one or more characters in this book?
+ Have you lived through similar situations?
+ Does the setting, plot, conflicts, problems, characters remind you of other books you've read?
+ Do the relationships, conflicts, feelings, or dialogue between characters remind you of similar experiences with your parents? siblings? friends? teachers?
+ Can you apply parts of this book to situations at school? at home? to community service projects?
+ What issues does this book raise that you read about in the newspaper, hear your parents discuss, or see on TV?

But of course, the memory of the atrocity will never be eradicated. Nor should it be. Lidice remains an overwhelming reminder of the way that wars can destroy the humanity of the people who wage them.

"I can support that with *Zlata's Diary,*" a student says. "And that's happening today in Bosnia, Kosovo, and China," another adds. And still another says, "The book *Red Scarf Girl* shows how during the Cultural Revolution in China the government tortured wealthy and educated adults." These connections reclaim an abundant flow of memories that students discuss.

2. I ask students, "Was hunger an experience confined to the Holocaust? Does starvation only occur in German concentration camps? Did the story of the people of Lidice link you to hunger experienced in today's world?" Students respond passionately and explain that there are millions of children in the United States who go hungry every day, and we aren't in a war. One child points to the biannual food drives to fill area food banks so poor families can eat. "Hunger," one boy points out, "is not just part of war. It is in our own community."

Some tell about the hunger in Biafra and the hunger in war-torn countries or countries with too large a population to adequately feed everyone.

Suggestions for Guided Practice

1. Use daily read-alouds to help students make connections to other books, to daily living, and to community and world issues.

2. Find a short story or folk tale everyone can read, and provide the questions that encourage/require students to link the story to other books, their lives, and world issues. (See margin box for a list of questions to adapt.)

3. Continue to foster these connections as you coach students alone, in pairs, or in small groups.

STRATEGY LESSON
Exploring Implied Meanings

ADAPT
for grades
5 and up

Introduction

Making inferences, exploring implied meanings, and drawing conclusions all relate to the same process: moving beyond the literal meaning of a story by linking prior knowledge and experiences to the text. All children make inferences based on the actions and words of others. When I questioned Lenny, a fifth grader who refused to go out during recess, he told me, "I always have to do what Jimmy says or I don't get included in the game, and I end up just watching." Lenny

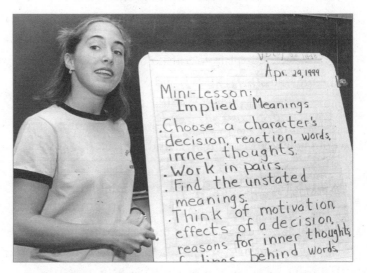

Eighth grader presents a mini-lesson on implied meanings to a group of students.

based his decision to skip recess by inferring that Jimmy was a bully and a boss and would continue to act that way. Like Lenny, we all make inferences based on the words and actions of others. Once students become aware of the inferences they make about classmates, friends, adults, and family, they can transfer this ability to literature.

Use the sample lessons that follow to help students move from making inferences about people in real life to making inferences about characters in books. Model how to study what characters say, what they do, and the decisions they make to draw conclusions about their personalities and motivations. Show how exploring the themes in a book starts with drawing general conclusions about the people and events and ends with relating the theme to oneself.

Materials

a book, folktale, myth, or story you've read aloud

Book: *Sadako and the Thousand Paper Cranes* by Eleanor Coerr

Grade: Fifth

Summary of pages 42 and 44

Sadako is in the hospital, ill with radiation sickness, and she meets nine-year-old Kenji for the first time. Kenji tells Sadako that he will die from leukemia soon. Trying to comfort her new friend, Sadako tells Kenji to fold paper cranes "so that a miracle can happen." Nurse Yasunaga overhears Kenji explain to Sadako that it's too late for doctors or miracles to save his life. When the nurse asks Kenji how he can know such things, Kenji replies, "I can read my blood count on the chart. Every day it gets worse."

Quickly, Nurse Yasunaga wheels Kenji out of the room, leaving Sadako to wonder what it would be like to be Kenji—ill and alone in the hospital with no family.

PART I: Interpreting Characters' Dialogue

1. Explain that by studying what characters say, it's possible to draw conclusions about their personalities and infer their motivations for actions and decisions. The author doesn't state these meanings; he implies them. Readers are like detectives, discovering the hidden meanings embedded in a character's words.

2. Select a rich dialogue between two or three characters. Fifth graders and I reread pages 42 and 44, the dialogue between Kenji, the nurse, and Sadako. I model how I read between the lines and draw conclusions about Kenji and Sadako: *Kenji is realistic about his leukemia. He says that he'll die soon. This shows he's accepted death. He backs his statement up by telling Sadako that he reads the blood counts on his chart and they are lower every day. Even the nurse doesn't know what to do with Kenji's honesty—the author says she's "flustered." I felt that way when my father told me that he was going to die. I felt confused and awkward as I tried to refute what I knew in my heart would happen.*

3. Ask students to identify the inferences in your think-aloud and what the characters said that made you draw these conclusions.

4. Have students point out the personal connection you made. I explain that making personal connections links the character's experiences to my life and can clarify the inference.

5. Invite students to offer additional thoughts about the character you discussed. A fifth grader points out that Kenji also says that the cranes and even the gods can't help him. He shows courage to Sadako, for Kenji doesn't cry, even though he knows he'll die soon.

6. Ask students to explain what conclusions they can draw about the other characters in the dialogue. A student focuses on the nurse and says: "She [the nurse] can't handle Kenji's honesty. She asks him how he could know he will die. Then she is caring about Sadako who is also very sick. I know that because the nurse wheels Kenji away so Sadako won't hear anymore."

When I ask, "Why does Sadako deny that Kenji has leukemia and then suggest that Kenji make paper cranes?" another student points out: "She first denies that Kenji has leukemia by saying, 'You weren't even born then.' I think she's trying to convince herself that she wasn't born then, either, and can't be that sick. Sadako puts thoughts of her illness aside and tries to comfort Kenji when she suggests he make cranes. But Sadako has still not connected Kenji's fate to her own, for she wonders what it would be like to be sick like Kenji and have no family."

PROMPTS THAT SUPPORT INFERRING FROM DIALOGUE AND INNER THOUGHTS

As you teach students to infer from characters' words, actions, and thoughts, you can scaffold their learning with these prompts:

✦ Why did the character say that [restate the words]?

✦ Why were the inner thoughts different from the spoken words?

✦ Why won't the character say her/his inner thoughts out loud?

✦ Does the situation or setting for the dialogue help you draw conclusions about the character's feelings? thoughts? personality?

✦ Using events that came before these words, explain what motivated the character to speak this way.

✦ How does the tone of voice you imagine for the character help you understand his or her mood? feelings?

✦ Try to visualize the character's expression and gestures. What can you infer from these?

✦ Can you select words the character says that enable you to infer feelings, attitude, personality, inner conflicts?

Summary of Page 45

Sadako continues folding paper cranes, hoping to reach one thousand so a miracle will happen and her life will be spared. She sends the prettiest crane to Kenji, hoping it will bring him luck. Late one evening, Sadako hears a bed being rolled down the hall. Gently, Nurse Yasunaga tells Sadako that Kenji died. Sobs rack Sadako's weak body. She asks the nurse if Kenji is now in the sky, on a star island. As Nurse Yasunaga assures Sadako that Kenji must be happy now, because he has shed his sick body and freed his spirit, Sadako recognizes that she will die next.

Suggestions for Guided Practice

1. Invite pairs to select a dialogue from a book they are studying in class.
2. Have pairs draw conclusions about the characters and share what they've learned with one another and other members of their reading group.
3. Have partners, over several days, share with the entire class. Ask students to explain the clues they used to read between the lines.
4. Continue modeling and practicing with students until they can interpret dialogue on their own. You can assess this by listening to pairs or individuals interpret dialogue from an independent reading book.

PART II: Interpreting Characters' Reactions to an Event [Complete on Another Day]

1. Choose a character's reaction to an event. I select Sadako's reactions to Kenji's death. The students and I reread page 45. I tell the students: *"Sadako sobs. I think she is crying for Kenji and for herself, because Sadako thinks, for a brief moment, that she will die next. It's hard to accept your own death, especially when you're as young as Sadako. I sobbed, in grade school, when my best friend died. The tears were also for myself and my own deep fear of dying."*
2. Have students point out the inferences and personal connections in your think-aloud.
3. Ask partners to find a character's reaction to an event and discuss what the reaction might mean or express about the character. Students should also explain the clues they used to make these inferences.
4. Have students share with classmates during two or three classes.
5. Ask reading groups to work in pairs to find characters' reactions to events in their books. Pairs search for implied meanings, think about how they made their inferences, and share with other group members.

6. Continue modeling and practicing until students can discover the implied meanings in characters' reactions to an event.

PART III: Interpreting a Character's Decisions
[Complete on Another Day]

1. Select an important decision a character made. I choose Sadako's decision to fold the one thousand paper cranes and to continue folding them until her death. I explain: *"The cranes symbolized life and hope, because the legend said that if a sick person folds one thousand cranes the gods will make her healthy again. Sadako longs for health and life and a chance to run again. Even after Kenji's death, whenever she lets herself think she might die, Sadako folds more birds. The cranes also show Sadako's courage and refusal to give in to death. Kenji refused to fold, but even when Sadako was near death, she tried to fold the cranes. Sadako's last image is the birds hanging from the ceiling above her bed. Perhaps the author wants us to think that death frees Sadako's spirit—like the birds she describes: beautiful and free. I admire people who face death bravely. My dad did. He talked to me and my brother about his dying and asked us to help him enjoy what time he had left."*

2. Ask pairs to select the inferences or implied meanings from your statements as well as the personal connections.

3. Invite pairs to select another decision from the book and explore what meanings are implied in the decision.

4. Over three or four days, ask pairs of students to share how they discovered implied meanings from a decision both selected.

Suggestions for Guided Practice

1. Have students work in pairs to select a character's important decision and discover the inferences they can draw about the decision.

2. Invite students to share with other group members.

3. Continue to model and have students practice exploring inferences that surround a character's decision.

Embrace Every Connection

Students' connections to the story will differ from yours, for prior experiences and knowledge determine the connections readers make. Accept all connections as long as students support them with the story.

What Good Readers Do When They Infer

+ Predict and revise predictions as they read.
+ Weave their background knowledge and information into the text to answer questions they continuously pose during reading.
+ Evaluate characters' decisions, motivations, talk, and the author's themes.
+ Draw conclusions about people, conflicts, settings, and information.
+ Interpret the book, basing interpretations on their own experience and the author's words.
+ Connect what they know to what they are learning as they read and adapt their background knowledge to the new understandings they've gained.

PART IV: Exploring the Themes in a Book or Story [Complete on Another Day]

1. Define the word *theme*. I explain that the themes in a book are large, general topics or ideas that the book explores through its characters, plot, and settings. Or, put another way, the theme is an unstated idea embedded in the story. A book can have a single theme or a few; several books can have the same or similar themes that grow out of different plots, settings, and characters' interactions.

2. Show students how *you* discover themes. First, reflect on a character's decisions and interactions with others, or on what forces change the character at the end, or on significant events in a book. Then, model how you take these specific details and create general statements. I point out that one of the themes in *Sadako and the Thousand Paper Cranes* is the importance of family and friends in helping people cope with serious illnesses. I knew this from the way Sadako's parents and her best friend, Chizuko, acted.

   I point out that in stating a theme, I use general language, such as *family, friends, people*, rather than naming specific characters.

3. Organize students into groups of four or five. Groups try to think of other themes or topics this book highlights. Groups of fifth graders offered these themes:
   + Keeping some hope can help you live your life when in your heart you know you will die;
   + The atom bomb can affect the children born of parents exposed to radiation;
   + A young life taken before dreams are realized is sad and painful.

4. Ask students to relate a theme to their lives, experiences, and/or other books.

HELPING STUDENTS UNDERSTAND THEME

Using specific details in a book about character, time, conflict, or relationships and creating general statements that express a theme is difficult for middle school students. I start with experiences from their lives, and together, we create themes from these. Share these with students as well as others you collect from your experiences with young adolescents.

Detail: Several students consistently arrive at school out of dress code. Though parents have come to school with a change of clothing and many students have repeatedly been sent home, a group persists in dressing inappropriately.
Theme: One way to protest rules is to repeatedly break them.

Detail: At a party, Sue, an outstanding citizen and student, is urged to drink. She refuses, saying that she has a headache and doesn't want any. Her peers insist she's a wus and afraid of what her parents will say. Sue gives in.
Theme: Peer pressure can make people do things they don't want to do.

First, I explain how I generalize the theme from the detail, pointing out that I don't use names or specific situations, but try to arrive at a statement that could apply to similar situations. Once students understand, through discussion, the differences between the theme and details, I invite them to use this thinking with the books they are reading.

Next, I encourage students to use details to discover themes from a read-aloud I've completed. I invite pairs of students to select details from *Bridge to Terabithia* by Katherine Paterson, then generalize to the theme, for I want students to see that a book contains many themes. What follows is the thinking of two pairs of sixth graders:

Detail: Brenda and Ellie whine about going to Millsburg for school shopping. When Mama says there's no money, they insist they want to just look around. They end up getting $5.00 by insisting their daddy promised it to them.
Theme: Some children can easily manipulate parents and get their way.

Detail: Jess denies Leslie drowned when his father tells him. He gets angry and insists it's a lie. Then he thinks about things Leslie said and things they did together.
Theme: When you love someone, accepting an unexpected death is tough. First there's denial, then anger.

Continue practicing with students until you feel they understand how to move from story details to a general theme statement.

AUTHORS LEAVE CLUES
THAT HELP READERS INFER

Authors leave clues that can support readers as they try to infer or read between the lines. Here are some clues that students can look for and use to discover the implied meanings embedded in a story.

Find the words the author uses to describe a character's facial expression, looks, demeanor, and gestures.

Example: "Dr. Viridian is tall and good-looking, like a doctor on TV, and has a smooth, soothing voice. He doesn't wear a lab coat or anything; he's casually dressed in expensive-looking clothes." From *The Night the Heads Came* by William Sleator, Puffin, 1996 (pages 24–25).

Study a character's inner thoughts—the words not spoken—and reflect on what these show about mood, feelings, and personality.

Example: "Sometimes she wondered where the tears that had flowed so freely the year before had gone. Why could she not weep for all those she loved who had died? Was it because their deaths seemed unreal? As though all those things had happened in some other lifetime?" From *Of Nightingales That Weep* by Katherine Paterson, HarperTrophy, 1974 (pages 150–151).

Consider the dialogue or speaker tags that authors include.

Example: "'Take Paddy somewhere safe!' Dad yells." From *Fire! My Parents' Story* by Jessie Haas, 1998, Greenwillow Books (page 21).

Study the other character in the dialogue and analyze reactions, words, and inner thoughts to draw conclusions about the character.

Example: Ob talks about May: "'All those years,' he said, 'every time we'd be packing up to go see the folks in Ohio, half of May would want to go and half of her would want to stay here. Couldn't make up her blame mind. She used to be afraid she'd lose this place if she left it for very long. Afraid it and the 'gigs would burn up or be washed away. She just didn't want to let this trailer out of her sight.'" From *Missing May* by Cynthia Rylant, Dell Yearling, 1992 (page 13).

Review a decision—the course of action a character decides to take—and decide what you can infer from the decision.

Example: "Then I'm running down the hall and it's like I'm Kicker again, ready to blast anybody who dares touch me, and I have to keep running, I'm skidding around the corners and bumping into walls, and not one can touch me even if they're brave enough to try, I just keep running and running until I get to these glass doors that say Medical Research." From *Freak the Mighty* by Rodman Philbrick, Scholastic, 1993, (page 155).

Think about the tone of voice of the character and what it means: is the voice quiet, laughing, shouting, sarcastic, fearful?

Example: "'Where did you learn to climb like that?' Coach Takahashi says, a hint of laughter in his voice." From *The Heart of a Chief* by Joseph Bruchac, Dial, 1998 (page 85).

EXPLORE IMPLIED MEANINGS WITH "THE INFERENCE GAME"

Students naturally make inferences in their daily lives. By playing "the inference game" with struggling readers, you can help them recognize that they are constantly drawing conclusions about family, friends, and teachers. Help students see that they base their conclusions on the talk and actions of these people.

The inference game offers mini-dramas that can link the inferences that students make every day to the inferences they can learn to make from books. Selected students dramatize situations, while their classmates—the audience—draw conclusions from the mini-drama. The game can be played as a whole-class or small-group activity.

Game Directions:

1. Write each mini-drama on an index card. Mini-dramas for the Inference Game include:

   ✦ Sit at your desk, yawn loudly, stretch, and put your head on the desk.

   ✦ Take a classmate's pen or pencil without asking.

   ✦ Three girls whisper in a group. A fourth girl tries to enter the group but is told to "bug off."

   ✦ Two students toss a ball. A third asks to play, but the first two do not answer. The third just hangs around and watches.

   ✦ A student carries books down the hallway. Another student walks up and knocks the books out of the student's arms, laughs, and walks away.

   ✦ A teacher gives directions to a class, and the class begins working. A student arrives five minutes later. The student is loud and disruptive.

   ✦ For two nights, Student A calls Student B to get the answers to the math homework. On the third night, Student A calls, but Student B refuses to give the answers. Student A then tells Student B not to expect to be invited to the big weekend party.

   ✦ Two students sit in the back of the classroom, pass notes, and talk.

   ✦ A student enters the classroom, crying.

2. Have one or more students perform the scene. Scenes require no rehearsals. The audience should not see what is on the card before the dramatization.

3. The audience can then draw inferences that offer explanations for the actors' behavior and words.

4. Prompt students with these questions: *What is the person thinking? feeling? How do you know that?*

STRATEGY LESSON
Cause/Effect

ADAPT
for grades
5 and up

Introduction

Since standardized tests and informal reading inventories assess students' ability to comprehend cause-and-effect relationships, it is an important thinking skill for students to understand. When using the cause-and-effect strategy during reading, readers infer from known and implied ideas in the text an effect or outcome. Sometimes a cause can result in many effects

I help eighth graders develop cause statements.

and an effect can become a cause (see margin box on page 178).

Materials

a book or story that you're reading aloud or one the class (or groups) is reading

Guidelines

1. Introduce cause/effect by explaining a *cause statement* and the term *effects*. Tell students that cause statements stem from actions and events, and effects are what happen as a result of the event or action. The event or action can be personal: *Michael didn't invite me to his party.* Or one character can cause another character to feel a certain way: *That slope is too hard for you to ski down.* Or the event can come from the environment: *An ice storm hit our city.*

2. Start with a cause statement from students' lives. For sixth graders, I write on the blackboard: "My room is very messy." Using examples from students' lives will help struggling readers understand the cause/effect relationship.

3. Invite students to generate a list of effects. Here are some effects sixth graders offered: *I have one*

Deepen Students' Knowledge of Cause/Effect

Eighth grader Amy showed me her list of effects for her cause statement (*Dare I disturb the universe?*) from Robert Cormier's *The Chocolate War.* "Lot's of these can be causes," she told me, "like brother Leon hated Jerry. [Pause.] I could do this for two others on my list: 1) Jerry becomes a social outcast; 2) Jerry decides to box with Emile Janza."

As students become adept at thinking in terms of cause and effect, many come to understand that an effect of one cause can become the cause for other effects.

hour to clean it; I can't go to the movies until I clean up; If I miss the movie my friend will be mad; I'm grounded for two weeks because it's [the room] been messy for a month.

4. Point out that often, effects that are events, such as "I have one hour to clean my room," can also be cause statements.

5. Have partners create their own cause statements and list the effects. Share with the class.

6. Continue using cause/effect examples from students' lives until they understand the relationship and can create their own cause statements.

Jaime Lockhart
To Kill a Mockingbird, Harper Lee

Cause:
Miss Maudie's house burned down.

Effect:
- Boo Radley came out and put a blanket around Scout without her knowing it.
- Miss Maudie was glad her house burned down.
- Since Miss Maudie had no home, she moved in with Stephanie Crawford

Cause:
Jem and Scout walked home alone at night after Scout's pagent.

Effect:
- Jem broke his arm when he was attacked by Mr. Ewell
- Boo Radley was finally revealed.
- Scout was saved by Boo Radley and they became friends.
- Atticus and Sheriff Tate realized Boo Radley killed Mr. Ewell but the sheriff refused to prosecute because he said it would be like "killing a mockingbird".

On Another Day

1. Introduce cause/effect using a book you've read aloud. I use *Black Like Me* by John Howard Griffin (Signet).

2. Write a cause statement on the blackboard. For *Black Like Me* I write: "John Griffin temporarily darkens his skin to pass as a black in the Deep South."

3. Have groups discuss the statement and jot down several effects. Here are some effects eighth graders offer:

   ✦ Has trouble finding places that will serve him food.

   ✦ It's tough finding a decent hotel to sleep and rest.

   ✦ Could only get menial jobs.

   ✦ Could only use bathrooms marked "colored." Not many of these.

   ✦ Had to sit in the back of buses.

   ✦ White women, especially older ones, gave him hate-filled stares—even when Griffin, dressed in a suit, walked by their churches on Sunday.

4. Invite groups to each write an original cause statement and list several effects. Share these.

Suggestions for Guided Practice

1. Move students to working on cause/effect from a book they've read with their reading group.

2. Organize students into pairs. Have each partner create a cause statement using their reading-group book.

3. Invite partners to share and discuss their cause statements and list of effects.

4. Turn the responsibility for the entire process over to students once they have demonstrated a clear understanding of the cause/effect relationship.

Standardized Test Link: Define Terms

Standardized tests require students to make inferences, draw conclusions, and figure out the effects of a cause. First, as you introduce and practice these reading-between-the-lines strategies, use this terminology. Knowing the correct words will enable students to better understand test questions that include these terms.

After completing mini-lessons and guided practice, work with small groups so students can observe one another's strategizing. You can also provide a framework of helpful, probing questions and suggestions (see pages 222–224).

MODELING READING STRATEGIES WITH PICTURE BOOKS

Because they are short and can be completed in one or two sessions, picture books make great model texts for strategy lessons. Choose books with themes that appeal to middle school students. On the pages that follow, I've listed some titles that I use again and again, and ones that students especially admire. In parentheses, I've listed other strategies you can model with these titles.

PREDICTING

White Wash by Ntzoake Shange, illustrator Michael Sporn, Walker, 1997.

Zeke Peppin by William Steig, HarperCollins, 1994. (visualizing)

The Lily Cupboard by Shulamith Levey Oppenheim, illustrator, Ronald Himler, HarperCollins, 1992 (making connections).

Peppe, The Lamplighter by Eliza Bartone, illustrator, Ted Lewin, Lothrop, Lee & Shepard, 1993. (inferring)

THE SENSES AND COMPREHENSION

From Slave Ship to Freedom Road by Julius Lester, illustrator, Rod Brown, Dial, 1998 (posing questions)

Vejigante, Masquerader by Lulu Delacre, Scholastic, 1993. (inferring)

Big Blue Whale by Nicola Davies, Candlewick, 1997.

The Librarian Who Measured the Earth by Katherine Lasky, illustrator Kevin Hawkes, Little Brown, 1994.

POSING QUESTIONS

Grandfather's Journey by Alan Say. Houghton Mifflin, 1993. (predicting, making connections)

My Father's Boat by Sherry Garland, illustrator, Ted Rand, Scholastic, 1998.

The Island of Skog by Steven Kellog, Dial, 1973. (predicting)

Wump World by Bill Peet, Houghton Mifflin, 1970. (making connections)

VOCABULARY IN CONTEXT

A Gathering of Garter Snakes by Bianca Lavies, Dial, 1993. (questioning)

Alvin Ailey by Andrea Davis Pinkney, illustrator, Brian Pinkney, Hyperion, 1995. (visualizing, making connections)

Autumn Across America by Seymour Simon, Hyperion, 1993. (partner readings, retellings)

Journey to Ellis Island: How My Father Came to America by Carol Bierman, illustrator Laurie McGaw, Hyperion, 1998. (inferring and making connections)

PARTNER READINGS AND RETELLINGS

The Hatseller and the Monkeys by Baba Wague Daikite, Scholastic, 1999.

Call Me Ahnighito by Pam Conrad, illustrator, Richard Egielski, HarperCollins, 1995.

Pablo Remembers by George Ancona, Lothrop, Lee & Shepard, 1993.

The Gods and Goddesses of Olympus by Aliki, HarperCollins, 1994.

SUMMARIZING AND SYNTHESIZING

Mirette on the High Wire by Emily Arnold McCully, Putnam, 1992. (predicting, making connections)

She's Wearing a Dead Bird on Her Head by Kathryn Lasky, illustrator, David Catrow, Hyperion, 1995. (making inferences and connections)

Georgia Music by Helen V. Griffith, illustrator, James Stevenson, Greenwillow, 1986.

An Octopus Is Amazing by Patricia Lauber, illustrator, Holly Keller, Crowell, 1990.

MAKING CONNECTIONS TO SELF, COMMUNITY, THE WORLD

Rose Blanche by Roberto Innocenti, Creative Education, 1990. (inferring, questioning)

Hiroshima No Pika by Toshi Maruki, Lothrop, Lee & Shepard, 1980. (visualizing, questioning)

Golem by David Wisniewski, Clarion, 1996.

The Wall by Eve Bunting, illustrator, Ronald Himler, Clarion, 1990.

MAKING INFERENCES

Going Home by Eve Bunting, illustrator David Diaz, HarperCollins, 1996.

Minty: A Story of Young Harriet Tubman by Alan Schroeder, illustrator Jerry Pinkney, Dial, 1996.

Terrible Things: An Allegory of the Holocaust by Eve Bunting, illustrator Stephen Gammell, The Jewish Publication Society, 1996. (making connections)

The Tale of Mandarin Ducks by Katherine Paterson, illustrators, Leo and Diane Dillon, Lodestar, 1990. (making connections)

DRAWING CONCLUSIONS ABOUT CHARACTERS

The Fortune Tellers by Lloyd Alexander, Dutton, 1992. (visualizing)

Boundless Grace by Mary Hoffman, illustrator, Caroline Binch, Dial, 1995. (making connections)

Missing May by Michael O. Tunnell, illustrator, Ted Rand, Greenwillow, 1997. (making inferences)

Through Grandpa's Eyes by Patricia MacLachlan, illustrator Deborah Kogan Ray, HarperCollins, 1980. (making inferences and connections, visualizing)

PAIRED READING

Russian Girl: Life in an Old Russian Town by Russ Kendall, Scholastic, 1994. (visualizing)

A Library of Congress Book: Inventors by Martin W. Sandler, HarperCollins, 1996.

From Slave Ship to Freedom Road by Julius Lester, illustrator Rod Brown, Dial, 1998.

Trapped by the Ice! Shackleton's Amazing Antarctic Adventure by Michael McCurdy, Walker, 1997.

READ, PAUSE, RETELL, REREAD

Serengeti Migration: Africa's Animals on the Move by Lisa Lindblad, photographer Sven-Olof Lindblad, Hyperion, 1994.

Sharks by Seymour Simon, HarperCollins, 1995.

Seven Brave Women by Betsey Hearne, illustrator Bethanne Andersen, Greenwillow, 1997.

Emergency! by Joy Masoff, Scholastic, 1999.

Pause and Reflect on:
Taking Time to Read Between the Lines

Reserving time to discuss books and explore implied meanings enables students to discover themes, construct new understandings, and recall plot details. The deeper students involve themselves in a story, the more likely they are to make book-to-book and book-to-personal-life connections. Such connections confirm the relevancy of reading for them. A struggling seventh-grade reader told me after reading *Bridge to Terabithia*, "When I saw that Jesse's dad didn't understand Jesse's need to paint, it helped me think about how my dad hates that I signed up for tap dance lessons. It's the first time a book meant so much to me." Reading attitudes changed for this young adolescent, who linked his life to a part of Jesse Aaron's life and felt validated.

🌿 Chapter 8

Ways to Connect Students to Books

"I'd rather be punished than read a book."   —Seventh Grader

The school bus parks in front of a fast-food restaurant. Nineteen boys and six girls from an eighth-grade class are on a field trip, visiting area factories. The boys dash into the restaurant and line up, ready to order. Several take out pocket combs and arrange their hair. While I quietly explain that combing hair in a restaurant is not acceptable, I notice the girls rush toward the restroom like lemmings racing toward the sea. Ten minutes pass; I decide to hurry the girls along. When I enter the small restroom, three are applying lipstick, one is spraying her hair, and two stand in a corner, pulling their shirts out and then tucking them into their jeans. "Which looks better?" Jenny asks me.

Like these eighth graders, middle school students constantly worry about their image and how peers perceive them. Between classes they dash to the lavatories, to inspect the progress of a zit or to comb their hair.

More than anything, adolescents want to be part of a popular group, have friends, and socialize during and after school. Confronting reading difficulties is not high on the agenda for these students—and changing their negative attitudes toward reading is a daunting challenge for teachers. Every year I relearn this lesson after I confer with students and hear comments like these:

"I never think about a book after I read. I'm glad I'm done." —*Eighth Grader*

"My mom says I have to read fifteen minutes. I set the timer and wait for it to ring."
—*Sixth Grader*

"I see nothing when I read—just words." —*Seventh Grader*

"I don't understand the words, so why bother?" —*Sixth Grader*

The research of Pearson et al (1992) and Schallert and Reed (1997) points out three factors that can turn students away from reading in the elementary grades and continue to impede on their learning when they enter middle school:

1. Students lack prior knowledge about the topic. Even if the text is readable, without prior knowledge, the attempt to comprehend will be frustrating for them (see Chapter 5).
2. Books that are too difficult for students to read block comprehension, because students struggle with decoding and can't focus on connecting what they know to the text.
3. Students' engagement with texts and their ability to untangle and understand confusing

parts is weak, because they are not using in-the-head strategies such as visualization, posing questions, and making personal connections.

This chapter focuses on three strategies that can draw middle school students into reading for pleasure and reading to learn:

1. Read aloud daily and reveal the in-the-head strategies you use to interact with books.
2. Choose books at students' instructional levels to improve reading.
3. Show students how to select books at their independent-reading levels so they can enjoy reading.

THINKING ALOUD DURING DAILY READ-ALOUDS

When I introduce a reading strategy and engage students in guided practice, I use daily read-alouds to model how I apply the strategy. While reading aloud, I pause and think out loud, so students know my inner thoughts, questions, reactions, and imaginings. It's crucial for them to observe that my mind and imagination constantly interact with the text. I want them to know that it's the interactions that make reading pleasurable and exciting! So, many times throughout the year I model these key strategies:

Personal connections to a character, event, decision, or setting: Once readers connect aspects of the story to their own lives, and to the lives of friends and family, the story hooks them, compelling them to read on. I bring in a Betsy Byars "Herculeah Jones" mystery and a P.D. James adult mystery and tell students that I connect to mysteries because one of my fantasies is playing detective, and I like to step into the sleuth's shoes and try to interpret the clues.

Images that pop into my mind: When I describe the process of visualizing a character, setting, or event, I use sensory words to describe what I see. I tell students, "Visualizing is like making my own movie, and the screen is my mind." While reading Louis Sachar's *Holes* (Farrar, Straus & Giroux), I share my mental picture of Stanley, tired and thirsty, spotting the boat in the middle of the desert, on page 154. I envision a half-rotted boat with a rusted motor, covered with hot, dry sand, and the name *Mary Lou* printed in red letters on the stern.

Questions the text raises: The questions I pose to myself often drive my reading because I'm longing to discover answers. I point out that as I continue to read, the text will answer some of my questions, but not all of them. Often, I bring in a book or magazine article that answers an unresolved question, and read and discuss it. This shows students that acting on curiosity is an important part of reading and learning.

One day I told my class that I had read a review of an opera that had horses and donkeys onstage. The review caused me to wonder what happens when horses have to relieve themselves while onstage, so I explored several books and articles to find an answer. I discovered that sometimes a poop-catcher is attached to an animal's rear. Other times, stagehands, dressed in costume, follow the animal and clean up, undetected, as the singers perform.

Predict and support: A close relative to questioning, making predictions about what will happen next in the story creates anticipation, and students continue reading to test their predictions against the unfolding story. When I pause and predict, I always offer some support, so students can observe how these strategies work together. For example, when I predict after chapter three that Jesse Aarons will become friends with Leslie Burke *(Bridge to Terabithia)*, I use the following support: She lives close by; he can't relate to his older sisters because they're prissy and interested only in clothes and makeup; she is a great runner and beats Jesse and his friends in the race; when Jesse steps off the bus and watches Leslie run, he thinks "beautiful," but puts the word out of his mind.

Making inferences: While reading dialogue or a character's inner thoughts or actions, I explain how I read between the lines and draw conclusions about personality and motivation. In *Bridge to Terabithia*, after Leslie beats Jesse (who's the fastest runner in his class) in a race at school, Jesse boards the school bus and sits next to his little sister, Maybelle. Since Jesse wouldn't ordinarily sit with Maybelle, his action tells me that he's avoiding Leslie; he doesn't want to face the girl who beat him. Jesse is having trouble accepting that he's not number one anymore.

Passages that confuse: All readers bump into sections of texts that confuse them. I'm up front about this, and it is a great relief and comfort to my students. To "unconfuse" myself, I reread a passage until I can say in my own words what I believe it means. Sometimes I reverse and read several sentences that preceded the confusing part. Whatever I do, I share my thoughts with students so they can eavesdrop on my reading process. One day I wrote on the chalkboard the title of Avi's story, "What Do Fish Have To Do With Anything?" because the group that read it thought the title was weird and had nothing to do with the story. I asked them to reread the exchange between Willie and his mom on the story's last page. Willie's mom called the police to rid their block of the homeless man because he was "pestering kids"; she doesn't want Willie to talk to the man again. Willie insists his mom doesn't have eyes. He tells her that she's blind like the fish in the cave. Willy's mom responds by asking, "What do fish have to do with anything?"—the story's title. Before I could share my thoughts, light bulbs went on in students' heads. The mom, they told me, is as blind as the cave fish to Willie's emotional needs, his loneliness, and to the friendship between Willie and the homeless man.

Free choice reading engages students.

Connections to other books: The ability to discover similarities between characters, themes, settings, and plots of different books not only adds to the excitement of reading, but also reflects a high level of thinking and literary analysis. When I verbalize the connections I've made to other books, I include what sparked the connection. For example, the unfair punishment of fictional Stanley Yelnats in *Holes* made me think of the unfair punishment of Ji-li, her family and her friends in *Red Scarf Girl,* an autobiographical account of a girl living through the Chinese Cultural Revolution. They were all unable to defend themselves and sought redemption.

Teacher Read-Aloud in Action

Following is a poem by Emily Dickinson, along with the think-aloud (in italics) that I present to my eighth graders. To enter into the emotions and images of a poem, it's important to read it aloud several times. I select a short poem and read it to the class, then I reread it, adding the think-aloud.

ROBB'S THINK-ALOUD FOR "INDIAN SUMMER" BY EMILY DICKINSON

These are the days when birds come back,
A very few, a bird or two
To take a backward look.

(Think aloud after first stanza.)
At this time of year, I can't wait to take a backward look. I love nature's deceit, and play along, believing that summer has returned.

These are the days when skies put on
The old, old sophistries of June,—
A blue and gold mistake.

(Think aloud after third stanza.)
Though I allow nature to deceive me, its creatures, such as the bee and trees that turn crimson and gold, are not tricked. But that won't prevent me from believing that summer is back.

Oh, fraud that cannot cheat the bee,
Almost thy plausibility
Induces my belief,

Till ranks of seeds their witness bear,
And softly through the altered air
Hurries a timid leaf!

(Think aloud at the end.)
I connect to the child who feels that nature's brief return to summer is like a sacrament— a holy and religious experience that returns annually.

Oh, sacrament of summer days,
Oh, last communion in the haze,
Permit a child to join,

The personal connections to this poem help me understand the images and references to Holy Communion in a poem about Indian summer. My connections bond me to this poem because I can link my experiences with Emily Dickinson's. It's this linkage that pulls me back to the poem again and again.

Thy sacred emblems to partake,
Thy consecrated bread to break,
Taste thine immortal wine!

On the next day, I reread the poem and explain the mental pictures, the images in my mind. Sometimes students have a burning need to share connections they make. Accept their comments and adjust your schedule, for these are "teachable moments."

Teaching Reading in Middle School

OTHER POEMS TO READ ALOUD

"Alligator on the Escalator" by Eve Merriam

"Bats" by Randall Jarrell

"Bishop Hatto" by Robert Southey

"Chinatown Games" by Wing Trek Lump

"Dear Neighbor God" by Rainer Maria Rilke

"Dream Variation" by Langston Hughes

"The Erl-King" by Johann Wolfgang von Goethe

"Finding A Poem" by Eve Merriam

"For My People" by Margaret Walker

"Frederick Douglass" by Robert Hayden

"A Half Blade of Grass" by Yevgeny Yevtushenko

"Incident" by Countee Cullen

"Jazz Fantasia" by Carl Sandburg

"Kite" by Valerie Worth

"Kubla Khan" by Samuel Taylor Coleridge

"La Belle Dame Sans Merci" by John Keats

"The Lake Isle of Inisfree" by William Butler Yeats

"Little Blanche" by Naomi Shihab Nye

"Migrants" by Dills Lying

"Nan Do in Grouse Point" by J. Patrick Lewis

"The Poet Stumbles Upon the Astronomer's Orchards" by Nancy Willard

"Pregnant Teenager On The Beady" by Mary Bills

"Recess" by Linda Pastan

"The Road Not Taken" by Robert Frost

"The Runaway" by Robert Frost

"Runner" by Don Lang Stein

"The Snake" by Emily Dickinson

"Things" by Eloise Greenfield

"The Tyger" by William Blake

"We Real Cool" by Gwendolyn Brooks

Tips for Modeling Strategies While Reading Aloud

I want struggling and reluctant readers to hear, again and again, how I apply reading strategies. Proficient readers benefit from hearing them, too, for as sixth grader Dominique said, "I enjoy comparing what you say to what's in my head."

Here are some tips for successful think-alouds while you read aloud:

1. Explain that this is a time when you share your process with students and that you will not always set aside time for such a lengthy discussion. Point out that students will have multiple opportunities to participate during and after reading-strategy mini-lessons.

2. Pause and think aloud two or three times, in a 10- to 15-minute read-aloud.

3. Start with personal connections, then move to visualizing. Without these, bonds between

reader and text will rarely form.

4. Spend several weeks modeling each strategy.

5. Integrate two strategies, such as predict-and-support and visualizing, in the same read-aloud once students have a clear understanding of each one.

6. Repeat strategies and think-alouds if students express confusion.

7. After the read-aloud, take a minute or two to explain why you use the strategy you're modeling. If you're working on the same strategy for several weeks, offer an explanation two or three times. Confirm that students can explain why the strategy is beneficial.

All the while you're modeling how you apply reading strategies, you're selecting books for instruction, and teaching students how to choose books at their independent levels. Finding a book that a student is burning to read and that he *can* read is the first step to helping students develop personal reading lives.

CHOOSING BOOKS THAT MEET ALL STUDENTS' DEVELOPMENTAL NEEDS

It's difficult to find one title that will be accessible to a class of students at diverse reading levels. Yet, the kinds of books that you and I choose for reading instruction can determine whether every student experiences success, becomes involved with a book, and improves in reading throughout the school year.

Many school districts require that teachers use a basal anthology or specific books that relate to required themes. However, in most middle school classes, those students who are reading below grade level will not be able to read these required texts independently. I know many middle school teachers who read these texts out loud while students follow along. Students will improve their listening skills and learn information by hearing you read. However, to improve reading, learners must consistently *read at their independent level.*

More fortunate teachers can order two or three grade levels of the district's anthology, and organize instructional groups that meet two or three times a week.

For me, a basal anthology is only one part of a reading program. Students, to become more proficient, should *read, read, read* at their independent level, where reading is comfortable and enjoyable. To accomplish this, I recommend varying the way you organize reading workshop, by including requirements, novel studies, core and extension books, text sets, and free-choice reading.

Teaching Reading in Middle School

A QUICK AND EASY READABILITY FORMULA

Leveling books to meet students' independent and instructional reading needs is one of my top priorities. The readability formula I recommend teachers use is McLaughlin's SMOG Formula [McLaughlin's acronym for Some Measure of Gobbledygook]. After you apply the steps listed below to four or five books, you'll remember the formula and find that it is an efficient way to predict independent reading levels.

The SMOG formula predicts readability necessary for 90 to 100 percent comprehension (Vaughan, Estes, 1986), which is considered the independent reading level of a book. For instructional reading comprehension levels, Estes and Vaughan recommend that you adjust the SMOG results by subtracting two years.

Here are the six steps in McLaughlin's formula:

1. Count 10 consecutive sentences in the beginning of the book, 10 in the middle, and 10 at the end.
2. Count every word of three or more syllables when the words are read aloud. Do this for the 30 sentences. If words are repeated, include them in the count.
3. Round the number of polysyllabic words to the nearest perfect square.
4. Take the lower of the two perfect squares if the number of polysyllabic words falls exactly between two perfect squares.
5. Take the square root of the nearest perfect square.
6. Determine the independent reading level by adding 3 to the estimated square root.
7. Subtract 2 from independent level to estimate instructional level.

Example: Number of polysyllabic words in 30 sentences: 32

The nearest perfect square is 36.

The square root of 36 is 6.

6 + 3 = 9 for the independent-reading level at 90–100% comprehension

9 - 2 = 7 for the approximate instructional level. A seventh grader reading on grade level can read this book *with the support of a teacher.*

NOVEL STUDIES:
INTRODUCE STUDENTS TO GREAT BOOKS

During a novel study, which lasts about three to six weeks, the entire class reads the same book, and there are times when I want all of my students to read a particular book because that title is not to be missed. (It's important, however, that whole-class novel studies aren't the exclusive instructional diet offered.) Chances are that not everyone will read the chosen novel with ease, but strategies such as paired reading, listening to the book on tape, or having an adult read the text aloud can provide varying levels of support students might require.

30 NOT-TO-BE-MISSED
MIDDLE SCHOOL TITLES

Here are some all-time favorites of students in grades five to eight. These books can be whole-class book studies as long as the book is on every student's instructional level.

The Amazing Potato by Milton Meltzer, HarperCollins, 1992.

Bridge to Terabithia by Katherine Paterson, Crowell, 1977.

The Chocolate War by Robert Cormier, Dell, 1986.

California Blue by David Klass, Scholastic, 1994.

Down River by Will Hobbs, Bantam, 1992.

The Endless Steppe by Esther Hautzig, Crowell, 1968.

Fahrenheit 451 by Ray Bradbury, Ballantine, 1953.

Freak the Mighty by Rodman Philbrick, Scholastic, 1993.

Gentlehands by M.E. Kerr, Bantam, 1981.

Ghosts of the West Coast by Ted Wood, Walker, 1999.

The Giver by Lois Lowry, Houghton Mifflin. 1993.

Glory Field by Walter Dean Myers, Scholastic, 1994.

Core and Extension Books: Use for Theme and Genre Studies

A core book should be accessible to everyone in the class. With this book that everyone can read, teachers engage students in applying reading strategies, show them how to conduct meaningful discussions, and model journal responses. As students read the core book, they also read books at their independent-reading levels.

Core books can introduce a theme or topic such as prejudice, peer pressure, family relationships, survival, or war. Introduce literary genres with a core book—genres such as realistic fiction, fantasy, mystery, or historical fiction. Launch an author study with a core book. A study of the books of Jean Craighead George was one that my sixth graders rated high. The core book for this author study was *The Cry of the Crow* (HarperCollins). In addition to reading the core book,

Hatchet by Gary Paulsen, Viking, 1987.

To Kill a Mockingbird by Harper Lee, Warner, 1988.

Lincoln: A Photobiography by Russel Friedman, Clarion, 1987.

Maniac Magee by Jerry Spinelli, HarperCollins, 1991.

My Brother Sam Is Dead by James and Christopher Collier, Macmillan, 1974.

The Mystery of Mammoth Bones by James Cross Goblin, HarperCollins, 1999.

No Promises in the Wind by Irene Hunt, Berkley, 1987.

Of Nightingales That Weep by Katherine Paterson, HarperTrophy, 1974.

One World, Many Religions: The Ways We Worship by Mary Pope Osbourne, Knopf, 1996.

The Outsiders by S.E. Hinton, Dell, 1967.

Parrot in the Oven by Victor Martinez, HarperCollins, 1998.

Rescue: The Story of How Gentiles Saved Jews in the Holocaust by Milton Meltzer, HarperTrophy, 1988.

Roll of Thunder, Hear My Cry by Mildred Taylor, Viking, 1976.

Shabanu: Daughter of the Wind by Suzanne Fisher-Staples, Knopf, 1989.

Tuck Everlasting by Natalie Babbitt, Farrar, Straus & Giroux, 1975.

Walkabout by James Marshall, Sundance, 1984.

The Wizard of Earthsea by Ursula K. Le Guin, Bantam, 1968.

pairs or groups selected three to five additional nonfiction and fiction titles by George. During an author study students have the opportunity to immerse themselves in one person's work and compare and contrast the writer's use of language, plot, setting, character, and themes. When I choose a core book for a whole-class themed novel study, I measure it against these seven criteria:

1. Struggling readers can read the text.

2. My reluctant readers will connect to the story.

3. The story addresses issues and problems that middle grade students find relevant and meaningful. Readers will understand the basic concepts, and also be introduced to new information that interests them, thereby increasing their background knowledge.

4. The text is an example of quality writing and provides students with an outstanding writing model.

5. Characters are not stereotyped.

6. Students will enjoy rereading all or parts of the story.

7. The story is worth thinking and talking about, for it can stimulate charged discussions and diverse interpretations.

Extending the theme study beyond the core book allows each student to read at his or her level. To offer all students choices for extension books, I ask our librarian to select theme-related titles two or three weeks prior to the study and provide her with my students' range of reading levels.

I arrange books on three or four tables, stacking them according to reading levels. Then I invite groups of students to choose books from a stack they find readable. Though titles and levels of difficulty vary, the genre or theme provides a common ground for pairs or small groups to discuss. This strategy offers students the opportunity to choose among books they can read independently, and improves reading, because students can make meaning using books they enjoy.

Text Sets: Variations on a Theme

Sometimes called multiple texts, these are sets of different titles related to a theme, such as peer pressure; a nonfiction topic, such as the American Revolution or whales; a genre study, such as mystery or different versions of a fairy tale. Text sets are beneficial because:

✦ Each student may read a different book, so everyone's knowledge is enriched by the variety of perspectives.

✦ Students can read about the same topic and find books at their reading levels.

✦ When many titles are read and shared, students become interested in reading books their classmates rated as tops.

✦ Teachers can find titles in their school and public libraries.

✦ Ordering five to seven copies of one title is an efficient use of school funds. The result is greater variety of books at varying reading levels.

20 WORTHWHILE CORE BOOKS THAT CAN REACH ALL READERS

Baby by Patricia MacLachan, Bantam, Doubleday, Dell, 1993.

The Book of Three by Lloyd Alexander, Bantam, Doubleday, Dell, 1984.

Boy: Tales of Childhood by Roald Dahl, Farrar, Straus & Giroux, 1984.

The Children's Story by James Clavell, Bantam, Doubleday, Dell, 1963.

The Dark Stairs by Betsy Byars, Puffin, 1997.

Dear Mr. Henshaw by Beverly Cleary, Morrow, 1983.

The Face in the Frost by John Bellairs, Macmillan Children's Books, 1991.

The Friendship by Mildred Taylor, Dial, 1989.

The Green Book by Jill Paton Walsh, Farrar, Straus & Giroux, 1982.

Hiroshima by Laurence Yep, Scholastic, 1985.

The Language of Goldfish by Zibby O'Neal, Puffin, 1990.

The Midwife's Apprentice by Karen Cushman, Houghton Mifflin, 1995.

Nightjohn by Gary Paulsen, Doubleday, 1993.

The Outsiders by S.E. Hinton, Dell, 1967.

The Pinballs by Betsy Byars, HarperCollins, 1987.

Sadako and the Thousand Paper Cranes by Eleanor Coerr, Dell, 1979.

Shades of Gray by Carolyn Reeder, Macmillan Children's Books, 1989.

Shiloh by Phyllis R. Naylor, Atheneum, 1991.

Stone Fox by John Reynolds Gardiner, HarperCollins, 1989.

What Jamie Saw by Carolyn Coman, Puffin, 1997.

The Window by Michael Dorris, Hyperion, 1997.

TEXT SETS REACH ALL READERS

Text Set: Author Study on Survival: Jean C. George

My Side of the Mountain, Dutton, 1988.

The Cry of the Crow, HarperCollins, 1980.

The Summer of the Falcon, HarperCollins, 1979.

Julie of the Wolves, HarperCollins, 1972.

Julie's Wolf Pack, HarperCollins, 1997.

The Talking Earth, HarperCollins, 1983.

Water Sky, HarperCollins, 1987.

Text Set: Growing Up

Baseball in April by Gary Soto, Harcourt Brace, 1990.

The Chocolate War by Robert Cormier, Dell, 1986.

The Contender by Robert Lipsyte, HarperCollins, 1967.

Downriver by Will Hobbs, Atheneum, 1991.

Glory Field by Walter Dean Myers, Scholastic, 1994.

The Moves Make the Man by Bruce Brooks, HarperCollins, 1984.

Nothing But the Truth by Avi, Avon, 1993.

Rites of Passage by Richard Wright, HarperCollins, 1994.

Scorpions by Walter Dean Myers, HarperCollins, 1988.

Words by Heart by Ouida Sebestyen, Bantam, 1968.

Text Set: War and Peace

Across Five Aprils by Irene Hunt, Follett, 1964.

The Diary of a Young Girl by Anne Frank, Doubleday, 1967.

The Endless Steppe by Esther Hautzig, Crowell, 1968.

Fallen Angels by Walter Dean Myers, Scholastic, 1988.

The Fighting Ground by Avi, HarperCollins, 1984.

The Foxman by Gary Paulsen, Puffin, 1977.

The Fragile Flag by Jane Langton, HarperCollins, 1984.

Hiroshima, No Pika by Toshi Maruki, Lothrop, Lee & Shepard, 1982.

Music and Drum: Poems of War and Peace, Hopes and Dreams, editor: Laura Robb, Philomel, 1996.

Traitor: The Case of Benedict Arnold by Jean Fritz, Putnam, 1981.

The Wall by Eve Bunting, Clarion, 1990.

The Wave by Todd Strasser, Dell, 1981.

No Pretty Pictures by Anita Lobel, Greenwillow, 1998.

FREE-CHOICE READING:
ALLOW IT TO RUN THE GAMUT

For students to develop a personal reading life and become lifelong readers, it's crucial to provide opportunities for them to select books that relate to their interests. By sampling a variety of books and magazines (see box), your middle school students will develop literary tastes. Like you and me, they will not always select a classic or a challenging title. Think of your own reading habits. At the beach, on vacation, or on a quiet weekend, you might turn to a mystery novel, a magazine, a collection of poems, or even a store catalog. Students deserve the same opportunities, for like adult readers, the situation and amount of time define their choice of book.

During middle school years, encourage students to explore literary and non-literary genres. Bring in a fashion or computer magazine, a mystery or fast-paced novel, and show students how you read for different purposes.

Write these suggestions on chart paper and discuss with students how to choose a book

---

MAGAZINES FOR MIDDLE SCHOOL STUDENTS

Teacher Resource
Magazines for Kids and Teens: A resource for parents, teachers, librarians, and kids!
Donald R. Stoll, editor, published by The Educational Press Association of America and the International Reading Association.

Content-area magazines middle school students enjoy
Cobblestone, a history magazine, Cobblestone Publishing, Inc., 7 School St., Peterborough, NH 03458.

Merlyn's Pen, publishes fiction by teens, Merlyn's Pen, Inc., 98 Main St., P.O. Box 1058, East Greenwich, RI 02818.

Read Magazine, a literary magazine, Weekly Reader Corp., 3001 Cindel Dr., Delran, NJ 08370.

Science World, Scholastic, Inc., 2931 East McCarty St., P.O. Box 3710, Jefferson City, MO 65102-9957.

Zoobooks, Wildlife Education Limited, 3590 Kettner Blvd., San Diego, CA 92101.

---

and predict whether or not they will enjoy it:

✦ Study the cover and title. Read the back cover or the summary inside the book's jacket.

✦ Read the chapter headings or table of contents.

✦ Browse through photographs or illustrations.

✦ Look for books about your hobbies, interests, or favorite sports.

✦ Explore other books written by an author you enjoyed.

✦ Ask friends, classmates, your teacher, and the librarian for recommendations.

Tips for Making That Book a Perfect Fit

Teach your students the five-finger method for determining if a book is too difficult (Glazer and Brown, 1993; Robb, 1996). Ask them to turn to any page and begin reading. If there are five words they can't pronounce or don't understand, then recommend that they read the book later.

Adapt the five-finger method for struggling readers by making it the two- or three-finger method, and help them choose another book if they can't pronounce or don't understand two or three words on a page.

As students check their selections, I spot-check able and struggling readers. I always observe my best readers first, so weaker students don't feel I'm spotlighting them.

Some students will insist on checking out a hard book. Let them, and suggest that they ask someone at home to read it aloud. You might even read the book aloud to the entire class!

A Book Is Too Easy If: You can pronounce and understand all the words and can retell everything you have read.

A Book Is Too Difficult If: You can't pronounce or don't know the meaning of five words on the page and you can't retell what you've just read.

A Book Is A Perfect Fit If: You can pronounce and understand all but one or two of the words and can retell most of what you have read.

Free-Choice Reading Contracts

Independent-reading contracts invite students to develop their own reading tastes because students choose their own books. Each month students set a goal—in writing—where they commit to reading a specific number of books. Often, struggling and reluctant readers can complete two to four books a month at their comfort level, improving fluency and comprehension. More able readers might opt to complete one very long book. Each month, students can negotiate with you the number of books they plan to read. You can use the contract form at right or adapt it. I have students store these in literature journals or in a reading folder.

Reading Contract

My goal is to read _____ books during the month of _____.

Student's Name _____

Teacher's Name _____

Students learn to pace themselves and can see positive growth as the year unfolds. I explain that if a student feels she won't meet a contract deadline date, she should negotiate new terms several days before the end of the month.

During and at the close of each month, I set aside time for students to record the books they've read on a reading log form headed with title, author, and date completed. They use contract books for book reviews and talks, teacher conferences, and projects.

When Students Choose Books That Are Too Difficult

"My weakest readers always choose books way beyond their reading level. How can I change this?" This is a question I'm often asked, and one I too wrestle with each year. The principle that guides the intervention strategy I've developed is to help a struggling reader maintain self-esteem.

I ask all students to show me their selections. If I notice an inappropriate choice, I approach that student with several readable books in hand and say: "That's a terrific book you've selected. But just in case you don't get into it, here are three others I've checked out for you. It's okay to put one book aside for another. I always do that when I'm bored."

Such negotiations honor the student's choice without being critical. I always offer other choices and close by sharing the fact that I change my mind after starting a book. Too often adults feel that students must complete books they've chosen, much like cleaning their dinner plates. However, if you reflect on your reading life, I'm sure you'll find that you readily put a book aside when you're not enjoying it.

Some struggling readers will refuse to take your suggestions and continue to check out books that are too difficult. There are times, however, when I must be patient and wait for trust to develop between the student and me before that student accepts titles I offer. My annual goal is to reach all readers in my workshop. I don't always attain that goal—but I never stop trying.

Pause and Reflect on:
Your Reading Workshop Journey

Before moving on to the next chapter, which discusses strategic-reading groups, evaluate where you are with reading workshop. Before you organize for group instruction, make sure your students can work independently on meaningful reading and writing experiences for 20 to 40 minutes.

Here is a question checklist I refer to during the opening weeks of school while I am introducing reading workshop, its routines, and guidelines.

1. Do I have a literacy folder for each student?
2. Have I collected, through a short "getting-to-know-you" conference and "all-about-me" letters, students' attitudes toward books and reading?
3. If conferences, students' records, and portfolios do not offer adequate information on students' reading expertise and attitudes, have I set aside time to administer Informal Reading Inventories?
4. Have I negotiated behavior guidelines for group work?
5. Have I established a series of "help" strategies for students?
6. Are routines and reading-and-writing guidelines clear enough for me to begin small-group work?
7. Am I balancing my goals for students with district requirements?
8. Do all students have many opportunities to enjoy books at their independent and comfort reading levels?
9. Am I modeling, during daily read-alouds, how I use strategies to connect to books?
10. Have I helped students learn how to work independently?

Teachers who have recently implemented reading workshop tell me that the list helps them think about these various elements. However, I want teachers to understand that it's fine if not all the elements are in place. Use the checklist to assess where you are and add new workshop experiences when you think that you can manage them without feeling overwhelmed and frustrated.

Chapter 9

Organizing and Guiding Strategic-Reading Groups

"Talking about books I can read has helped me enjoy reading."
—Fifth Grader

In 1991, I taught a class of 16 struggling readers at Johnson Williams Middle School in Clarke County, Virginia. The seventh and eighth graders in this class had failed the Virginia Literacy Test in Reading at least twice. All had attended summer school because they had failed reading in sixth and/or seventh grade. Standardized tests showed that students were two to four years below grade level. Teachers and administrators felt that every student in this class was capable of learning to read. In addition to their five-times-a-week double period of reading/writing workshop, students met with me for two, weekly 45-minute periods.

I entered this class with three beliefs: 1) For students to personally connect to books, they had to read at their comfort level, which is about one or two years below their independent level. 2) If I armed students with reading strategies—and strategies for decoding and figuring out the meaning of unfamiliar words—they could and would improve. 3) Since reading is a social experience, with students discussing and collaborating and supporting one another, students should sit in groups.

On the first day, I seated students in groups of four, and opened class by reading aloud "The Elevator," a short story by William Sleator. Within minutes I noticed students whispering, kicking, punching, taking pencils, yawning, or tuning out with their heads on their desks. Daunted and shaken, I completed the story and asked students to write, in journals, their feelings toward reading. Twelve students turned in blank pages or pages covered with drawings. Three wrote, "I HATE it," and a fourth wrote, "I never do it." During this time, two students were yelling at each other, several kicked one another under the desks, and their victims shouted and whined, "He's kicking me!"

As soon as the bell rang, students literally stampeded out of the class, shouting: "What kind of teaching is this anyway?" and "What are we gonna learn from you reading to us? This is dumb!" Their comments were not what I had hoped for. Though I'd mentally prepared myself for negative reactions, their words and behavior stung.

Over the next weeks, these seventh and eighth graders taught me some important lessons:

✦ Grouping students who have never worked collaboratively can result in unproductive behaviors.

My Solution: I moved students into rows, brought them together for partner work, then separated them into rows again. This continued until March, when students had created behavior guidelines and had enough collaborative experiences to cooperate in small groups.

- Supporting readers who have struggled for years is difficult because students' self-esteem is so low that they cover up their inability to read with unruly behavior.

My Solution: Build community by doing the following: Actively listen to students and honor their frustration and anger—don't try to change them with words and lectures. Accept students where they are and offer materials they can read. Make participation voluntary. Give students choices and let them put aside books that don't engage them. Involve students in setting goals for themselves.

- Reading aloud can utterly bore students.

My Solution: Choose action-packed stories such as *Captain Murderer* by Charles Dickens, retold by George Harland. Movies and MTV are what these students watch. To engage them, start with fast-paced stories, filled with mystery and suspense and adventure.

- Reading easy books students perceive as "babyish" can turn them further away from reading.

My Solution: I developed projects with teachers of kindergarten through grade three— projects that asked students to read easy books to younger children; to prepare annotated bibliographies for teachers of books related to themes such as oceans, weather or friends; or to tape books for listening centers in primary classrooms (see pages 227–242).

- Looking for a quick transformation in students' attitude toward reading and learning is an unreal expectation.

My Solution: Keep offering strategic mini-lessons and guided practice. Teach students to monitor their own progress by having them self-evaluate, and debrief by discussing what worked and what can be improved. Give yourself a break and remember that struggling readers have a long history of reading and learning difficulties. Most of them need and deserve many years of support to replace negative outlooks with positive ones.

RESPONSIVE GROUPING

Learners improve at different rates. Therefore, responsive grouping, where you work with students who have common needs, is the key to moving all readers forward. Once students understand and apply a strategy, such as finding support for predictions or using context clues to figure out a word's meaning, it's time to move them to a group that's working on another strategy.

Responsive grouping is dynamic and changes throughout the year. It's how teachers group students for strategic reading. When students gain control over a strategy, they move into a different group (see pages 206–209). Such grouping results from the careful observation of students as they respond to mini-lessons, practice strategies, read silently, discuss and write about books, and self-evaluate. You'll also gather important information as you hold brief one-on-one conferences.

I jot down my observations on sticky-notes. Each note has the date, student's name, and whether it's a one-on-one, small-group strategic lesson, journal entry, etc. I store notes in students' literacy folders (see page 94).

The observations that follow were taken over two weeks for eighth grader Randy, who was reading three years below grade level. Taking notes is a manageable task because these are jots, not complex paragraphs.

It's clear from these observations that Randy can make personal connections and figure out words in context in *Stone Fox,* a book at his instructional level. However, supporting predictions is an area that needs more attention, so I've moved Randy to a group that will work on that strategy.

Collecting pages of Post-its—with your observations—is a way for you, students, and parents to see progress over time.

Randy   1/6/97
SSR · 30 min.
· reading book for 3rd grade buddy
· focused
· laughs
· showed Tyler a part – read it aloud softly
· stayed focused

Randy   1/9/97
Journal - Predict/Support "Seventh Grade" - Baseball in April.
· logical predictions
· support from R's own experience
Goal: work on finding support in the story. Move to group working on this strategy.

Randy   1/13/97
Group Discussion
Stone Fox - Chapters 1+2
· personal connection to his own grandpa when sick — told how he felt when saw grandpa in bed
· Understood Willy's words "No! - We're a family." Talked about family sticking together

Observational notes on Randy.

WHAT TEACHERS NEED TO KNOW
ABOUT GROUPING

The research in early reading of Marie Clay, Irene Fountas, and Gay Su Pinnell has dramatically changed the static, traditional methods of grouping students for instruction. Clay says in *Reading: The Patterning of Complex Behaviour* (1979), "Groups will change as children find their own pace and level." Once a child understands and uses a strategy for reading, such as self-monitoring for meaning, it's time to move that child into another group to practice and internalize other strategies.

Fountas and Pinnell elaborated on Clay's flexible grouping concept in *Guided Reading: Good First Teaching for All Children* (1996). They named the kind of grouping Clay described "dynamic grouping." Fountas and Pinnell base dynamic grouping on three assumptions about primary children: 1) In each class there is a wide range of experience and knowledge among children; 2) all children differ in their knowledge of and level of skills; 3) children progress at varying rates. Although these researchers were dealing with emergent and beginning readers, middle school teachers know from their experience that the three assumptions about primary children also apply to readers in grades five to eight.

For middle school readers to progress, grouping must be responsive, based on the progress and needs of each child, because *every child's progress and needs will always differ.*

The question, then, that faces all teachers is, "How do I monitor the progress of each child so I can respond to his/her reading needs by changing group membership?" All three researchers agree that teachers must systematically observe their students, gather data, and use the data to make decisions that benefit children. For children in kindergarten to grade two, systematic observation occurs during the taking of running records, where teachers can closely observe students' reading strategies. Teachers use the data collected from running records to select appropriate reading materials and to regroup students as they progress.

In the middle grades, I find that running records are appropriate for students who are at the emergent and beginning stages of reading, or who are disfluent and reading in a halting manner. But with proficient readers, instead of running records, I use the reading inventory symbols to complete a modified miscue or error analysis of students' oral reading (see page 252). At the October 1999 Keystone Reading Association Conference, Irene Fountas, in her keynote address, also suggested that instead of using running records for third-grade proficient readers, teachers should assess their reading with a modified miscue analysis.

For me, systematic observation of students in grades five on up includes: error analyses of oral reading, patterns observed by studying several standardized tests, observations during small-group and brief one-on-one lessons, journal entries, conferences, and students' self-evaluations (see Chapter 11). The student profile that follows illustrates how teachers can use collected data to make instructional decisions that can move struggling readers forward.

SUGGESTIONS FOR DETERMINING WHEN A STUDENT CAN APPLY A STRATEGY AND MOVE TO ANOTHER GROUP

Interact with and observe students as they work in pairs, groups, or independently. As you read students' self-evaluations and journal responses you'll gain valuable information about whether or not students can apply the strategy. This information will help you decide who is ready to move to another group to be coached on a different strategy.

Such decision-making requires that you use your observational notes, interactions with students, and theoretical knowledge of reading to make informed decisions. Will you always make the decision that's best for a student? Probably not, and that's acceptable, as long as you revise your thinking and do what's best for each reader.

Fifth graders prepare their group presentation of a novel.

On page 208 I share my observational notes on Kayla, an eighth grader, so you can observe how I made the decision to move her to a different group. Reading slightly below grade level, Kayla is presently part of a group of three students working on figuring out vocabulary, using context clues. In her first "Reading Strategy

Teaching Reading in Middle School

A COMPARISON OF RESPONSIVE AND TRADITIONAL GROUPING

Responsive Grouping	Traditional Grouping
✦ Students grouped by assessment of a specific strategy.	✦ Students grouped by general assessments such as standardized testing.
✦ Responds to students' needs and changes as these needs change.	✦ Static and unchanging for long periods of time.
✦ Strategies practiced for before, during, and after reading with a variety of genres.	✦ Selections limited to basal. Worksheets for specific skills.
✦ Books chosen for the group at their instructional level.	✦ Students move through a grade-level basal whether or not they read above or below grade level.
✦ Students read the whole book or story silently. Reading is in meaningful chunks or groups of chapters.	✦ Round robin oral reading.
✦ Students discuss the book and search for as many interpretations as the text supports.	✦ Students read to find the correct answer.
✦ Varied vocabulary with an emphasis on solving word problems while reading.	✦ Controlled vocabulary.
✦ Students practice and apply strategies that enable them to connect to and think deeply about texts.	✦ Students complete worksheets that have little to do with the story in the basal.
✦ Students learn to apply word-solving strategies to real books.	✦ Students practice skills with worksheets. The transfer to real word skills to books is rarely made.
✦ Evaluation based on careful observations of student's reading in a variety of situations.	✦ Evaluation based on skills sheets and basal reading tests.

Checklist" (see page 102), next to the statement, "I identify unfamiliar words and use context clues to figure out their meanings," Kayla wrote: *I skip these.* Her honest reaction helped me decide to monitor Kayla when I presented this strategy lesson to the class. What follows are transcriptions of my shorthand notes and an evaluation of Kayla's progress.

Guided Practice: Kayla works with partner. Partner does 90% of work. *[I'm thinking, tomorrow I'll sit with Kayla and Kendra and try to engage both.]*
Next day, Kayla needs lots of prompting to read ahead, reverse and reread, find key words, phrases.

Robb's Decision: Group Kayla with two other students who need more practice. The group reads "Pets," a short story by Avi from *What Do Fish Have To Do With Anything?* As they read, students record tough words on sticky-notes and when we meet, I coach students, supporting their use of context clues.

Strategic–Reading Group: First Meeting. Words: *compelled*, p. 124; *indignantly* and *haunts*, p. 125. Kayla uses clues such as "returning to her favorite sleeping spot" to define *haunts* as *favorite places.* Said that it was like *haunted* because the cat was always in those places and haunted them. Group had trouble with *indignantly.*

Second Meeting: Words: *cringing*, p.131; *primly*, 132; *plaintive*, p. 139. Kayla explains *plaintive* using the situation and the plot. She was excited to be able to do it and said, "It's fun looking for clues."

One-on-One Meeting: Kayla thinks aloud and shows me how she figures out meaning of *bemused* from p. 141 of "Pets." When I ask her to explain some strategies she used, Kayla has trouble expressing ideas with words. We discuss these strategies, and find examples of clues in the sentence, the situation, reading ahead, and reversing and rereading from words the group discussed at second and third meetings.

Group Practices Independently: Kayla participates. Shows how she figured out words from the "situation." She uses the word "situation" to tell others that the situation the character was in provided clues for figuring out the word's meaning.

Journal Entry: Able to explain words from context alone. Did this with free-reading book *The Cabin Faced West* by Jean Fritz. Used sticky-notes to jot tough words: When Kayla finished reading a section, she returned to the sticky-notes and text to figure out the words' meanings.

One-on-One: Uses journal notes to show me how she figured out each word. Able to say things like *read ahead, read before, think of what's happening,* etc.

How I Decided to Move Kayla to a Group Practicing Summarizing: Observing Kayla and her group as they practiced, led me to believe that she was internalizing the strategies. Her journal work corroborated my hunch. During our last one-on-one meeting, Kayla was able to explain several ways to use context clues, and she used her journal work to show me. It's time to move Kayla to a group practicing summarizing. I notice that Kayla's book reviews open with retellings, rather than short introductory summary paragraphs. Two groups are presently working on learning to summarize, which is a challenge since students need to understand the point or theme of the story and be able to select three to four key points to summarize.

Use your understanding of your own reading process, theoretical knowledge gained from reading professional books and journals, and careful observations of your students to decide when it's appropriate to move students to different groups. The guidelines that follow help me focus on where students are and ways I can scaffold their learning.

GUIDELINES FOR THINKING ABOUT STUDENTS' REACTIONS TO STRATEGY LESSONS AND FOLLOW-UP PRACTICE

✦ During mini-lessons, make careful mental notes of students who appear confused, detached, or uninterested, or who say, "Oh, that's easy for me."

✦ Circulate during guided practice and note students who are not working or participating with a partner. If students are writing, note those who write little or whose responses appear confused.

✦ In a small- or whole-group situation, middle school students rarely ask for help. They think it's uncool and damaging to their self-image and standing with peers. During my first free moment, I jot down students' names and the title of the mini-lesson. As soon as possible, I work in a small group or one-on-one with these students, basing that decision on what I already know about these learners.

✦ Some students process a demonstration better when they are in a group of three or four or alone. Being closer to the material and teacher also supports their listening and learning. I'll redo a mini-lesson for them.

✦ Other students might shut down because the material seems too hard or fears and anxieties about reading cloud their ability to process. These students benefit from five- to ten-minute one-on-one support meetings. These individual sessions allow me to clarify a strategy, build self-esteem, and provide the scaffolding that can move the student forward.

✦ In one-on-one meetings, I assess how well students can talk about a strategy. Those who cannot discuss the strategy and explain how they use it probably require more scaffolding from you or a peer.

✦ One-on-one meetings also acknowledge that the strategic reading experiences each learner needs differ from student to student. For example, two students struggle with the prediction strategy—one needs coaching to make logical predictions using information in the text, the other with skimming to find support. Brief individual meetings can bring them further along before placing them in a group.

As you carefully observe students in various settings, you'll also be thinking about managing a workshop where students work alone, in pairs, and in small groups.

A Bird's-Eye View of a 90-Minute Workshop in Action

To give you a sense of how to manage a classroom that is grouped for strategic reading, here is a snapshot of a typical day in an eighth-grade reading-writing workshop. It's similar in structure to workshops in grades five through seven. Twenty-five students arrive; and they sit in heterogeneous clusters of five.

Class Openers: 20 minutes

✦ As students arrive, they take out their homework and reading books and set up their response journals with name and date.

✦ Students and I hand out the spelling and writing folders, and sometimes portfolios, stored in three separate crates.

♦ While students prepare their materials, I read aloud for 10 minutes from Rosemary Sutcliffe's *Black Ships Before Troy: The Story of the Iliad,* Delacorte, 1993.

Whole-Class Gathering

Review workshop schedule, including meeting with the strategic-reading group working on inferring, and the group working on decoding multisyllable words; choices for students working independently, in pairs, or in groups; mini-lesson for 12 students (a large group having difficulty supporting predictions with specific details).

Strategy-lesson: 10 minutes

I gather a group for a strategy-lesson (other times it's a whole-class strategy-lesson).

Topic: Finding support from the story for predictions.

Students not part of this strategy-lesson work on:

1. Journal response;

2. Independent silent reading;

3. Partners work on tough words.

Strategic Reading For Two Groups: 45 minutes (devote 20 minutes for each group, with five minutes for making the transition to the second group)

♦ *The Chocolate War* Group: five students read this book; teacher directs the lesson.

Teaching for: Drawing conclusions about characters from dialogue, decisions, and actions.

♦ *The Great Gilly Hopkins* Group: six students read this book; teacher directs the lesson.

Teaching for: Skimming Chapters 1 to 4 to find support for predictions made at the end of Chapter 4.

Some days I work with one group and hold one-on-one meetings with five to six other students. While I work with groups, students look at the chalkboard where I've listed three choices of activities:

Your Top Priority:

1. Journal response on free-choice book must be completed by tomorrow. Response topic: The main character's problem; the actions taken to solve it; the outcome.

Other Choices:

2. Students work with a partner or in a small group (that I've organized) for two to four weeks and help one another figure out the meaning of tough words in their books.

3. Independent reading.

Final 10 Minutes of Workshop:

While the strategic-reading group members who have just finished meeting with me complete the "top priority" journal response, and the rest of the class continues working, I confer, one-on-one, with a student for five minutes. Students copy homework during last five minutes. While they do this, I bring closure to the workshop by making three or four upbeat statements about what I noticed that day, such as:

✦ I noticed that the noise levels were low enough for me to help groups.

✦ I noticed that all of you were involved with your work.

✦ I noticed that several asked classmates for help.

✦ I noticed that everyone has turned in a completed journal response.

More About Guiding Strategic-Reading Groups

After students have practiced a strategy during guided practice, you'll be able to separate the class into two groups: those who can read independently and continue to apply the strategy, and those who require support. Some students will improve with brief individual conferences, while others will benefit from practicing a reading or fix-it strategy in a small group.

You can differentiate instruction when you organize students into small groups whose membership changes as students improve or backtrack. Let's look at the groups in a fifth grade class of 25 students in October, and then again in November.

Fifth Grade Strategic-Reading Groups in October

Students' Names	Strategy
Maria, Josh, Gina	Word Meanings in Context
Tony, Rob, Chantell, José, Liz	Support for Predictions
Lynn, Carla, Darnell, Arnie	Personal Connections
James, Bobby, Dominique	Logical Predictions
Emily, Lissa, Mark, Sean, Shauna, Ann	Pronouncing Multisyllable Words
Ryan, David, Mena, Rosie	Making Inferences

Fifth Grade Strategic-Reading Groups in November

Six weeks later, note how the membership and teaching for strategies changed:

Students' Names	Strategy
Carla, Sean, Liz, Maria, Josh, Ann	Adjusting Predictions
Chantell, José, James, Dominique	Support for Predictions
Gina, Lynn, Arnie, Darnell	Logical Predictions
Shauna, Lissa, Emily, Mark, Bobby	Pronouncing Multisyllable Words
Ryan, David, Mena, Rosie, Tony, Rob	Making Inferences

TEACHING STRATEGIES-ON-THE-RUN

While students read silently I circulate around the room, teaching strategies-on-the-run during short one-on-one conferences. My personal goal is to visit all struggling readers, which usually number from four to seven, and several others.

During these meetings, students and I discuss strategies. I ask one student to read a short passage aloud so I can listen to fluency, then another reads while I observe unfamiliar word-solving strategies. I pause to work on making logical predictions with yet another student. My next stop is with a student who shows me how she used Pocahontas's decision to tell Captain Smith about the impending attack by her father to draw conclusions about the Indian princess *(Pocahontas and the Strangers* by Clyde Bulla). In all these interactions, I'm coaching students and leading them to independence.

It's the variety of instruction—demonstrations, think-alouds, read-alouds, small strategic group work, and on-the-run meetings—that improves students' reading. Within all these experiences, students have opportunities to observe my reading process, the reading process and problem-solving strategies of classmates, and to independently reflect on and practice a strategy with me.

STRATEGY IN ACTION
Seventh-Grade Strategic-Reading Group:
Supporting Predictions

Materials:

The Pinballs by Betsy Byars (HarperTrophy, 1977)

Background Information

During the first two months of school, the class has been studying the predict/support/
confirm/adjust strategy. First, I modeled the strategy during four mini-lessons for the entire
class, and invited students to participate. Then on subsequent days, I had two additional mini-
lessons with a group of four struggling readers, because they had remained silent observers
during collaborative sessions. At the same time, other students worked in groups of three or
four and practiced the strategy using these books that deal with growing up: *The Great Gilly
Hopkins* and *Lyddie* by Katherine Paterson, *The Midwife's Apprentice* by Karen Cushman,
Maniac Magee by Jerry Spinelli, and *The Outsiders* by S.E. Hinton.

   The Pinballs is the book that four struggling readers are using. To develop an understanding of the terms, *foster children* and *pinballs,* students brainstormed lists of what they knew.

Foster Children	Pinballs
✦ they change homes	✦ a game you play
✦ nobody wants them	✦ you bounce a ball around
✦ can go on drugs	
✦ change schools a lot	
✦ real parents might be sick or poor	

   The four have enough background knowledge to discuss these terms and enlarge
their understanding prior to reading this book about three foster children placed in the
same home. While students read, we will return to these lists and add what they are
learning about foster homes, foster parents, foster children, and why the book is named
The Pinballs.

   After studying the cover and title, and reading Chapter 1, I asked each student to predict,
in a journal, what the book will be about, and to support their predictions. Group members

offered no evidence for their predictions. What follows are the four students' predictions and my analysis of them.

Seventh-Grade Students' Predictions and Support

Student 1: I predict its about kids. *[Problem: Too general]*

Student 2: Its abot fastr [foster] kids. *[Problem: Too general]*

Student 3: Carlies mean. *[Problem: An observation, not a prediction]*

Student 4: Harvey Thomas J. and Carlie will be frends. *[Solid prediction]*

At this point, I believe that five to ten minutes of one-to-one will be more beneficial than working with the group again. The transcription that follows shows the prompts I used to help Students 1 and 2 make predictions. I worked with Student 3 separately because she needed support in understanding the structure of a prediction. A brief meeting with Student 4 enabled him to find support. During the next class the four students shared their predictions and support with each other and explained how they had improved.

Note how I point out to students what they are doing well and the progress I've observed. This is crucial for these reasons:

+ It builds confidence.
+ It points out progress.
+ It's only possible for students to construct deeper understandings based on what they *can do.*
+ It makes the strategies they use visible.

Transcription of Meeting With Students 1 and 2

Robb: I'm pleased that you used what you learned in the first chapter to predict that the story will focus on three children. Pointing out that these are foster children makes the prediction more specific. I'd like you to look at the cover picture first and tell me what you learn about the three.

Student 1: Carlie looks away.

Robb: What does that show?

Student 1: She's not part of the others.

Student 2: Yeah. Like she's alone.

Robb: What are the boys doing?

Students' Rewrites of Predictions and Support

Student 1:

Its about 3 kids in the same foster home 2 boys and a girl. The boys will be frends but not the girl. The boys laf and tak on the cover. The girl looks away.

Student 2:

2 boys and a girl are put in a fastr home. I predict there lifes will be like pinballs. The book is the pinballs and thats proof that it will show how the 3 are moved arond.

Student 2: Talking and smiling. Having fun.

Robb: I am pleased with the inferences or conclusions you made using the cover picture. Now let's think about foster children and the word *pinballs*. [pause] What do you know about the word *pinball*?

Student 2: It's a game that you can move a ball all around.

Robb: How does the game relate to foster children?

Student 1: They both get moved around.

Robb: Good connecting! Now use our discussions to make your predictions more specific to this book and show where the evidence came from.

Students work on rewrites (see margin) while I confer with Student 3.

Transcription of Meeting With Student 3

Robb: How did you know Carlie was mean? The author never used that word.

Student 3: The way she talked to the woman—I forgot her name.

Robb: Mrs. Mason. You did something that's really difficult. You drew a conclusion about Carlie based on what she said. Find that part and show me.

Student 3: Here, at the end—pages 6 and 7. [She reads.]

Robb: You know how to find your evidence. That's terrific. Let's see if we can turn your observation into a prediction—what the story will be about.

Student 3: What do I do?

Robb: Tell me what you think will happen to Carlie, using your excellent observation.

Student 3: She'll get into trouble.

Robb: With whom? How?

Student 3: She'll be mean to Mrs. Mason and the boys and then she'll be alone because they won't want to be talked to that way. [She turns to the cover and looks at the illustration.]

Robb: Does the cover give evidence for your prediction?

Student 3: Well, Carlie looks off—she's not part of the talk the boys do.

Robb: Excellent. Now see if you can also use the cover to support your prediction about Carlie getting into trouble.

STRATEGY IN ACTION
Sixth-Grade Teaching Strategies-on-the-Run

Materials
Students' free-choice books, which are on their independent reading levels.

Background Information
Forty minutes have been reserved for independent reading. This is an ideal time to meet with students and support them as they apply strategies while reading. The six struggling readers in this class have been working on self-monitoring, so they can evaluate how much they recall and understand. Several students have resisted rereading, claiming, "It doesn't help," or "I'll forget it anyway."

Transcription of Three On-the-Run Meetings
I meet with Richard, who is reading Walter Wick's *A Drop of Water* (Scholastic). Up until third grade, Richard defined reading as, "Looking at the pictures" or "Getting someone else to read it to you." He's made a great deal of progress, but needs to see the purpose of *rereading*, a fix-it strategy he resists using. Richard checked out this book for a science project.

Robb: How do you feel about this book?

Richard: I like the way the pictures help. I think I'll do some of the experiments.

Robb: Sounds like you might be able to teach your classmates some experiments as part of your project. [Richard nods.] [I see that Richard is on page 18.] Have you read about "Molecules in Motion"?

Richard: Not yet. I just finished bubbles.

STUDENT BEHAVIORS

Following are characteristics of readers at varying levels of proficiency with the predict/support strategy, as well as tips for helping students who struggle with it.

Students Who Understand the Predict/Support Strategy:

✦ Make logical predictions that grow out of the title, plot, setting, characters, and illustrations. They're not searching for the "right" prediction, but for one they can support with the part of text they've read.

✦ Use detailed, specific examples that they can locate in the story—not general statements—to support predictions.

✦ Make inferences based on what happens and what characters say and do.

✦ Reread and skim to find support.

Students Who Don't Understand the Predict/Support Strategy:

✦ Resist making predictions.

✦ Predict but provide no evidence.

✦ Use evidence only from their personal experience—not the story.

✦ Make predictions that are not a logical outgrowth of what they've read.

✦ Use general statements for evidence instead of detailed, specific support.

✦ Resist locating details in the story to support their predictions.

✦ Don't reread to find support.

Try These Strategies to Help Students Who Don't Get It:

✦ Ask students why they are having difficulty. Often students can tell you information such as: The book's too hard; I can't concentrate; I don't know how to skim; My predictions are always dumb.

✦ Make sure students recall the story. Have them retell the plot.

✦ Think aloud in one-on-one conferences and model how you go about predicting and finding evidence.

✦ Have students redo their predictions in class with your help.

Robb: Tell me what you learned.

Richard: [Very long pause] Bubbles you blow look like drops of water. [Long pause] That's all I remember.

Robb: That's an important fact, and a good beginning. I have trouble remembering information that's new, especially after one read. Reread one paragraph at a time and tell what you recall.

Richard: [After rereading first paragraph] Soap bubbles are beautiful and almost perfect spheres. The liquid a bubble's made of is five hundred times thinner than one of my hairs.

Robb: That was great! You remembered every detail. What I really like was the way you connect the bubble to your hair. Try the next three paragraphs. [Richard completes these. He has to reread one of them twice.] Did rereading help?

Richard: A lot. But it takes too much time.

Robb: Then return to the sections you need for your project. Reread those so you can present ideas in your own words.

Next I meet with Gina, who has difficulty selecting the important details from a textbook in science and history. Gina and I have been setting purposes together before reading easy nonfiction texts on animals (Gina adores animals.) "Knowing the purposes," Gina says, "helps me decide what to pick out that's important." Yesterday Gina and I set purposes for reading *Wolves* by Seymour Simon (HarperCollins).

Gina: I really like this book—especially the photographs.

Robb: They are spectacular. Do you have a favorite? [Gina shows me the photo of sleeping cubs.]

Gina: They look so content, and I like the way they snuggle together.

Robb: I'm glad you enjoyed this book. Do you recall the purposes we set for reading?

Gina: I wrote them down. [She opens her journal and reads.] To show how wolves are like people and to show the social structure of the wolf pack. Look. [Gina points to two lists written under each purpose.] I was able to find important information.

Robb: Can you tell me what you did? [Gina nods.]

Gina: First I read the whole book. I read over the purposes, and leafed through the pages, looking for information about how wolves are like us and their social structure. I started to do both and that didn't work. So I did one purpose and then the second.

Robb: You're right. It's easier to focus on one purpose at a time. Your list shows me that you were able to choose details that support each purpose. You've made a lot of progress and you are able to tell me the strategies you used.

Gina: Sometimes teachers don't help you set purposes. Then what do I do?

Robb: Preview the pages in the textbook, read the chapter title, and try to set purposes yourself. Bring your science textbook tomorrow and we'll practice together.

After meeting with four struggling readers, I visit Shauna, a proficient reader, who is working on identifying themes in books she's completed. Taking specific details and turning these into general thematic statements has been difficult for her. Recently Shauna completed Ji-Li Jiang's *Red Scarf Girl*. This is how she described one of the book's themes in her journal: *"Ji-li learns that her family is more precious that being a Red Guard or an 'educable child' or recognized by the Communist party."*

Shauna: I know this is too specific to the story—it's what Ji-li learns.

Robb: Knowing what you have to rethink is terrific. Once you can do that, you can revise. Remember, I suggested two openings: *The book's purpose is…* or *One of the themes is…*

Shauna: [Long pause to think] One of the themes is that it's better to have the love and support of your family than be recognized by the party or group in power.

Robb: Good. Using one of the openings really helped. You took the *Communist Party* and made that general. Good. The situation can happen in any form of government.

Shauna: I need to use "one of the themes" so I don't write about a character.

Robb: Before revising another theme statement and showing it to me, can you connect the theme to your own life or another book?

Shauna: Now I just want my friends, not Mom and Dad, to tell me I'm okay and that they approve of what I wear and do. This book made me think about my mom and my brother and see that they are an important part of my life, too.

When you hold strategy-on-the-run conferences frequently, you can meet each student's unique needs, offer individualized feedback, and reinforce reading for strategies. It's also an opportunity to decide whether or not a student requires a longer conference or follow-up conference or both.

HOW TO USE
READING-STRATEGY PROMPTS

Support students with the prompts on the next page as you work on reading-for-strategies with small groups and individuals. I urge you to keep the list of prompts with you while meeting with students, for it is difficult to listen carefully to what students say, observe their physical reactions, and remember every prompt. Over time you'll put aside the list because these prompts, and those you develop, will be part of your teaching repertoire.

Tips for Prompting Students

The goal is to help students internalize these prompts and apply them to their reading when you're not there. Prompts work best when you're coaching one-on-one or pairs. You can foster this journey toward independence by following these steps:

1. Before inviting students to think in groups or alone, model how you synthesize, summarize, make personal connections, etc.

2. After saying the same prompt two or three times, tell students that next time you want them to prompt themselves.

3. Once you feel students understand the prompt, ask them to remember and use it "inside your minds" rather than wait for you to jump in.

4. During paired reading, have students use a prompt sheet to prompt one another.

PROMPTS FOR USING READING STRATEGIES

To support personal connections:

✦ How are you like one of the characters?

✦ How is the family like your family?

✦ Have you had similar experiences?

✦ Is there an event or place that reminded you of your experiences?

✦ I liked the way you connected your life to the story.

To support visualization:

✦ Tell me what you see when you read this part.

✦ How does the character walk? dress? What does he/she look like?

✦ Can you find parts in the story that help you see what a place or character is like?

✦ What story details helped you create a mental picture?

✦ Where did you have trouble making mental pictures?

To support self-questioning:

✦ What will happen next?

✦ How will the character solve his/her problem?

✦ What have you learned that'll help you understand a character, a decision, a conflict?

✦ What did you learn from the pictures? diagrams? charts?

✦ Did you read the captions?

✦ I like the way you raise questions and read on to explore answers.

To support self-monitoring:

✦ What information do you remember?

✦ Did the passage make sense?

✦ Did a word or phrase stump you?

✦ Reread that and see if it makes sense.

✦ Reread and see if you remember more.

✦ Look for that character's name, a specific place, et cetera, to find what to reread.

✦ Have you previewed this chapter?

✦ What do you already know about this topic?

...MORE PROMPTS FOR USING READING STRATEGIES

To support making predictions:

✦ Does your prediction tell what will happen next?

✦ What information from the book did you use to predict?

✦ Can you make your prediction more specific to the story?

To support finding specific evidence:

✦ Did you use the title and cover illustration?

✦ What can you use from these chapters to support your prediction?

✦ Reread these pages to find some support.

✦ I like the way you used specific details for evidence.

To support inferring or drawing conclusions:

✦ What do you learn from the character's words on page ___?

✦ What do the inner thoughts show you about the character?

✦ Can you infer what the character might do based on this event?

✦ Think of three decisions a character made and explain what the decisions taught you about the character.

✦ What specific adjectives or phrases describe the character's behavior?

✦ How are these characters alike? different?

✦ How are these books alike? different?

✦ What effects resulted from that event? decision? conflict?

To support exploring themes:

✦ Use the events to decide what the author was saying about friends, parents, fear, survival, peer pressure, et cetera.

✦ What is the author trying to tell you about an historical period?

✦ What have you learned about people, families, hopes, dreams, money?

✦ To help you generalize, start with "One of the themes is..." or "One of the purposes of the story is..."

...MORE PROMPTS FOR USING READING STRATEGIES

To support synthesizing or summarizing:

✦ Are you retelling or summarizing?

✦ Can you choose two, three, or four key events?

✦ Explain these main events in your own words.

✦ What is the purpose of the chapter? the entire book?

✦ What can you find in this textbook or nonfiction book to help set purposes?

✦ Summarize the points that relate to the purpose.

✦ Can you separate the literal information about the character from the conclusions you drew in your summary?

✦ Can you give several effects of that decision? event? conflict?

✦ Can you show how these two characters are alike? different?

To support determining what's important in a text:

✦ What did you learn from previewing this textbook or nonfiction book?

✦ Can you find key sentences that contain important details?

✦ Can you locate key words?

✦ Can you think of several ideas in a chapter or the entire book that are important to remember? How did you make your decisions?

✦ Did you set purposes before reading?

✦ Can you skim to find information that supports the purposes?

✦ Can you tell me what's important on this page? in this chapter? How did you know that?

To support fluency:

✦ Listen to me read, then you reread the phrase the same way.

✦ Pause at commas and end-of-sentence punctuation.

✦ Read in chunks or groups of words.

✦ Reread the sentence a bit faster.

✦ Let the punctuation guide your expression.

✦ Can you make those words sound the way the character feels?

✦ I like the way you read as if you are that character.

PROMPTS FOR FIGURING OUT
UNFAMILIAR WORDS

Use these prompts to build students' word-solving strategies, help them explore meaning, and figure out how to pronounce a word. Again, keep the prompting list with you as you meet with students.

To use context clues to figure out meanings:

◆ Reread the sentence. Look for ideas and words that offer meaning clues.

◆ Read two or three sentences that came before the one that stumped you to find meaning clues.

◆ Read two or three sentences that come after the one that stumped you to find meaning clues.

◆ Find the base or root word and think of its meaning.

◆ Have you seen or heard that word in another situation or book? What do you recall?

◆ Think of the plot at this point and see if that offers some meaning clues.

To help students notice errors and pronounce words:

◆ Did that sound right?

◆ Find the part that was not right.

◆ Take a good look at the beginning, middle, and end of the word.

◆ Does what you say match the letters you see?

◆ Can you think of another word it looks like?

◆ Why did you stop?

◆ Can you say the word in chunks or syllables?

◆ Does the word have a prefix? Say it.

◆ Does the word have a suffix? Say it.

◆ Can you say what's left of the word?

Pause and Reflect on:
Strategies and a Personal Reading Life

Teaching-for-strategies is a complex process because it requires that you reflect on students' reading processes and constantly make, adjust, and update decisions about how to group them for instruction. Responsive grouping can reach all readers and support the development of strategies that enable students to connect to and think deeply about books.

When you offer students strategies that stimulate thinking and wondering, and strategies that help them solve word problems, you arm them with tools that will nurture their personal reading lives. The result is lifelong readers who turn to books for pleasure, entertainment, and information. You won't always see the progress your students make. Eighth grader Wendy spent a year with me in a class for struggling readers. She gained many strategies and read books, for the first time, from beginning to end. Three years later I received this letter in the mail from Wendy.

The next day I visited Wendy at Clarke County High School. I wanted to thank her for writing, tell her how pleased I was that she had begun to enjoy reading, and give her several books. During that visit Wendy told me that she had applied to a two-year college in our area and hoped to work with young children. What I learned from Wendy was never to feel discouraged, for progress and changes in attitude have no time constraints. As I coach students and scaffold their reading, I try to remember that time is the partner of improvement. I might not see a dramatic changeover during the year a student is with me, but, hopefully, progress will come as their journey continues.

Mrs. Robb,

I hope remembere me. You worked with me to help me or to inslerence me to read more. I wanted to thank you for incouraging me to read. I remember when I first ~~went~~ went into your class. I hate to read, but now I read when ever I get a chance. I wrote to say thank you. You were my favorite teacher. I miss you. I hope we see each other soon.

Your friend always, Wendy Linster

 Be happy

❧ Chapter 10
Cross-Grade Projects
Support Struggling Readers

"I learn so much when I help younger students,
and I feel good about me." —Eighth Grader

In the August/September issue of *Reading Today* (1999), Carol Minnick Santa, president of the International Reading Association, tells the story of Dusty, a high school junior who has just become a reader. When Sylvia, Dusty's tutor, gave him easy-to-read books from her daughter's first-grade classroom, she placed them in a brown paper bag and stuffed the bag in Dusty's knapsack. Keenly aware that Dusty's peers would mock him for reading "baby" books, Sylvia protected her student.

Students like Dusty, non-readers in middle and high school, benefit from intensive one-on-one reading instruction. However, once adolescents can read continuous texts, another way to draw them into reading is through cross-grade experiences that invite them to read and write with, talk to, and teach young children (Boyd and Galda, 1997; Robb, 1993).

By pairing struggling adolescent readers with younger buddies, you invite older students to read "easy" books for real and meaningful purposes. Reading many texts at their comfort level can only improve these students' fluency and comprehension and enlarge their vocabulary. A cross-grade reading buddies project is easy to manage when a middle school is near an elementary school or when both are in the same building.

One group of students can work with their buddies while the rest of the class reads extension books or works on journal responses. There are also times when my entire class is involved in a cross-grade project, talking, drawing, and writing about books younger students invite older ones to read.

The bonds that form between older and younger students can change attitudes toward reading. A group of struggling eighth-grade readers at Johnson Williams Middle School read twice a week to kindergarten children. Older students diligently reread their picture books to one another until the reading was fluent; they practiced how to introduce a book and involve a young child in the story. Their preparation for reading to young children focused on the importance of posing questions, making predictions, and talking about the story and illustrations, thereby reinforcing reading strategies they themselves needed.

The first time 18 kindergartners walked shyly into their school's multipurpose room, older students gently grasped their hands and led them to chairs or a comfortable place on the floor. When the bell rang, eighth graders spontaneously lifted their buddies and carried them back to their classrooms. This ritual became a tradition, and as the weeks passed, I watched friendships develop from sharing stories. At the last session, the local newspaper came to interview students. Ben told the reporter, when asked how he felt about books: "Well, the more you read 'em, the more you begin to like 'em." And I'll add, "Especially when you *can* read 'em."

The following story about Randy will offer insights into one young adolescent's pain about school and learning, and illustrate how reading with younger students can develop self-esteem and the desire to read for pleasure.

Randy's Story

Randy entered Powhatan School in sixth grade. He had spent his first six years in a county elementary school. Though Randy was reading three years below grade level, the testing with a school psychologist did not reveal a learning disability. His scores indicated a low-average IQ. His standardized test scores were consistently low on verbal, math aptitude, and applications.

Athletic, a good conversationalist, and a charmer with deep-blue eyes and a shock of black curls, Randy's appealing looks and manner worked to his advantage. He was also refreshingly candid, saying, "I hate reading and school."

Randy's parents had pushed him to achieve. On school nights, they devoted two or three hours to helping Randy read, write, and study for tests. During fifth grade Randy began to rebel against the homework routine. At school, he was silent, almost sullen. At home, completing schoolwork became an ordeal—in fact, Randy refused to do it.

Randy made progress at Powhatan with the support of a reading specialist and by working in texts he could read. By the time he entered eighth grade, the Informal Reading Inventory that I administered placed Randy two years below grade level. Randy wrote on his "What's hard?" sheet: *Reading history and science and math books. They're all too hard. I get angry with them [the books]. I hate having my mom or dad read to me every night.* During a "getting-to-know-you" conference, I praised Randy for closing his reading gap, pointing out that when he came to Powhatan, he was reading three years below grade level. My words did not comfort Randy. "I still can't read," was his response.

Randy, and 10 other eighth graders reading below grade level, were part of my 90-minute reading-writing workshop, which met three times a week. I also worked with these struggling readers four additional periods a week on reading-for-strategies and vocabulary-building.

The experience that seemed to change Randy's attitude and build his confidence was a buddy reading program with third graders. My goal for Randy and his 10 classmates was to have them read dozens of easy books without feeling I had put them in "baby books." I wanted them to "knock off" book after book. The program I developed invited Randy to teach third graders how to read for strategies, using books the third graders selected (see pages 231–234). Through teaching, I hoped Randy would gain a deeper understanding of reading strategies. In four weeks Randy read eight books. "These are pretty good," he told me. "I'm reading stuff I never read when I was in third grade."

In January Randy and his classmates composed a piece for their portfolios that described their progress in reading. It took three years to turn Randy around—but he was finally becoming a reader. Note that I say "becoming." In my gut, I knew Randy was developing the strategies and positive feelings that would guide his way into what Frank Smith called "the club of readers" (1978).

The two mini-lessons that follow prepare students for cross-grade projects that can engage older, struggling readers with texts they can read because the books have been selected for primary children. Reading and rereading easy books is one way to develop fluency, for students can read in meaningful chunks instead of a halting, word-to-word pattern.

> ### Reading
>
> RANDY   Jan. 23, 1997
>
> Through Jan 22 I have read 13 books. This is more books that I have read any other year. My books are enjoyabe because they are on my level. I don't have a certain kind of book I like to read but I do like Goose bumps.
>
> When we first came to school It took me a long time to read but now It dose not take me very long. I read faster now. When I read I know what I read, I used to never reread but know I do and I understad the book I read more.

MORE TIPS FOR DEVELOPING READING FLUENCY

Always use materials at students' independent-reading levels.

"Echo-Read" Poetry: The teacher reads one or two lines, then the student reads the same lines, following the rhythm and inflection of the teacher.

Memorize Poetry: Ask students to read a poem many times, memorize it, then recite it.

Present Short Plays or Readers Theater Scripts: Students choose characters, read the play silently and discuss the personality of their character. Have students reread and practice their parts until they can project character with their voices. Groups present plays to their class or to younger students.

Tape-Record Readings: Invite students to tape an early reading and a later reading of the same passage. Between readings, have students reread the passage until they have gained fluency. Invite students to compare the readings and discuss how they achieved fluency.

MINI-LESSON
Organizing Reading Buddies

ADAPT
for grades
5 and up

Introduction

When you collaborate with teachers of younger children and create meaningful reasons for struggling readers to read texts at their comfort level, you're providing older students with opportunities to improve fluency and practice the strategies they are learning (Cunningham and Allington, 1999). These learning experiences also allow older students to observe and process how younger ones apply reading strategies and talk about books.

Materials

picture books or easy chapter books that primary children are reading; chart paper; marker pen

Time Commitment
for each book read, three
or four 30-minute ses-
sions with paired older
and younger students

Guidelines

1. Invite a primary class
   to buddy-read with
   your students. I invite
   third graders to read
   with 11 eighth-
   grade students who

Eighth grader reads to kindergarten children.

read several years below grade level. Each eighth grader works with two third graders.

2. Prepare eighth graders for their first meeting with third-grade students. Eighth graders
   decided to interview their buddies to discover their interests, likes, dislikes, favorite sports,
   subjects, etc. Students prepared questions to help start their conversations. Older students
   took notes during these interviews, recording information to use in future conversations.

3. Have older buddies write letters to third graders, inviting them to select books they've
   completed—books eighth graders will now read.

Ryan

Wesley Hillyard   February 3, 1997
      Ryan is a 3rd grader who loves
to collect arrow heades, he has 7 arrowheads
in all. His favorite parts of school are Art,
Sports, rescess and lunch. Ryan plays baseball
and his favorite team is the orids. His favorite
kinds of books to read are "scare yourself to
death books" such as Goosebumps, and mysteries
like Sherlock Homs. He says next time "I hope
we can finish out book descousion quickly, so
we can talk more next time!"

232

4. Allow older students to read third-grade titles as contract- and free-reading books.

5. Prepare older students to discuss books with their buddies. My students used strategies we'd been practicing, such as: 1) connect the title to the book; 2) find your favorite part, read it, and explain why you enjoyed it; 3) find a character or situation that you connected to and explain why; 4) discuss the genre and give examples.

> Wes   February 5, 1997
>
> Ryan
>
> Ryan liked his book very much, he said that his book had alot of his intrest in it. His favorit parts were Gawain and the lowthly lady, and The Kitchen Nights, because it was magical, and it teaches you a good lesson. His favorit charactor in the book was Sir Lanselot.
>
> Ryan was very fun to work with, he was very talkative, and alwas had alot to say, Expecily when his favorit park of the book to read was a whole chapter! If I got to pick there grades or this project, both of them most certently will get an A!

6. Help older students understand that they are teachers. Explain and guide them through a discussion of what that means. By assuming the role of "teacher," older students gained deeper insights into reading strategies and observed how they supported their buddies.

7. Continue having buddies read and discuss the books younger students choose. This project can be short, focusing on one title, or can continue for several weeks, using many books.

8. Ask older students to write summaries of the high points of each discussion.

Extending the Project

9. Review the predict/support/adjust/confirm strategy by having buddies read a book that's new for both. Place sticky-notes after the first chapter, in the middle, and before the last chapter. With a picture book, place sticky-notes after the first three to four pages, halfway through, and two or three pages before the end.

10. Have older students write their buddy's name and the title of the book at the top of the sticky-note. Under the heading, print "Predict," leave a large space, and write "Support."

11. Have older students help young ones complete each sticky-note, using the title, illustrations,

and story for support. Older buddies teach younger ones how to find specific support, by skimming the story.

12. Reread sticky-notes after completing the book to confirm or adjust predictions and support.

Anne   Feb. 6, 1997

I really think that the 8th grade - 3rd grade reading project was a good idea. It was fun, and we were still learning. My partner was really friendly. I felt really comfotable. Two of my friends were in my group so it was easy to talk

Dear Tyler,   2-6-97
I liked what we talked about! I liked the book! Did you? It's weird that you were my secret buddy before! You are cool! I realy like to draw. Here is a picture at the bottom! Your buddy,
                Hunter

#6 Richard   feb. 6, 1997
1. I lirnd a lot about my butty
2. It was fun beckas he was my 8th grader butty.
3. I felt good beus I had a frend whith me.

Third graders write to their buddies about the project.

MINI-LESSON
Annotated Book Lists

ADAPT
for grades
5 and up

Introduction

When you involve struggling readers in reading, selecting, and annotating books for a primary grade's themed study, you are asking them to read easy books for authentic and important purposes. At the same time, older students develop literary tastes and these four strategies: 1) Selecting and noting important information for annotated summaries; 2) Synthesizing a passage by summarizing it in their own words; 3) Developing reading fluency by practicing with easy-to-read books; 4) Transforming notes into clear and concise summaries.

Materials

books centered around a theme, such as weather or oceans or a genre, such as predictable books or nonfiction; copies of annotated lists of books: children's, teacher's, and parent's choices, or annotated lists from professional magazines such as the IRA's *The Reading Teacher* or ALA's *Book Links;* chart paper; marker pen

Guidelines

1. Ask a primary teacher to write a letter to your students, asking for their help in finding books related by theme or genre.

2. Prepare older students for the project. Have them read book annotations and work in groups to establish guidelines for annotating. Here are sixth graders' criteria: 1) Title, author, illustrator, publisher; 2) Must be short; 3) Contains a brief summary; 4) Why is the book special?

3. Have older students write back, accepting the invitation. This is an authentic and meaningful way to review friendly-letter writing.

4. Ask students to meet with the school librarian for help in locating books.

5. Allow older students to read all of the books as free-choice reading books.

6. Divide the books among students so each has several to reread and annotate (see sample annotations in margin box on next page).

7. Work with students to proofread and edit annotations.

8. Enter annotations into a computer.

9. Have students deliver the annotated list to the primary teacher.

Students' Annotations for Easy-to-Read Mysteries

Detective Dinosaur Lost and Found by James Skofield, pictures by R.W. Alley, HarperCollins. Detective Dinosaur and Officer Pterodactyl have 3 mystery adventures. They find Baby Penny, a lost dinosaur, Cadet Kitty finds them. When Detective Dinosaur is lost and sad, Officer Pterodactyl finds him. The book is funny and has a key for saying hard words in front.

Young Cam Jansen and the Ice Skate Mystery by David A. Adler, illustrated by Susanna Natti, Viking. At the ice skating rink, Cam's friend Eric loses his locker key and detective Cam helps Eric figure out what happened to the key. The story shows that having a good memory can help detectives.

10. Extend this project by having each older student select a favorite book, prepare a short book talk, and present it to younger students. Or, have each older student select a favorite title and read it to a younger child.

Though cross-grade projects are ideal for engaging older students in reading, they require support all year long if they are to improve. However, by the middle grades, teaching and supporting struggling readers presents a unique challenge; it is often difficult for these students to set aside their anger and frustration and let you into their lives. A yearlong effort is key. To help you along the way, I present the following time line for the assessments I use to inform my instruction of struggling readers throughout the year.

A TIME LINE FOR SUPPORTING STRUGGLING READERS

The following time line is only an approximation and will vary from student to student. It contains the highlights of my interactions with struggling readers. During the course of a school year there will be times when you accomplish more and times when you accomplish less. That's fine. The goal here is to build students' confidence through meaningful reading experiences and interactions with a teacher, hopefully improving their understanding and use of reading strategies.

August

Using all information available about students you will teach when the school year starts, list those who read two or more years below grade level. If the students come from your school district, speak to last year's teachers and gather information about each student.

236

September

1. Take two or three weeks to get to know all students.

2. Read aloud action-packed adventure and horror stories such as *Nightmares* by R.L. Stine (HarperCollins). The "Harry Potter" books by J. K. Rowling also engage struggling and proficient readers because, as eighth grader Michael wrote in his book review, "You're never bored, and you can't wait to start the next chapter because adventure is sure to come."

   Through read-alouds, you'll engage high-risk students in story, and develop their ability to connect to characters and to visualize favorite parts. Moreover, the more struggling readers hear literary language and syntax, the better equipped they'll be to enjoy reading.

3. Through conferences, try to establish a relationship with struggling readers. Once you have rapport, hopefully by the last week of September, negotiate with each student a time to administer a complete Informal Reading Inventory. If your school has a reading specialist, try to obtain support for the student from her.

October through December:

1. Discuss the results of the reading inventory with each student. I don't point out that they're reading however many number of years below grade level; students are aware of their deficiencies. What I do mention are their strengths, and I identify one or two areas that can be improved through our one-on-one meetings and during guided strategic reading with others.

   Here are excerpts of exchanges between me and a sixth and seventh grader.

Robb Discusses Reading Inventory Results with Thomas, a Sixth Grader

Robb: I noticed that you really tried to read with expression. You also self-corrected some words that would have really confused the meaning of the passage.

Thomas: I'm pretty good with easy books. But I can't read the science and history books. I look at words and guess.

Robb: I noticed that you did that on these passages.

Thomas: Yeah.

Robb: You and I will work on word sorts with tough multisyllable words. It can help you look beyond the first letter and think about the whole word.

Robb Discusses Reading Inventory Results with Vicki, a Seventh Grader

Robb: I noticed how you concentrated and tried.

Vicki: Uh-huh.

Robb: In this passage [third-grade level] you self-corrected three times. That's a strategy we can build on.

Vicki: Yeah. I can't believe I did that. It was cool, and it made sense.

Robb: That's another great strategy—knowing when something makes sense or when it's confusing.

Vicki: How can I read better?

Robb: We'll work on figuring out the meanings of words and strategies to help you say multisyllable words.

2. Three times a week I work one-on-one with these students. I can accomplish more in 10 to 15 minutes of individual conferences than in 20-minute group conferences because I am concentrating on each student's individual needs.

3. Twice a week I group two or three struggling readers who can benefit from working together. Today I pair Lisa and Maria to work on recalling and retelling chunks of text; Mark and Ricardo practice raising questions before and during reading.

4. Struggling students join secure readers during book discussions which focus on a theme or genre. That way every student can read a different book and use the theme or genre structure as the basis for discussion.

5. With each student, review progress made. Use response journals, reading folders, portfolios, and your observational notes.

6. During these months I work individually with struggling readers to find books they'll enjoy—books that don't appear babyish. The school's librarian is also on the lookout for books that might engage these readers. A series that struggling readers enjoy is Scholastic's *Dear America* books, fictional diaries of young Americans. The diary format makes the reading easy, and students enjoy seeing history through the eyes of someone close to their age.

Eighth grader Tyler, a student in my reading-writing workshop, checked out thick volumes of history and brought in novels by Isaac Asimov for free reading. Not until mid-November, when Tyler failed for the second time to fulfill his reading contract, could I get him to try a book I suggested. He told me he liked science fiction but could never get through books by Piers Anthony, Isaac Asimov, or Arthur C. Clarke. One Thursday I handed Tyler *The Book of Three* by Lloyd Alexander and told him that this was the first book of a series called *The Chronicles of Prydain*. He dutifully took the book, and I wondered if he would even open the cover. The next Monday Tyler came straight from the bus to my office to tell me that this was the best book he'd ever read. "Could I help him find the others?" he asked. After completing the five books in the series, Tyler started reading at home and during workshop choice time at school. Two other books that Tyler rated as tops were *Tangerine* by Edward Bloor and *Gentlehands* by M.E. Kerr.

Putting "the right book" into students' hands can capture their imagination and inspire the desire to find another and yet another book. At the 1999 Keystone State Reading Conference in Hershey, Pennsylvania, Irene Fountas, in her speech "Raising the Literacy Achievement of All Learners—What Will it Take?" discussed research that correlated the number of books students read with their progress. She emphasized the importance of reading many books—of students gaining "reading mileage" to improve reading. To become competent readers, students need several years of high-quality reading instruction: this means 15 to 20 minutes a day of reading with an expert at their instructional level. Fountas stressed that during these daily meetings students should learn how to apply a strategy with increasing skill so they can continue to process texts with ease. In addition, children must read books at their independent level at school and at home. The box on the next page lists some titles that students rate highly—titles for independent and teacher-supported reading.

7. Every four to six weeks, do an error analysis of students' oral reading (pages 248–255). First try a passage at students' instructional levels; then try one above, as some students might be able to move into more challenging texts. Always review results with students. This is the ideal moment to point out progress and establish new goals.

January through March

1. Continue group and individual instruction.
2. With each student, review progress made. Use response journals, reading folders, portfolios, and your observational notes. Jot down what you've discussed and file in student's literacy folder.
3. Organize a cross-grade project or ask your librarian to invite students to evaluate new books she has purchased for the library—books they can read.

BOOKS THAT HOOK READERS

Boy: Tales of Childhood by Roald Dahl, Puffin, 1984.

The Cartoonist by Betsy Byars, Puffin, 1987.

Dear Mr. Henshaw by Beverly Cleary, Morrow, 1983.

I'm Not Who You Think I Am by Peg Kehret, Dutton, 1999.

Journey by Patricia MacLachlan, Delacorte, 1991.

Knights of the Kitchen Table by Jon Sceiszka. Viking, 1991.

The Language of Goldfish by Zibby O'Neal, Puffin, 1990.

The Music of Dolphins by Karen Hesse, Scholastic, 1996.

The Not-so-Jolly Roger by Jon Sceiszka. Viking, 1991.

Protecting Marie by Kevin Henkes, Greenwillow, 1995.

Strider by Beverly Cleary, Morrow, 1991.

Then Again, Maybe I Won't by Judy Blume, Dell, 1971.

Your Mother Was a Neanderthal by Jon Sceiszka. Viking, 1993.

2095 by Jon Sceiszka. Viking, 1995.

4. Students can record books on tape for primary grades. This experience provides opportunities for students to practice rereading and develop fluency. Taping stories builds confidence, for students complete projects that others will use and enjoy.

5. Reassess students' oral and silent reading with an Informal Reading Inventory. Use the information you gathered to plan instruction for the last two months of school.

Sample Assessment

Thomas's instructional level went from fourth to fifth grade. He was more successful at decoding multisyllable words because he took the time to look at the entire word; sometimes he recognized the root or base word; he took off prefixes and suffixes and looked for small words in a large word. We'll continue word sorting, but emphasize using context clues to figure out a word's meaning—an area where Thomas needs additional practice.

Sample Assessment

Vicki's instructional level went from fourth to fifth grade; her independent reading level moved up from third to fourth. She has improved greatly in figuring out the meanings of unfamiliar words, using clues in the story. We will focus on word sorting and studying prefixes, suffixes, and roots to help Vicki pronounce multisyllable words.

April through June

1. Decide whether students will benefit from more group or individual instruction. Organize workshop so you can meet these students' needs.

2. Continue to engage students in cross-grade projects.

3. Near the end of May, help students take a long look at their year; ask them to point out progress. Add positive feedback to this conversation and help students see the importance of reading throughout the summer.

4. Before these students leave for summer vacation, I help them check out six to ten books. I explain that they don't have to read a book they dislike, but I hope that they will read at least six books. It's important for middle grade students to understand that a summer without reading can diminish the progress they've made. I also ask students to keep a list of the books and magazines they read over summer break.

Pause and Reflect on:
Supporting Struggling Readers

Consistent one-on-one tutoring with a reading specialist is the most effective way to transform young adolescents who cannot read into readers (Santa, 1999). However, this growth in reading must be supported by continuous, multiple reading experiences, custom-made for each struggling reader. Once students can read easy books, inviting them to work with primary children allows them to read at their independent level while maintaining their self-esteem. Most struggling readers in middle school have avoided reading for several years. Providing cross-grade reading projects enables them to read and enjoy outstanding books they missed when they were younger. As reading buddies work together, they enjoy reading and learn from one another. Eighth grader Tyler's journal entry reveals what he learned:

> *Hunter was very talkative today. He loves to read all kins of sports books. This year Hunter has read 86 books!! [September to February] He likes to read when he is in bed or when he is bord. His interests are skate bording and playing every spot imaginible. Hunter says he really likes it when we read the same book and talk about it. He says he looks foward to me coming and its more fun when we work on a book then he doing it alone. I think Hunter looks up to me. I told him I like reading with him alot.*

Tyler's final comments illustrate the bonds that develop between younger and older students who have grown to care about reading together. Strong friendships form as students read, write, and talk about books. Older students feel needed and important, for they are responsible for their own learning and the learning of younger children. With cross-grade reading projects low-achieving students can feel the pleasure they bring to others and have an authentic reason to practice their reading.

🍂 Chapter 11

Assessment, Interpretation, and Evaluation

"I collect all this information about students, and I don't know what I'm supposed to do with it" — Second-Year Sixth-Grade Teacher

It's 7:30 A.M. and I'm at school early so I can reread the literacy folders of four struggling readers and plan the kinds of interventions we'll work on next week. The seventh-grade teacher enters, holding a file folder. This is her fourth year of teaching.

"I need your help," she says. "Do you have some time?"

"Of course," I reply.

"It's Boomer," she says, spreading the contents of the folder out on a cluster of empty desks. "The science teacher told me that he's failed four vocabulary quizzes and he doesn't complete his homework questions. The standardized testing from last spring has Boomer at the bottom of the fourth quartile in reading comprehension and vocabulary."

"That's only one measure," I caution. "What have you collected in the literacy folder?"

Here are the assessments we reviewed and our interpretation or evaluation of each:

1. **Oral Reading:** marked error pattern or miscues (see page 252) of the first two pages of Chapter 1 of *Chancy and the Grand Rascal* by Sid Fleischman. Had no idea what the word "Rascal" meant.

   Read words accurately except needed help on *precisely, infernally,* and some of the unusual names. Read through three commas and several end-of-sentence punctuation marks. Little expression. When asked to go back and reread sections with these words and explain their meaning, he couldn't: *kin, infernally, limber-jointed, speckled, yearning, reckoned.* Could not predict what story might be about.

2. **One Journal Entry:** an unprompted response to *Captain Murderer* by Dickens, Boomer wrote: *I lik it when you read cause Im NOT reading. I lik to feel scard. Its the first good story I heard.*

3. **What's Easy? What's Hard?:** Boomer wrote that all reading was easy. "I read very hard books."

4. **Observational Notes:** 9/8: Boomer checked out *Redwall* by Brian Jacques. Refused to check out *Dear Mr. Henshaw* along with *Redwall*—I hoped he would have an alternative to try. 9/10: Independent Reading—Boomer goes to bathroom; leafs through book; doodles in journal; yawns many times; reads pages in different parts of book; 10/4: silent during group book discussions; 10/5: says *One Day in the Woods* too easy when we meet to work on figuring out the meaning of unfamiliar words; he guesses; resists looking for clues.

5. **Notes from a Getting-to-Know-You Conference:** hates school—it's boring; gets nothing from reading, can read the words, but it's boring. Only good part is being with friends; likes to play basketball and help his dad on his farm; hates homework; likes movies and TV.

6. **Gansky Spelling Inventory (1993):** placed Boomer at the early within word pattern stage.

Here's how his teacher and I interpreted, evaluated, and decided on possible interventions, based on the assessments in Boomer's literacy folder. We filed our ideas in Boomer's folder, recording them in short, to-the-point bulleted phrases.

Interpretation: Boomer covers up his reading difficulties by checking out hard books so classmates will think he can read well. Yet, in our interview, Boomer says he hates reading because it's boring. The real clue is "gets nothing from reading." Boomer's retelling of the Chancy passage was sketchy, even though he read the passage silently and made few errors reading out loud.

Based on his oral reading Boomer seems to have a deficit in vocabulary knowledge, and that could account for his inability to comprehend the passage and retell and predict. He did not understand that Chancy was not living with his real "kin" because he did not know what the word *kin* meant. Standardized testing and the science teacher's observations support this interpretation.

Evaluation and Possible Interventions: During one-on-one and group instruction times, focus on strategies for figuring out word meanings and work on introducing key vocabulary before reading. Have Boomer examine short passages and select words he doesn't understand—work on these. With entire class, work on roots, prefixes, and suffixes to provide additional word-meaning support. Also, make sure Boomer has enough prior knowledge about a topic—before reading.

This literacy story illustrates how a range of assessments, from informal to formal, enables teachers to draw conclusions about a student's learning and formulate a plan of support.

Is There a Difference Between Assessment and Evaluation?

Assessments are the data you have collected about a student. Included are standardized tests, teacher-made tests and quizzes, oral reading error analysis, journal entries, book logs, conferences, interviews, writing samples, spelling inventories, teacher's observational notes, student's self-evaluations, interest and attitude surveys, etc. When you collect a range of assessments, the

Teacher Resources for Assessment and Evaluation

Invitations: Changing as Teachers and Learners K–12 by Regie Routman, Heinemann, 1991.

Literacy Portfolios: Using Assessment to Guide Instruction by Roberta B. Weiner and Judith H. Cohen, Merrill, 1994.

Practical Aspects of Authentic Assessment: Putting The Pieces Together by Bonnie C. Hill and Cynthia Ruptic, Christopher Gordon, 1994.

Reading Assessment: Principles and Practices for Elementary Teachers, edited by Shelby J. Barrentine, IRA, 1999.

picture of the child's strong points and weak areas is more accurate than if you rely on one or two measures. A range of assessments offers an image of the child in many situations, on different days; such an image will be closer to reality than relying on one test or one teacher observation.

Assessments guide teachers' thinking about a child and help us comprehend the learning process and style of each individual in our classroom. A range of assessments, taken over time, enables us to interpret the data, draw conclusions about a child, and respond to each middle school student's instructional and emotional needs.

Evaluation, for me, means transforming the interpretations of assessment data into possible interventions that can improve learning. The reason I qualify interventions with "possible" is that some strategies might not benefit the student, so I must search for other supportive frameworks. The interventions that walk hand-in-hand with evaluation constitute a plan of action which drives instruction. Action facilitates change, growth, and progress—what we want for everyone we teach.

However, the ongoing collection of data, followed by interpreting and evaluating that data for a class of 25 to 35 students, is a challenge for experienced teachers, daunting for first-year teachers.

It Takes Time to Develop the Expertise to Assess, Interpret, and Evaluate

Assessments that monitor students' daily performance and go beyond teacher-made tests and quizzes and standardized testing programs make great demands on teachers' time. You'll become adept at interpreting and evaluating these assessments over time, as you continue to teach, to read professional books and articles on assessment and evaluation (see resource box at left and on the next page), attend conferences, observe how experienced teachers interpret and evaluate data, and develop your own theory of how children learn. A workshop environment is the ideal structure for ongoing, performance-based assessment, because when students work independently in pairs, groups, or alone, you are free to confer and assess.

Gaining the experience and knowledge base necessary to make informed decisions about students is an ongoing, never-ending journey. Every year professional journals, such as *The Reading Teacher, Language Arts, The New Advocate, Phi Delta Kappan, Education Leadership,* and *The Journal of Reading,* present the newest research on reading, writing, and thinking, offering glimpses into classrooms to illustrate how research affects practice. Keeping abreast of research, combined with observing the children you teach in various learning situations, will improve your ability to make informed decisions and plan interventions.

As you organize flexible strategic-reading groups and decide when it's beneficial to meet one-on-one with a student to provide support, you can use the chart below as a guide. It lists

READING EXPERIENCE	POSSIBLE ASSESSMENTS
Determining Student's View of Self as Reader	Interviews; What's Easy? What's Hard? reading and interest surveys; all-about-me letters; observational notes
Reading for Strategies	Oral reading; miscue patterns; guided-reading groups; debriefing; conferences; self-evaluations; checklists; response to mini-lessons; interviews
Book Selection	Book logs; journal entries; oral reading; retellings; book conferences; book talks; observational notes
Oral Reading	Error or miscue analysis; taped recording for fluency; Readers Theater
Reading Comprehension	One-on-one conferences; journal entries; book discussions; book talks; book reviews; critical essays; tests; quizzes; strategic-reading groups
Free-Choice Reading	Book logs; journal entries; book conferences; book reviews; book discussions; observational notes
Self-evaluation of Progress	Checklists; narratives that analyze progress over time; debriefings

specific learning events in reading workshop and a range of assessments that can help you monitor these events. The chart includes possible assessments that you can choose from.

The assessment suggestions I've included in this chapter are practical and develop middle school students' ability to self-evaluate and make decisions about learning goals.

A MANAGEABLE METHOD OF ASSESSING STUDENTS' ORAL READING

By the end of the first six to eight weeks of school, I have listened to each student read orally and marked the errors or miscues (see page 252). I do this during free-choice time while students read silently, work on a journal entry, or quietly discuss a book. It takes about 10 to 20 minutes to complete each assessment; the more you do, the faster you'll complete each one. Each free-choice time, I try to meet with two or three students in a quiet corner of the room. I start with students whose standardized test scores indicate they are reading below grade level. So that students working independently understand why their cooperation is necessary, I explain the purpose for this assessment.

Here's how I conduct these meetings:

1. **Bring Selections From Three Reading Levels:** At the start of the year, it's difficult to know students' independent or instructional levels, especially with students new to your school. I ask students to bring their free-reading book, as I've already shown them how to find a book that's just right. I also bring two books or two passages from a graded basal or the graded passages in the Woods and Moe *Analytical Reading Inventory* (see top of page 252). I photocopy one passage that is about a year below and another that is one year above the student's book. This way, if the student's book is too easy or too difficult, I can use one of the passages I brought.

2. **Keep a Copy of the Miscue Key Nearby:** Until you have done this many times and know the symbols, keep the miscue key next to you. I always tell students how the key helps me.

3. **Photocopy the Passage:** Because you'll be marking the errors, you will need a copy of the text the students will read.

4. **Provide Background Information:** Offer a one- or two-sentence summary of the passage and help the student access prior knowledge and experience about the topic.

5. Have Student Read the Passage Out Loud:

Explain that you will be marking the passage in order to learn more about the student's word recognition and knowledge. Say that you are doing this to find ways to support the student's reading.

Touch felt his back stiffen [go]. His great-uncle meant to bully him. "I've been known to curse," he answered firmly.

"Be warned. I'll fine you five cents a word for swearing. I go by the law books, chapter and verse!"

"Yes, sir."

"Let's not waste time. I expect you came seeking your inheritance."

Touch was caught by enormous surprise. An inheritance? He didn't know that he had one. But in as even a voice as he could manage, he said, "You seen clear through me, Judge. That's what I came [come] for."

The judge cracked a thin smile. "You're a shifty-eyed boy."

"I didn't know that, sir," Touch replied coolly. [cool like]

"Did your pa tell you I offered to bring him up in the law? In my own footsteps!"

"No, sir."

"But the ungrateful fool ran off to sea, leaving his [help] affairs in my hands. And now here's his whelp on my doorstep." The judge was breathing like a bel-[be] lows. "Don't expect me to take pity and put a roof over your orphan head. And feed you until you're grown."

22

"No, sir," replied Touch, with immense relief. [much]

"I won't have a brat underfoot."

"Can't blame you," said Touch. "Boys are terrible [pests] pesky to have around. Now you've found me out, being shifty and all, I'll pick up whatever Pa left me and be on my way." [go] 233 words (10 errors)

"Your inheritance is spent."

"Not by me, it wasn't," said Touch quickly.

"Don't get cheeky with me," snapped the judge. "I'll have you arrested for breaking the law."

"What law?"

"Whistling on the Sabbath."

"You've got the days of the week mixed up, Judge. It ain't Sunday. And the only thing whistling is the wind. You might as well arrest God Himself."

The old man squared his shoulders. "You put your foot in the law now! Blaspheming Our Lord!"

Touch saw that he'd fallen into a trap. The judge had a mind crisscrossed with spiderwebs, as the blacksmith had said.

"In a court of law, I'd fine you two dollars," said the judge. "But I'll suspend the judgment on your solemn promise to say your prayers dutifully and watch your tongue."

23

6. **Ask Student to Reread the Passage Silently:** I do this so students can relax and focus on meaning, and hopefully retell the selection with rich details.

7. **Choose Three to Five Words and Ask Student to Explain Their Meanings:** By middle school, many comprehension difficulties are due to limited vocabularies and students' inability to use context, syntactic, and semantic clues (see page 225) to figure out the meanings of unfamiliar words.

8. **Have Student Retell:** Ask students to retell everything they recall from the passage.

What to Look for in Retellings

Retelling enables you to assess students' recall and comprehension of a passage. To retell, students must synthesize the text into their own words, and organize and order details.

It's helpful to prompt students before and after retellings:

Open with: *Take some time to think about the passage. I'd like you to retell everything you remember, and I will record your words.*

After the student stops: *Can you recall more details?* or *Would you like to add anything?* [If the student asks you to read back the dictated retelling, do so and make a note of the request.]

RETELLING: NARRATIVE

Student's Name _____ Date _____

Record of Student's Retelling:

Elements in Student's Retelling	Teacher's Notes
☐ Identified Main Character	
☐ Told Main Character's Problem	
☐ Settings: Time and Place	
☐ Rising Action: Plot Details	
☐ Mentioned Other Characters	

Student's Speaking Patterns: (Answer yes or no. Give examples when helpful.)

Spoke in complete sentences.

Told details in chronological order.

Added details when asked for more.

Additional Comments:

On the previous page is a form I have developed to document retellings for narrative texts. These records can be added to students' literacy folders. Documentation ensures that I'll recall the event accurately and can use it to negotiate goals with a student, as well as to discuss issues with parents and supervisors.

THE THREE CUEING SYSTEMS

While reading, students use a variety of cues or signals contained in the unfamiliar word or the text surrounding that word (Gillet and Temple, 1990). A knowledge of these cueing systems will enable you to better analyze students' miscues and decide how to help your students obtain effective strategies for coping with tough words.

1 Graphophonic: This refers to the relationship between the letters in a word and the sounds they make. It's helpful to determine if readers are missing, and not self-correcting, the letter-sound relationships at the beginning, middle, or end of words. Or are they substituting words that have no sounds in common, such as *this* for *every*? You can support students who consistently don't attend to specific parts of words through word sorting, studying word parts such as prefixes, suffixes, and roots. A great resource for activities is *Words Their Way: Word Study for Phonics, Vocabulary, and Spelling Instruction* by Bear, Invernizzi, Johnston, and Templeton (Merrill, 1996).

2 Syntactic: This grammar-related cueing system has to do with how language works and the order of words in a sentence. An example of a syntactic miscue is when the reader substitutes a word that is a different part of speech or a nonword. For example, the text reads: *The girl cried for hours.* The students reads: *The girl sad for hours.* Here the student substituted an adjective, *sad*, for the verb, *cried*. Repair strategies can include improving students' understanding of sentence structure by focusing their attention on difficult sentences (Barr et al. 1990). These strategies can improve deficits in syntax: 1) Read aloud daily, so students hear literary language; 2) Have students read a variety of genres; 3) Offer many opportunities for students to write, speak, and listen. Hearing and using language will develop competence with the syntactic cueing system.

3 Semantic: These cues are meaning-related. Meaning-related miscues spotlight the reader's ability to attend to the meaning of the text. Kenneth and Yetta Goodman point out

continued on page 253

ORAL READING MISCUE CODE

This is the code from Mary Lynn Woods' and Alden J. Moe's *Analytical Reading Inventory*, Saddle River, NJ: Merrill, 1999, sixth edition.

The four miscues that follow are counted as errors.

Code	Meaning	Example
O	Omitted word. Circle the word.	A loud (explosion) caused the fire in the old house.
I	Insertion. Write inserted word or words.	Flames spewed ^big^ sparks that destroyed other buildings.
S	Substitution. Write the substitution which can be a real word or nonword.	The moose stood silently in the ^grass^ meadow, watching the prey.
A	Aided word. Draw a diagonal through the word you helped student pronounce.	The therapeutic dose was taken every four hours.

The four miscues that follow are not counted as errors.

Code	Meaning	Example
Rp	Repetition. Underline the repeated words. If repeated more than once, underline for each repetition.	The coyote tensed its muscles before leaping on the unsuspecting rabbit.
SC	Self-corrected. Readers often repeat a word or phrase or pause and use semantic or context clues to self-correct.	home SC The house is near the mall. SC Mud (spattered) her new tricycle.
/	Hesitates. If a student reads haltingly, making many hesitations, mark those, for it indicates a lack of fluency.	During the/circus,/the monkeys jumped/from horse to horse while/ dogs did/cartwheels/on the mat.
X	Ignores punctuation. Use the x for punctuation within a sentence or when they ignore end of sentence punctuation. This indicates they are not monitoring meaning.	Sitting by the fire,x the old dog yawned and scratched his neck.x Suddenly, the cat, sitting nearby,x leaped on the dog's back.

See opposite page for more on scoring the passage.

Teaching Reading in Middle School

(1969; 1999, see page 251) that many miscues do not affect or impede comprehension. However, readers who make many substitutions need to have their attention drawn to the structure of the word and the letter-sound relationships. Subtle differences in meaning can occur when a student reads *laughed* for *snickered* or *fussed* for *fumed*. Therefore, offer fix-it strategies to students whose miscues change the meaning of a passage and to those who repeatedly substitute words with similar meanings. Word sorting, analysis of word parts, webbing words related to a root, and a comparison of the letters of the word in the text with the substituted word are effective fix-it strategies.

The "Strategy in Action" that follows illustrates how I apply a knowledge of the three cueing systems to interpret oral reading miscues. After interpreting the information gained from oral reading and the student's retelling of the passage, I evaluate these assessments and design possible instructional interventions.

Another Informal Reading Inventory

In addition to the Woods and Moe *Analytical Reading Inventory,* many teachers use the *Qualitative Reading Inventory-II* by Lauren Leslie and JoAnne Caldwell, Longman, 1995.

SCORING THE PASSAGE

To interpret the oral reading miscue analysis, I use the criteria that Woods and Moe set. For a quick comprehension assessment, I have students retell the passage after they reread it silently.

Independent: Student makes no more than one error in 100 words and offers a detailed retelling of the passage that shows about 90 percent recall. Sometimes a student might retell the passage in great detail and make two or three errors. Use your judgment and knowledge about the student to decide whether or not the student can read at this level with confidence and pleasure.

Instructional: student makes no more than five errors in 100 words and the retelling reveals comprehension of about 75 percent of the passage.

Frustration: student makes many miscues, 10 or more per 100 words, and cannot retell or can only retell a small portion of the text.

STRATEGY IN ACTION
Eighth Grader's Oral Reading Miscues

David brought *The Midnight Horse* by Sid Fleischman to our meeting. Before class he had checked out a copy from the library, read a page at random, and felt comfortable reading it.

The SMOG formula (see page 191) placed *The Midnight Horse* at a seventh-grade independent-reading level. I expected David to read the text with few errors; however, David made 10 errors after reading 233 words (see page 249 for David's error analysis).

Interpretation: Formulating and thinking about questions the marked oral passage raises helps me interpret this assessment. I also review the retelling and other assessments, including standardized test scores that I have in the student's literacy folder. Here are the questions I asked myself about David's oral reading, and the ideas that the questions generated:

Oral Reading: Why doesn't David know when a miscue confuses the meaning? (Ask him this at a conference.) Did he have difficulty with *inheritance* and *bellows* because the words were split between two lines? (Copy the sentence with *bellows* and have him read it.) Does he need support strategies for pronouncing multisyllable words? (Ask David to read a page from his science text, which is on grade level.) What is David's instructional level? Should I have him read an eighth-grade passage?

Retelling: Detailed; recalled

RETELLING

Student's Name David   Date 2/17/99

Record of Student's Retelling:

Touch discovers he has an inheritance from his great-uncle, the Judge. The Judge tells Touch that Touch's Pa was a fool who ran off to sea and left his affairs in the Judge's hands. Touch tries to get his inheritance and acts cool. But the Judge says it's spent. The Judge is mean and spiteful and tries to threaten David by telling the boy he broke the law. I'd hate to deal with such a miserable person - and a relation!

Elements in Student's Retelling	Teacher's Notes
Identified Main Character	✓
Told Main Character's Problem	✓
Settings: Time and Place	Judge's place
Rising Action: Plot Details	✓
Mentioned Other Characters	

Student's Speaking Patterns: Answer *yes* or *no*. Give examples when important.

Spoke in complete sentences.   most of the time

Told details in chronological order.   yes

Added details when you asked for more.   yes

Additional Comments:
David drew conclusions about the Judge's personality and added David's feelings. Told in chronological order.

---

most of the plot; identified both characters; used complete sentences for most of it.

Vocabulary in Context: David could explain the meaning of *inheritance* and *blaspheming*.

Evaluation: David read *bellow* correctly when the word wasn't divided at the end of the sentence. Since his retelling showed good comprehension of the passage, I believe that David can select books he can read. We'll work on these strategies: reading words divided at the ends of sentences; decoding multisyllable words and strategies that help; comparing words David guesses with what is in the text—*much* for *immense*—carefully looking at the features; work on building vocabulary in a group using roots, prefixes, suffixes, and using context clues in the text.

Which Students Do I Reassess?

It's impossible for me to frequently reassess all 25 students I teach. Therefore, I set priorities and focus on students reading below grade level, doing an error analysis of their oral reading about every four to six weeks. Usually, out of 25 students, five to eight read below grade level.

I monitor grade-level students' choice of books, and assess them each trimester; proficient readers are assessed twice a year. My goal is to identify their strengths and deficits and help them improve through small strategic-reading group work, one-on-one conferences, and debriefings, where students reflect on and analyze reading strategies.

DEBRIEFINGS

Debriefings offer students opportunities to exchange experiences with and understandings of how reading strategies work for them. First, I think–aloud and model how I debrief after practiving skimming with fiction and nonfiction:

> *Skimming with the history textbook was easier than with the novel. The textbook had boldface headings and words and captions that helped me find the place I needed to reread. With the novel, I had trouble remembering whether I'd find the question's answer in the beginning or middle of the book. Then, I had to search for a key word in the question. That took more time because the word was repeated many times and I had to reread three times until I found the place I wanted. But once I got to the right place, I was able to answer the question using story details. My goal will be to gain better recall of a novel's plot so I can pinpoint the section I need to skim.*

Next, I invite students to comment on what I said and they notice that I point out what worked, what was a challenge or difficult, and set one goal.

To scaffold debriefings, I start students working in pairs, then in small groups. As I circulate, I'm identifying those who need one-on-one support from me. Writing questions (see bottom of this page and top of page 257) on the chalkboard before students debrief helps guide their thinking and goal-setting.

When to Debrief

Initiate debriefings once students have practiced a strategy and have enough experience to reflect on and talk about the strategy. My one rule of thumb is to make sure students have debriefed after guided practice and applying the strategy in their strategic-reading groups.

Listen carefully during debriefings, for you will be able to identify students who really understand the strategy and those who are confused. Sometimes students who "get it" remain silent or contribute little. Make a note of these students and have a brief meeting with each one to evaluate the level of understanding they have gained.

Make Those Debriefings Productive

Since debriefing is a learned process, your job is to model how it works with the entire class before setting up small debriefing groups.

During debriefings, students share all their reactions and questions and confusions *without being judged*. The goal is to collect as many ideas as possible on applying a strategy.

Questions Stimulate Debriefing Conversations

Posing questions often starts students discussing how a strategy worked and supported their recall and comprehension. Collect students' questions about a strategy after mini-lessons and after strategic-reading groups meet. Add questions that you feel will be helpful. Here are some sample open-ended debriefing questions:

- ✦ Did you adapt or change the strategy? How?
- ✦ How did the strategy improve your reading?
- ✦ Did the strategy improve your recall? comprehension?

+ Did the strategy connect you to the book? How?

+ Did the strategy help you solve word problems? How?

+ Did the strategy "unconfuse" you? How?

STRATEGY IN ACTION
Debriefing in a Fifth-Grade Classroom

Twenty-four fifth graders sitting in groups of four discuss their experiences with posing questions before and during reading. Each group reads a different book by Jean Craighead George. First, groups exchange thoughts and feelings, referring to their response journals and several open-ended debriefing questions written on chart paper. Below is a debriefing with the group that read *The Talking Earth*.

Fifth Graders Debrief

Sarah: My question, "How could the earth talk?" really made me want to read on and find out what that meant.

Juan: I wondered what the otter had to do with the story and why the girl had a pole. [cover illustration]

Mario: Yeah. The questions I asked when I read did the same for me. It's kind of like predicting. I wanted to see if I could find an answer.

Julia: I asked a question when I didn't understand. [opens book to page 22] I didn't know what *mirage, phenomenon,* and *fathom* meant, and Sarah helped.

Mario: That happened to me on page eighty-three. I wanted to know more about *animal communication*. How did the panther know its mate was dead? It [the book] doesn't say.

Debriefing tuned these students into the benefits of questioning. Their exchange was successful because all four had practiced and thought about posing questions.

Many times debriefings don't run smoothly, and that's to be expected. A seventh-grade group debriefed their experiences with skimming. One student insisted, "Skimming is dumb—it's busywork." Another added, "I'd rather guess if I don't know it." Three out of five comments were negative and revealed that students did not view skimming as a helpful strategy. Their comments informed my decision to work one-on-one with them.

Derailed debriefings inform our teaching, spotlighting what didn't work, while pinpointing students who require additional support. Usually, as I circulate around the room and listen to each group, I can identify students who are confused or who don't really understand a strategy's benefits.

STRATEGY IN ACTION
Debriefing in a Sixth-Grade Classroom

Sixth graders have observed two mini-lessons on generating their own literature group discussion questions; the entire class collaborated, creating open-ended questions for a short story the teacher read aloud. Next, the teacher invited each group of five students to create open-ended discussion questions for their book. Each group had a different novel that related to a survival theme. The teacher invited groups to collaborate and create six to eight open-ended questions after reading half the book and again after finishing it. The debriefing occurred at the halfway mark, as the teacher wanted to assess students' reactions to creating their own questions. After groups exchanged ideas, the teacher collected these on chart paper. Here are some responses:

1. I had to reread parts. You have to know it [the story] to make good questions.
2. I like discussing our questions. [pause] It's what means a lot to us.
3. It's boring.
4. I think testing a question for factual or open [ended] is hard.
5. I needed to remember more details—it was hard.

This information enabled the teacher to identify students who would benefit from one-on-one conferences. Responses 3 to 5 also raised the question: Do students have enough prior knowledge to read their novels independently? Debriefing not only informs students, but it enables teachers to draw conclusions about students' ability to verbalize their understanding of a reading strategy.

Students' Debriefing Comments Can Teach the Teachers

Sometimes I invite students to summarize their debriefing remarks; other times I jot down, on sticky-notes, comments that appear significant. The students' insights and queries that follow illustrate how you and I can learn from this process and plan meaningful interventions.

Teaching Reading in Middle School

"It's hard for me to look back and find support. It takes forever. I start rereading every word. Everyone finds the stuff [support] before me." —Grade 7

Intervention: One-on-one work with skimming, using chapter headings and skimming for key words in each question.

"I reread but my mind still wanders, and I don't remember much." —Grade 6

Intervention: Practice Read/Pause/Retell/Reread in small chunks—one to three sentences—until student can concentrate. Gradually add more text.

"This book is boring. I can read the words, but it makes me want to sleep." —Grade 5

Intervention: Check if book is on independent-reading level. Build background knowledge or change book to a more familiar topic.

With debriefing, teachers can respond to students because strengths and needs have been highlighted. Students learn about themselves and from one another as they reflect on their reading process alone and exchange ideas with peers. The debriefing strategy builds background experiences for the thorough self-examination that self-evaluation leads to.

THE BENEFITS OF SELF-EVALUATION

It's the middle of April and as I circulate around the room, I remark to myself that part of my eighth-grade workshop looks and sounds chaotic. Five students discussing *Words By Heart* (by Ouida Sebesteyen) argue loudly over the ending of the story. A group of three students, who should be building words with roots, prefixes, and suffixes, are chatting with a classmate who should be typing the final draft of her original myth. Independent reading has deteriorated into talking about a weekend bowling party. I flick the lights (the signal for silence) and ask students to return to their seats. Quickly, I pass out sheets of composition paper and invite these eighth graders to tell me why I stopped workshop. Blunt honesty characterizes their responses, for students know that I use this self-evaluative strategy to engage their cooperation, not to punish.

+ "We talked about who was coming to the party. We should have done our work, but it was fun talking about the bowling party."
+ "I meant to read today, but I got to talking."

◆ "We argued and shouted because we didn't agree. It's hard to value what someone else says if you really believe in your idea."

These statements represent three important benefits of self-evaluation for students. Self-evaluation…

1. increases self-awareness, enabling middle school students to confront and deal with learning issues and issues related to working with peers;

2. develops, over time, a deeper understanding of an issue, situation, or process, and empowers students to make decisions about their learning;

3. enables the teacher to keep self-evaluations and review them with students in order to negotiate reasonable goals about using choice time.

In a safe environment, students are honest because they understand that they will use these self-evaluations to set specific goals for workshop. In addition to reflecting on their behavior during workshop, I invite students to think deeply about these aspects of self-evaluation: 1) workshop goals students have set; 2) reading strategies; 3) response journals; 4) progress in reading.

SETTING AND EVALUATING WORKSHOP GOALS

During the past week, several eighth graders have not used free-choice time wisely. To help them focus on their work, I invited students to set written goals for what they hoped to accomplish, and to evaluate these goals at the end of workshop. Adam wrote: "Today I plan to read for 20 minutes and then work on my book of poems for 20 minutes." Five minutes before the class ended, I asked students to reread and evaluate their goals. Adam wrote: "I talked a lot this workshop and then spent time daydreaming after Mrs. Robb asked me to reread my goals. I didn't feel like working.

Tomorrow, I will do more if I don't talk." Like adults, middle school students have days when they don't feel like working. Confronting students with their own words helps me deal with this issue without being judgmental.

The next day, as I circulated among students during choice time, I asked Adam to reread his self-evaluation and establish new goals, which he met (see Adam's self-evaluation on page 260). However, accomplishing a turnabout is not always this easy. Sometimes I sit with one student or a small group, help them organize their work, set priorities, and provide support as they read or write.

Use the form on the next page to focus students' thinking on their use of choice time during workshop.

NAME William   DATE Apr 16, 1997

My plan for today's workshop is to:
Do my Book Review on The Kingdom by the Sea
I also need to write a poem.
Then I'll read.

What did I accomplish?
finished Book review
Wrote poem

How can I use my work time to complete more   Poem revising
use more time

Goals for next workshop class:
revise poems

Self-evaluations reveal students' honest appraisals.

NAME Mary   DATE April 29, 1996

My plan for today's workshop is to:
Read 20 pages and really do it, not stop every five minutes.

What did I accomplish?
I read exactly 20 pages in the Book A Island Like You

How can I use my work time to complete more of writing ?
Maybe by splitting the time equally between reading and writing.

Goals for next workshop class:
To split the time somewhat equally between reading and writing

Self-Evaluation of Choice Time

Name _____ Date _____

My plan for today's workshop is to:

What did I accomplish?

How can I use my work time to accomplish more?

Goals for next workshop class:

Evaluating Reading Strategies

After students practice and seem to understand a strategy, invite them to reflect on how the strategy supports their comprehension and recall. Once students can express how rereading, using context clues, brainstorming, visualizing, etc., can improve their understanding and remembering, they will see a purpose for using these strategies.

Before inviting students to self-evaluate in writing, set aside time to engage students in a lively discussion about the strategy:

+ Organize students into small groups of four to six.
+ Have students discuss a strategy they've been practicing.
+ Encourage them to exchange ways the strategy supports their reading.
+ Instead of publicly debriefing, ask them to write these thoughts in their journals.

Exchanges enable students to hear how others employed a strategy and helps students recognize that strategies can be great reading problem-solvers. The comments that follow illustrate the benefits of reflective self-evaluation:

> *"I never reread before we practiced. If I didn't get it first time around, I waited for the teacher to discuss the chapter."* —*Grade 7*

> *"I used to just skip over hard words. Sometimes I still do that. But lots of times I can find a clue and know what it [the word] means."* —*Grade 5*

> *"I thought the smart ones never had to reread. I learned that they do it a lot; they just don't tell everyone. I've started rereading in science where the book is hard. It takes a long time and sometimes I can't do all of the pages, but it helps."* —*Grade 6*

> *"Once I saw that I'm making inferences all the time, I could look at characters and events and discover unstated meanings in books."* —*Grade 8*

My daughter, Anina, uses the self-evaluation form I developed for the predict/support/ adjust/strategy. Students complete the form on page 264 after finishing a prediction book log (see page 157). After a student self-evaluates, Anina and the student confer, and she completes the form by adding the student's comments as well as her comments and recommendations. The student sets a goal for the next prediction book log. (File evaluations in students' literacy folders.) Discuss with students goals that need fine-tuning. Anina helped David see that it was fine to need adjustments, as long as predictions were logical.

Student's Self-Evaluation Checklist
for Predict-and-Support

Name _____ Date _____

Directions:

This checklist will help you think about the way you made predictions and about the characters and events in the book. After you read each item, try and recall how often you did it. Write O for often, S for sometimes, and R for rarely.

Title _____

Author _____

Key: **O**=Often   **S**=Sometimes   **R**=Rarely

After completing chapter I

_____ I used the title and cover as support.

_____ I used information in the first chapter as support.

_____ I used my own knowledge of how stories work.

_____ I used my own experiences to support predictions.

_____ Predicting made me want to continue the book.

_____ At this point, my predictions could be off target.

Halfway through the book

_____ My prediction was based on what had already happened.

_____ I used examples from the story as support.

_____ I find myself predicting as I read more and more of the story.

_____ Making predictions makes the reading enjoyable.

After completing the book

_____ I reread parts of the book so I could adjust off-target predictions.

_____ I gave examples from the story to support my adjustments.

_____ I confirmed predictions that were on target.

Student's Comments:

Teacher's Comments and Recommendations:

Student's Goal for the Next Book:

Student's Self-Evaluation Checklist for Predict and Support

Name _David Thomas_   Date _10/27/99_

Directions:

This checklist will help you think about the way you made predictions about the characters and events in the book.

After you read each item, try and recall how often you did it. Write **O** for often, **S** for sometimes, and **R** for rarely.

Title _I Hadn't Meant To Tell You This_

Author _By Jacqueline Woodson_

Key:	O=Often;	S=Sometimes;	R=Rarely

After Completing Chapter 1

__O__ I used the title and cover as support.

__S__ I used information in the first chapter as support.

__O__ I used my own knowledge of how stories work.

__S__ I used my own experiences to support predictions.

__R__ Predicting made me want to continue the book.

__O__ At this point, my predictions could be off target.

Halfway Through the Book

__S__ My prediction was based on what had already happened.

__S__ I used examples from the story as support.

__R__ I find myself predicting as I read more and more of the story.

__R__ Making predictions makes the reading enjoyable.

After Completing the Book

__R__ I reread parts of the book so I could adjust off-target predictions.

__S__ I gave examples from the story to support my adjustments.

__S__ I confirmed predictions that were on target.

Student's Comments: I think this story was very good. I liked it because you can replay it to real life. I say you can use this book for real life because when you tell people stuff you have to think ahead of times where it will wined up.

Teacher's Comments and Recommendations: Excellent job - your support is much better on this Report than on the last one. I think you should be aware of this - David. You do make predictions As I read aloud - Iwonder if you are doing

Student's Goal for the Next Book: For my next book I want to try to get " No adjustment needed". Just like I did in this book.

it and not listening to yourself?

24

STUDENTS EVALUATE THEIR RESPONSE JOURNALS

Middle school reading-writing workshop teachers meet with more than one hundred students each week. It is impossible to read and comment on each one's response journal. I read students' entries as I circulate around the room, taking notes that I file in their literacy folders. Sometimes I ask students to place a marker on an entry they want me to read; other times I randomly select an entry.

Several times a year I invite students to self-evaluate a section of their journals that relates to a study of a theme or literary genre. I tell students they will be self-evaluating their journals prior to starting the study and explain that we will develop guidelines for entries.

Before students review their entries, we establish and list on chart paper the criteria I want them to apply to their self-evaluations. Criteria vary with each study and grow out of mini-lessons and guidelines negotiated for class notes and students' responses to the reading.

Four groups of seventh graders read different books about survival. Students and I set these criteria for giving themselves a grade and defending their grading. Each entry must have:

- ◆ Name, date, and a heading that identifies the entry.
- ◆ Class notes taken from the chart paper and the chalkboard.
- ◆ Journal responses that illustrated students' independent thinking as they read and responded after completing four or five chapters.
- ◆ Summaries of the collaborative thinking of group discussions.

Here are a few self-evaluations that reveal how students take this responsibility seriously. If a student gave herself a high grade for poor work, I'll review the criteria and

> Self-Evaluation
>
> I did date each entry. I took all the class notes. I worked well by myself and In a group.
>
> GRADE: B or C
>
> I think I should get a B or C. I think this cause I kept all the notes and dated everything. I also worked well with others and by myself. The negative reasons this grade is because I didn't keep up with my notebook, didn't turn it in on notebook check days. Also because I came to class unprepared and without my journal. I also didn't pay attention in class sometimes and just started to draw when I should have payed attention.

entries with that student in a brief conference. My goal? To help the student see her strengths and areas that did not meet the criteria. I always conclude these meetings by asking the student how she could have improved her work. On sticky-notes, I jot down suggestions in the journal so they can be reviewed before starting the next self-evaluation journal project.

Seventh graders evaluate their journals, offering reasons for the grade they chose.

June 2, 1993

Self Evaluation

Did you?

Date each entry
Take Notes - Class
Do Independent Thinking
Do Collaborative Thinking

Grade: Reasons
Participation → Talk
Listening
Sharing with whole class

I think I should get an A. I don't say this because I want a good grade but I say this because I dated each entry, took all of the notes or got them If I were sick, did my own Independent and Collaborative (with Cheyenna) Thinking. I participated in class and shared my feelings. I also listened and felt that some of the things a classmate said was very interesting. I also shared when I could or when I was asked to. I really enjoyed this class. _con tinued on back_

6/2/93   Tannette McGlashan

What might a close brush with death make me feel?

*My idea still wouldn't change because I still feel the same way.

Self Evaluation
Date each entry
Notes - Class
Independent thinking
Collaborative thinking

: I think I should get an A+ because I dated my entrys, listened, took notes, I was good with independent + collaborative thinking as I did my paragraphs they got longer and longer, I participated in group and class talks, and

Reflecting on and Writing About Reading Progress

Two or three times a year, I invite students to think about their progress in reading. This is a difficult task for middle school students, especially those in grades five and six. However, if you provide questions for them to consider and use as a springboard for brainstorming, they can take a long look at their progress and even pinpoint some needs.

Select questions from the following list that reflect what you and students have focused on. Write these on the chalkboard and invite students to think about how the questions apply to their reading. Then, have students brainstorm a list of ideas to include in a narrative about their reading process.

The sample self-evaluations of reading that I've included highlight the differences between eighth and fifth graders. Eighth graders write more and are able to explain their progress and process in greater depth.

Information in these pieces can become topics for one-on-one strategy meetings, can be used at conferences with students and parents, and can help you understand how students perceive their progress.

Fifth (top right), sixth (below) and eighth graders (below right) write about progress in reading.

Shantell   Dec. 3, 1998

   This year is the First year I started rereading. I stop to think— do I remember? I have started doing this and its easier to read a book especialy in science and history. I also reread chapters in books I am liking. I read Bridge to Terabithia and I reread the part where Jesses dad tells that Leslie is dead. I cried every time.
   I learned that even teachers reread. It helps me Figure out hard parts. I remember more. This year has been important to my reading cause I reread and stop and think about the story.

Rebekah   Reading Self Evaluation   May 10, 1999

   I like to read all types of books, but my favorite are mysteries and science fiction. I also like some history books like we have had to read in history class. This year I found a series of books that take place in the 1800s. They are by Miriam Grace Monfredo and are very good. I like to read in the evening or when there is nothing very exciting to do. My favorite places to read are in my room and in my living room chair with my cats.
   Strategies I use are looking at titles and reading the cover. By doing this I can usually figure out very easily if I like it. My strengths as a reader are speed and understanding. I can read fast and still follow a confusing plot scheme or scene changes. My goal is to read more often. If something exciting is going on, I forget about reading, and I need to remember. I also want to try some other types of books

Reading in 6th grade   May 12

   In 6th grade reading I learned so much, and read so many books. We did not just read the books we discussed, story parts, themes and interpretive questions. I think this helped us actually read the book and make it stick in your head. We read free reading books also, and kept a reading log. One of my favorite books that we did was Jip by Katherine Paterson the activities we did were making predictions and telling if your prediction was right. We also did vocabulary where we wrot down vocabulary and page number of word we didn't know.
   Some other books we read were Lyddie, The Great Gilly Hopkins both by Katherine Paterson, Henry Sugar by Roald Dahl, Hatchet by Gary Paulson, Junior Great Books, and Slave Dancer. For all these books we read we did different activities. I also like this activities because I enjoy reading.

Questions That Encourage Students to Brainstorm Ideas About Their Progress in Reading

✦ What strategies do I use before I read? How do these help?

✦ How do I activate my prior knowledge and experiences?

✦ What do I do when I can't pronounce a word?

✦ How do I figure out the meaning of an unfamiliar word?

✦ How do I help myself recall information?

✦ Can I select the important details in a chapter? a book?

✦ Do I reread? When? Why?

✦ What kinds of free-choice books do I select?

✦ Do I choose to read at home? Why?

✦ What can I do if a word or passage confuses me?

✦ Do I set purposes? Why?

✦ Do I connect my life and experiences to the book?

✦ When do I skim? How does this help me?

✦ Do I enjoy reading? Why? Why not?

✦ Can I discover inferences? the main idea? themes?

✦ Do my journal entries have specific examples to support my ideas?

Teaching students to self-evaluate provides me with insights into their reading—insights I might never have discerned if I had not encouraged reflection. Students' self-evaluations, combined with my observational notes and notes taken at conferences and strategic-reading group lessons, supply me with enough information to complete a checklist that monitors students' application of reading strategies.

A Checklist for Teachers: Monitor Students' Strategizing Progress

The following reproducible invites you to monitor students' progress three times each year: in the fall, shortly after the New Year, and during the final month of school.

Use these evaluations as you confer with students and parents, and pass them on to next year's teacher.

Teacher Evaluation of Reading Strategies

Name _____ Date _____

Before-Reading Strategies	Practicing	Developing	Independent
Brainstorm/Categorize			
Predict/Support			
Skim			
Pose Questions			
Fast–Write			
During-Reading Strategies			
Personal Connections			
Predict/Support/Adjust			
Use Prior Knowledge			
Self-Question			
Identify Confusing Parts			
Self-Monitor for Understanding			
Use Context Clues for Vocabulary			
Visualize			
Reread			
Infer			
Pause/Recall			
After-Reading Strategies			
Evaluate/Adjust Predictions			
Skim			
Reread			
Question			
Compare/Contrast			
Cause/Effect			
Draw Conclusions			
Identify Themes			

Additional Comments:

Performance-based assessments and self-evaluations enable you to plan instruction and negotiate goals with students. However, the reality we all face is that most school districts require that teachers give reading tests to measure students' progress.

HOW CAN I TEST STUDENTS' READING?

Every six weeks I test students' reading by having them read a short story, folktale, myth, or nonfiction selection on their independent-reading level. The purpose of these tests is to observe how well students apply what we are studying to their reading. Students usually read different selections because independent-reading levels vary. I choose stories from graded basal readers or from my file of stories from magazines and anthologies that I have leveled using the SMOG formula.

If my class is studying the structure of short stories, the test will include questions like these:

+ Name the protagonist and two or three problems this character faced.
+ Identify three antagonistic forces and show how each worked against the protagonist.
+ What is the climax? the denouement? Defend your choice.
+ Select one problem and show how the protagonist solved it.

If we are studying character development and how dialogue, inner thoughts, decisions, setting, conflicts, and other characters affect the protagonist's personality, I pose these questions:

+ Discuss two decisions the protagonist made and explain what these decisions taught you about this character.
+ Pick two settings in the story and explain how the character reacted to these settings. Explain what you learned about the character from these reactions.
+ Read the dialogue and inner thoughts on page [xx] of the story. What personality traits do these reveal?
+ Explain the conflict between the protagonist and another character and show what you learned about each character from the way they dealt with the conflict.
+ Show how interactions between a minor character and the protagonist reveal personality traits of each.

During the year we study different literary genres. A reading test can also assess students' knowledge of a genre's structure. If we're studying myths or fairy tales or science fiction, I'll ask students to select the elements in the selection that identify the genre.

The key to students' success on these teacher-made tests is finding materials that students can read, so that thinking can occur. When evaluating these tests, I look for students' ability to select details that support their answers to the question. Because I assess students when I'm sure that they can experience success, students find these reading tests a positive experience. I always struggle when trying to assign a letter or number grade to these assessments, because I'm keener on monitoring progress than labeling results. However, the reality all teachers face is that most school districts require grades.

Some Problems That Grading Poses

At a graduate class on assessment, I organized 50 teachers into groups of five and asked each group to brainstorm a list of the problems testing and grading raised. Their list spotlighted frustrations that students and teachers experience with a test and grade-driven curriculum:

- ✦ It's often subjective.
- ✦ Provides a limited picture of achievement and progress.
- ✦ Encourages teaching to a test.
- ✦ Affects learners' motivation by creating stress and frustration.
- ✦ Assumes all students in a class can learn the same material and read and write at the same level.
- ✦ Believes that all students should be measured the same way.
- ✦ Views learning as the ability to test well.
- ✦ Doesn't consider the child as a learner at home, in school, and in the community.
- ✦ Excludes talent in music, art, and dance.

Members of the class agreed that learners are more than the sum of their scores on several reading quizzes and tests. The problem we wrestled with was how to assign a fair grade to performance-based assessments. There are no easy answers. However, most agreed that in addition to the teacher-made and standardized tests districts required, it was possible to include performance-based assessments as long as teachers had a rubric, a clear set of guidelines or criteria for establishing the grade.

Though I am required to assign a letter grade to students' work, I also write a long narrative. A variety of assessments—information in students' literacy folders, their self-evaluations, my observations—enable me to write about each student, highlighting progress over each marking period. Though I often grumble while I work on the narratives because they're time-consuming, I would never abandon them. The information they present clarifies my understandings and provides students and parents with data that considers and emphasizes daily learning and progress.

IF I'M A BEGINNING TEACHER, WHERE DO I START?

Since it's crucial for teachers to gain insight into how students read and solve problems the text poses, I recommend that teachers become proficient with the error analysis of oral reading. While developing that skill, you can also teach students how to self-evaluate and include their personal insights in the decisions you make about grouping and what strategies to teach.

Pause and Reflect on:
Assessment and Evaluation

In order to reach all middle school readers, it's crucial that we collect information about their reading lives and attitudes toward learning and reading. During the first six to eight weeks, get to know the differences in reading expertise among your students. Confer, interview, and assess their oral reading and comprehension. With this information, frame learning experiences that meet the diverse needs of each student and build confidence, independence, and reading expertise.

Closing Reflections on Guiding Students' Reading

"Children cannot keep up with a standard set of instruction, will not learn the same things from a standard lesson, and will not learn the same amount in the same lesson time."
—Marie Clay (1993)

arie Clay's words hurled me back in time to my first year of teaching in a rural elementary school in Virginia. A wall of windows brightened the institutional-green classroom. Thirty five wooden desks, nailed to the floor in five neat rows, shouted, "No group work in this room!" Budgets were tight, and sixth-grade basal readers, science and social studies textbooks, all with accompanying workbooks, were my teaching materials. No pencils, no paper, no crayons. The principal assured me that the students would bring these supplies to school.

Thirty-three students, ranging in age from 12 to 15, entered my classroom on the first day. I quickly learned that though every child was given the same basal reader, 12 students could not read the stories or complete the workbook pages, and five were bored with the book. The basal was just right for only half my class.

Though I knew little about teaching reading, I quickly recognized that this one-size-fits-all program, based on whole-group instruction, would not support my sixth graders' diverse reading levels. Even more frustrating was the pacing system that required me to complete a reading unit and the basal test by a specific date. Whether or not children learned seemed unimportant; covering the material was the primary goal.

Marie Clay's words force us to consider the effects of the standardization of teaching and learning: a small group improves; students reading below grade level regress; and proficient readers are bored. Clay calls for "interactive teaching" to replace standardization (1993).

Similar to a conversation, interactive teaching invites teacher and students to listen, exchange ideas, and ask questions about the meaning of those ideas. The interactive teacher does not set out to "teach something" to a student, to lecture and fill that student with knowledge. Interactive teachers do the following:

1. Listen carefully to what students say.
2. Observe students in a variety of learning experiences.
3. Respond to what students show teachers they need.
4. Discover student's knowledge base and level of expertise.
5. Create learning experiences that accept students where they are and gently move them forward.
6. Find materials students can read and enjoy.
7. Monitor each student's progress.
8. Negotiate goals with students.
9. Teach the whole group, small groups, and meet one-on-one.

10. Reflect on students' work and their own interactions with other students to plan appropriate interventions.

Reading workshop is the ideal environment for interactive teaching. Workshop allows teachers to support middle school students who arrive at school with varied levels of reading competence. During workshop, teachers can meet with small groups and individuals when students work independently.

Becoming an interactive teacher who can reach all readers in a classroom is a journey without a destination. We try new strategies, revise them, and try again. Our students change throughout the year, and we must adapt our interactions to these changes. We must offer books they can read, without a hidden agenda of what we want them to learn from that book. Katherine Paterson expressed this humble respect for readers in her essay "The Spying Heart."

> *I'm so concerned that the reader be free to come to a book from his own experience and take from the book what he can and will. I don't want anyone telling a child what he should get out of one of my books or any book I care about, for that matter.*

My hope for all the students I teach is that I can help them choose books that reach the roots of their imaginations and souls, connect them deeply to the life and experiences of a character, and leave them asking wistfully, "Why did this book have to end?"

Bibliography
of Professional Books and Articles

"Adolescent literacy comes of age." 1999. In *Reading Today.* Newark: DE. vol. 17 (1). August/September.

Allington, Richard L. 1983. "The Reading Instruction Provided Readers of Abilities" In *The Elementary School Journal.* vol. 83, pp. 548–559.

Alvermann, Donna E. 2000. "Classroom Talk About Texts: Is it Dear, Cheap, or a Bargain at Any Price?" In *Reading for Meaning: Fostering Comprehension in the Middle Grades.* Newark, Delaware: The International Reading Association.

Alvermann, Donna E. 1984. "Second Graders Strategic Reading Preferences While Reading Basal Stories" In *Journal of Educational Research.* vol. 77, pp 184–189.

Alvermann, Donna E. and Stephen F. Phelps. 1998. *Content Reading and Literacy: Succeeding in Today's Diverse Classrooms,* second edition. Boston, MA: Allyn and Bacon.

Anderson, Richard. 1984. "Role of Reader's Schema in Comprehension, Learning and Memory." In *Learning to Read in American Schools.* Richard Anderson, Jean Osborne, and Robert Tierney, eds. Hillsdale, NJ: Lawrence Erlbaum Associates.

Atwell, Nancie. 1987, 1999. *In the Middle: Writing, Reading, and Learning With Adolescents.* Portsmouth, NH: Heinemann.

Barr, Rebecca, Marilyn Sadow and Camille Blachowicz. 1990. *Reading Diagnosis For Teachers: An Instructional Approach.* New York: Longman.

Barrentine, Shelby J. 1999. *Reading Assessment: Principles and Practices for Elementary Teachers.* Newark, DE: International Reading Association.

Baumann, James F., Leah A. Jones, and Nancy Seifert-Kessell. 1993. "Using Think-Alouds to Enhance Children's Comprehension Monitoring Abilities." In *The Reading Teacher,* November, vol. 47, pp. 187–199.

Bomer, Randy. 1998. "Conferring with Struggling Readers: The Test of Our Craft, Courage, and Hope." In *The New Advocate*, vol.12 (1). Boston, MA: Christopher-Gordon.

Boyd, Fenice B. and Lee Galda. 1997. "Lessons Taught and Learned: How Cross-Aged Talk About Books Helped Struggling Adolescents Develop Their Own Literacy." In *Peer Talk in the Classroom: Learning From Research,* Jeanne R. Paratore and Rachel L. McCormack, eds. Newark, DE: International Reading Association.

Calkins, Lucy McCormick, with Shelley Harwayne. 1991. *Living Between the Lines.* Portsmouth, NH: Heinemann.

Clay, Marie. 1979. *The Early Detection of Reading Difficulties.* Portsmouth, NH: Heinemann.

Clay, Marie. 1993. "Marie Clay Responds..." In *Reading in Virginia*, vol. XVIII.

Clay, Marie. 1979. *Reading: The Patterning of Complex Behaviour.* Portsmouth, NH: Heinemann.

Cunningham, Patricia M. and Richard Allington. 1999. *Classrooms that Work.* New York: Longman.

Dowhower, Sarah L. .1999. "Supporting a Strategic Stance in the Classroom: A Comprehension Framework for Helping Teachers Help Students to be Strategic." In *The Reading Teacher,* vol. 57, pp. 672–688.

Edelsky, Carol, Bess Altwerger and Barbara Flores. 1991. *Whole Language, What's the Difference?* Portsmouth, NH: Heinemann.

Estes, Thomas H. and Joseph L. Vaughan. 1986. *Reading and Reasoning Beyond the Primary Grades.* Boston, MA: Allyn and Bacon.

Fielding, Linda G. and P. David Pearson, 1994. "Reading Comprehension: What Works." In *Educational Leadership,* vol. 51 (5), pp. 1–7. Alexandria, VA.

Fielding, Linda G. and Cathy M. Roller. 1998. "Theory Becomes Practice at the Point of Interaction." In *Primary Voices K-6.* Urbana, IL. vol. 7 (1).

Fountas, Irene and Gay Su Pinnell. 1996. *Guided Reading: Good First Teaching For All Children.* Portsmouth, NH: Heinemann, 1996.

Gambrell, Linda B. 1996. "What Research Reveals About Discussion." In *Lively Discussions! Fostering Engaged Reading,* Linda B. Gambrell and Janice F. Almasi, eds. Newark, DE: International Reading Association.

Gansky, Kathy. 1993. *Developmental Spelling Analysis: A Qualitative Measure of Assessment and Instructional Planning.* Barboursville, VA: Gansky.

Gardner, Ruth. 1992. "Metacognition and Self-Monitoring Strategies." In *What Research Has to Say About Reading Instruction,* second edition. S. Jay Reading Association.

Gillet, Jean Wallace and Charles Temple. 1990. *Understanding Reading Problems: Assessment and Instruction,* third edition. New York: HarperCollins.

Glazer, Susan Mandel and Carol Smullen Brown. 1993. *Portfolios and Beyond: Collaborative Assessment in Reading and Writing.* Norwood, MA: Christopher-Gordon.

Goodman, Kenneth, Yetta Goodman, and Wendy Hood (eds.). 1989. *The Whole Language Evaluation Book.* Portsmouth, NH: Heinemann.

Goodman, Yetta. 1985. "Kidwatching: Observing Children in the Classroom." In *Observing the Language Learner,* edited by Angela Jaguar and M. Trinka Smith-Burke, Newark, DE: International Reading Association.

Goodman, Yetta. 1996. "Revaluing Readers While Readers Revalue Themselves: Retrospective Miscue Analysis." In *Reading Assessment: Principles and Practices for Elementary School Teachers.* Newark, DE: International Reading Association.

Graves, Donald. 1983. *Writing: Teachers & Children At Work.* Portsmouth, NH: Heinemann.

Graves, Michael F. and Bonnie Graves. 1994. *Scaffolding Reading Experiences: Designs for Students Success.* Norwood, MA: Christopher-Gordon.

Graves, Michael F. 2000. "Vocabulary Program to Complement and Bolster a Middle-Grade Comprehension Program." In *Reading for Meaning: Fostering Comprehension in the Middle Grades.* Newark, Delaware: The International Reading Association.

Guice, Sherry and Richard Allington, Peter Johnston, Kim Baker, and Nancy Michelson. 1996. "Access?: Books, Children, and Literature-Based Curriculum in Schools," In *The New Advocate,* vol. 9 (3), pp. 197–207.

Hansen, Jane. 1987. *When Writers Read.* Portsmouth, NH: Heinemann.

Holdaway, Don. 1980. *The Foundations of Literacy.* Portsmouth, NH: Heinemann.

Hynds, Susan. 1997. *On the Brink: Negotiating Literature and Life With Adolescents.* Newark, DE: The International Reading Association.

Keene, Ellin Oliver and Susan Zimmerman. 1997. *Mosaic of Thought.* Portsmouth, NH: Heinemann.

Kohn, Alfie. "Choices for Children: Why and How to Let Students Decide." In *Phi Delta Kappan,* September 1993.

Lapp, Diane and James Flood, Wendy Ranck-Buhr, Janice Van Dyke, Sara Spacek. 1996. "'Do Your Really Just Want Us to Talk About This Book?': A Closer Look at Book Clubs as an Instructional Tool." *In Lively Discussions! Fostering Engaged Reading,* Linda B. Gambrell and Janice F. Almasi, eds. Newark, DE: International Reading Association.

Lytle, Susan L. 1982. "Exploring Comprehension Style: A Study of Twelfth Grade Readers' Transactions with Text." Ph.D. diss., University of Pennsylvania.

Minsky, Marvin. 1975. "A Framework for Representing Knowledge." In *The Psychology of Computer Vision,* edited by P.H. Winston. New York: McGraw-Hill.

Ogle, Donna M. 1986. "K-W-L: A Teaching Model That Develops Active Reading of an Expository Text." In *The Reading Teacher,* February, vol. 39, pp. 564–570.

Ogle, Donna, M. 1988/1999. "Implementing Strategic Reading." In *Educational Leadership,* December/January, pp. 47–60.

Paris, Scott G., Marjorie Y. Lipson, and Karen K. Wixon. 1983. "Becoming a Strategic Reader." In *Contemporary Educational Psychology,* vol. 8, pp. 293-316.

Paterson, Katherine. 1989. "The Spying Heart." In *The Spying Heart: More Thoughts on Reading And Writing Books for Children.* New York: Lodestar.

Pearson, P. David, L.R. Roehler, J.A. Dole, and G.G. Duffy. 1992. "Developing Expertise in Reading Comprehension." In *What Research Has to Say About Reading Instruction,* second edition. J. Samuels and A. Farstrup, eds., Newark, DE: International Reading Association.

Rico, Gabriele L. 1983. *Writing the Natural Way: Using Right-Brain Techniques to Release Your Expressive Powers.* Los Angeles, CA: J. P. Tarcher.

Robb, Laura. 1993. "A Cause for Celebration: Reading and Writing with At-Risk Students. In *The New Advocate,* vol. 6 (1). Boston, MA: Christopher-Gordon.

Robb, Laura. 1991. "Building Bridges: Eighth and Third Grades Read Together." In *The New Advocate,* vol. 4 (4). Boston, MA: Christopher-Gordon.

Robb, Laura. 1998. *Easy-to-Manage Reading & Writing Conferences.* New York: Scholastic.

Robb, Laura. 1999. *Easy Mini-Lessons for Building Vocabulary.* New York: Scholastic.

Robb, Laura. 1998. *Reach All Readers: Guidelines for Teaching a Class of Struggling, Reluctant, and Secure Readers in Grades 6–8.* Littleton, MA: Sundance.

Robb, Laura. 1995. *Reading Strategies That Work: Helping Your Students Become Better Readers.* New York: Scholastic.

Robb, Laura. 1994. *Whole Language, Whole Learners: Creating a Literature-Centered Classroom.* New York: Morrow.

Rosenblatt, Louise. *Literature as Exploration,* 4th ed. 1983. New York: The Modern Language Association of America.

Rosenblatt, Louise. 1978. *The Reader, the Text, the Poem: The Transactional Theory of the Literary Work.* Carbondale, IL: SIU Press.

Routman, Regie. 1991. *Invitations: Changing as Teachers and Learners K–12.* Portsmouth, NH: Heinemann.

Ruddell, Robert B. and Norman J. Unrau. 1997. "The Role of Responsive Teaching in Focusing Reader Intention and Developing Reader Motivation." In *Reading Engagement: Motivating Readers Through Integrated Instruction.,* John T. Guthrie and Allan Wigfield, eds. Newark, DE: International Reading Association.

Ryder, Randall J. and Michael F. Graves. 1998. *Reading and Learning in Content Areas,* second edition. Saddle River, NJ: Merrill.

Santa, Carol Minnick. 1999. "Watching Dusty Read." In *Reading Today.* Newark, DE: International Reading Association. August/September.

Schunk, Dale H. and Barry J. Zimmerman. 1997. "Developing Self-Efficacious Readers and Writers: The Role of Social and Self-Regulatory Processes." In *Reading Engagement: Motivating Readers Through Integrated Instruction,* John T. Guthrie and Allan Wigfield, eds. Newark, DE: International Reading Association.

Schallert, Diane L., Joylyn H. Reed, and E.T. Goetz. 1992. "Exploring the Reciprocal Relationship Among Comprehensibility, Interestingness, and Involvement in Academic Reading Tasks." Paper presented at the annual meeting of the American Educational Research Association, San Franscisco, CA.

Schallert, Diane Lemonnier and Joylyn Hailey Reed. 1997. "The Pull of Text and the Process of Involvement in Reading." In *Reading Engagement: Motivating Readers Through Integrated Instruction,* John T. Guthrie and Allan Wigfield, eds. Newark, DE: International Reading Association.

Smith, Frank. 1978. *Reading Without Nonsense.* New York: Teachers College Press.

Stauffer, Russel G. 1975. *Directing the Reading-Thinking Process.* New York: Harper & Row.

Strickland, Dorothy. 1987. "Literature: Key Element in the Language and Reading Program." In *Children's Literature in the Reading Program,* Bernice E. Cullinan, ed.

Sweet, Anne P. 1997. "Teacher Perceptions of Student Motivation and Their Relation to Literacy Learning." In *Reading Engagement: Motivating Readers Through Integrated Instruction,* John T. Guthrie and Allan Wigfield, eds. Newark, DE: International Reading Association.

Vacca, Richard T. and Vacca, Jo Anne L. 2000. *Content Area Reading: Literacy and Learning Across the Curriculum,* sixth edition. New York: Longman.

Vygotsky, Lev S. 1978. *Mind in Society: The Development of Higher Psychological Processes.* Cambridge, MA: Harvard University Press.

Wasserman, Selma. 1999. "Shazam! You're a Teacher: Facing the Illusory Quest for Certainty in Classroom Practice." In *Phi Delta Kappan,* February, pp. 464–468.

Wells, Gordon. 1986. *The Meaning Makers: Children Learning Language and Using Language to Learn.* Portsmouth, NH: Heinemann.

Wigfield, Allan. 1997. "Children's Motivation for Reading and Reading Engagement." In *Reading Engagement: Motivating Readers Through Integrated Instruction,* John T. Guthrie and Allan Wigfield, eds. Newark, DE: International Reading Association.

Bibliography
of Children's Books

Adler, David A. 1998. *Young Cam Jansen and the Ice Skate Mystery*, illustrated by Susanna Natti. New York: Henry Holt

Alexander, Lloyd. 1964. *The Book of Three.* New York: Henry Holt

Avi. 1984. *The Fighting Ground.* New York: Lippincott.

Avi. 1997. *What Do Fish Have To Do With Anything? And Other Stories.* Boston, MA: Candlewick.

Babbit, Natalie. 1975. *Tuck Everlasting.* New York: Farrar, Straus & Giroux.

Bloor, Edward. 1997. *Tangerine.* New York: Harcourt.

Bowen, Gary. 1994. *Stranded at Plimoth Plantation, 1626.* New York: HarperCollins.

Bulla, Clyde Robert. 1971. *Pocahontas and the Strangers.* New York: Scholastic.

Burnett, Frances Hodgson. 1932. *The Secret Garden,* illustrated by Tasha Tudor. New York: Lippincott.

Coerr, Eleanor. 1977. *Sadako and the Thousand Paper Cranes.* New York: Dell Yearling.

Coles, Robert, reteller. 1996. *The Story of Ruby Bridges.* New York: Scholastic.

Coman, Carolyn. 1997. *What Jamie Saw.* New York: Puffin.

Cormier, Robert. 1874. *The Chocolate War.* New York: Pantheon.

Cushman, Karen. 1996. *The Midwife's Apprentice.* New York: Clarion.

Dahl, Roald. 1959. "The Landlady." In *Kiss, Kiss.* New York: Knopf.

Davies, Nicola. 1997. *Big Blue Whale,* illustrated by Nick Maland. Cambridge, MA: Candlewick.

Dickens, Charles. 1886. Harland, T. reteller, *Captain Murderer.* Morrow.

Ehrlich, Amy, reteller. 1982. *The Snow Queen by Hans Christian Andersen,* illustrated by Susan Jeffers. New York: Dial.

Elvsin, Bernard. 1969. *Ulysses.* New York: Bantam, Doubleday, Dell.

Filipovic, Zlata. 1994. *Zlata's Diary: A Child's Life in Sarajevo.* New York: Viking.

Fleischman, Paul. 1980. *The Half-a-Moon-Inn.* New York: Harper & Row.

Fleischman, Sid. 1990. *The Midnight Horse.* New York: Dell Yearling.

Fleischman, Sid. 1997. *Chancy and the Grand Rascal.* New York: Beech Tree.

Fritz, Jean. 1987. *The Cabin Faced West.* New York: Puffin.

George, Jean Craighead. 1980. *The Cry of the Crow.* New York: Harper & Row.

George, Jean Craighead. 1983. *The Talking Earth,* New York: HarperCollins.

Griffin, John Howard. 1969. *Black Like Me.* New York: Signet.

Guiterman, Arthur. "Ancient History." In *Knock at a Star: A Child's Introduction to Poetry,* edited by X.J. Kennedy and Dorothy M. Kennedy. Boston, MA: Little, Brown.

Haas, Jessie.1998. *Fire! My Parents' Story.* New York: Greenwillow.

Hinton, S.E. 1968. *The Outsiders.* New York: Viking.

Hunt, Irene. 1987. *No Promises in the Wind.* New York: Berkley.

Jacques, Brian. 1986. *Redwall.* New York: Avon.

Jiang, Ji-Li. 1997. *Red Scarf Girl: A Memoir of the Cultural Revolution*. New York: HarperTrophy.

Kerr, M.E. 1994. *Deliver Us From Evie*. New York: HarperCollins.

Kerr, M.E. 1981. *Gentlehands*. New York: Bantam.

Klass, David. (1994). *California Blue*. New York: Scholastic.

Leapman, Michael. 1998. *Witnesses to War: Eight True-Life Stories of Nazi Persecution*. New York: Viking.

MacLachlan, Patricia. 1980. *Through Grandpa's Eyes*. New York: HarperCollins.

Marshall, James Vance. 1984. *Walkabout*. Littleton, MA: Sundance.

McCully, Emily Arnold. 1996. *The Bobbin Girl*. New York: Dial.

Myers, Anna. 1997. *The Keeping Room*. New York: Walker.

Nye, Robert. 1968. *Beowulf: A New Telling*. New York: Dell.

Paterson, Katherine. 1977. *Bridge to Terabithia*. New York: Crowell.

Paterson, Katherine. 1978. *The Great Gilly Hopkins*. New York: Crowell.

Paterson, Katherine. 1996. *Jip, His Story*. New York: Puffin.

Paterson, Katherine. *Lyddie*. 1991. New York: Viking.

Paulsen, Gary. 1987. *Hatchet*. New York: Viking.

Paulsen, Gary. 1991. *The River*. New York: Dell.

Rowling, J.K. 1997. *Harry Potter and the Sorcerer's Stone*. New York: Scholastic.

Rowling, J.K. 1999. *Harry Potter and the Chamber of Secrets*. New York: Scholastic.

Rowling, J.K. 1999. *Harry Potter and the Prisoner of Azkaban*. New York: Scholastic.

Sachar, Louis. 1998. *Holes*. New York: Farrar, Straus & Giroux.

Sebestyen, Ouida. 1979. *Words By Heart*. New York: Dell.

Scieszka, Jon. 1991. *The Not So Jolly Roger*. New York: Viking.

Scieszka, Jon. 1996. *Tut Tut*. New York: Viking.

Simon, Seymour. 1997. *The Brain*. New York: Morrow.

Simon. Seymour. 1976. *The Paper Airplane Book*. New York: Puffin.

Simon, Seymour. 1994. *Comets, Meteors, and Asteroids*. New York: Morrow.

Skofield, James. 1998. *Detective Dinosaur Lost and Found,* pictures by R.W. Alley. New York: HarperTrophy.

Soto, Gary. 1990. *Baseball in April and Other Stories*. New York: Odyssey Books.

Spinelli, Jerry. 1991. *Maniac Magee*. New York: HarperCollins.

Strasser, Todd. 1981. *The Wave*. New York: Dell.

Taylor, Mildred D. 1976. *Roll of Thunder, Hear My Cry*. New York: Viking.

Taylor, Mildred D. 1987. *The Friendship*. New York: Puffin.

Taylor, Mildred D. 1995. *The Well*. New York: Dial.

Van Leeuwen, Jean. 1996. *Blue Sky, Butterfly*. New York: Puffin.

White, E.B. 1952. *Charlotte's Web*. New York: Harper & Row.

Wick, Walter. 1997. *A Drop of Water*. New York: Scholastic.

Wolff, Virginia Euwer. 1998. *Bat 6*. New York: Scholastic.

Woodson, Jacqueline. 1994. *I Hadn't Meant to Tell You This*. New York: Delacorte.

Yep, Laurence. 1995. *Hiroshima*. New York: Scholastic.

Yolen, Jane. 1999. *The Devil's Arithmetic*. New York: Puffin.

Yolen, Jane and Martin H. Greenberg, editors. *Things That Go Bump in the Night*. "The Elevator" by William Sleator. New York: HarperCollins, 1989.

READING SURVEY

Name _____ Date _____

Fill in the blanks.

1. What words pop into your mind when you think of reading a book?
_____

2. Do you read at home? _____ How often do you read at home? _____

3. Where's your favorite place to read at home? _____ At school? _____

4. How do you find books you love to read? _____

5. Besides books, what other types of materials do you read? _____
_____ Why do you enjoy these? _____

6. Do you own a library card? _____ How often do you visit the library to
check out books? _____

Complete these sentences.

7. My favorite author is _____

8. The best book I read is _____

9. The best book someone read to me is _____

10. The topics I enjoy reading about are _____

11. I watch TV for _____ hours a day because _____

12. The things I'm great at as a reader are _____

13. Things I need to work on to improve my reading are _____

14. I use these strategies as I read: _____

15. I enjoy talking about books because _____

16. I enjoy responding to books in discussions because _____

17. I enjoy responding to books in my journal because _____

18. I can choose books that I can read for enjoyment because _____

ELEVEN QUESTIONS ABOUT READING

Directions: Read the questions that follow. On separate paper, take notes for each question. For each question, write your notes up in a paragraph. If you can't answer a question, write: *I don't know.*

1. Why do you read?

2. What benefits do you see in reading? How do you think reading helps you in your daily life?

3. What do you do well as a reader?

4. Do you read for pleasure at home? How often? What do you enjoy reading?

5. How does reading make you feel?

6. How do you select a book to read for enjoyment?

7. What do you do with the book before you start reading it?

8. As you read, are you aware of any strategies you use when you don't understand a word? a passage?

9. When you finish a book, what do you do?

10. What are some of your favorite books?

11. Do you have a favorite author? Why do you enjoy this author's book?

PARENT/GUARDIAN INFORMATION SHEET

Child's Name _____ Date _____

Parent/Guardian _____

Teacher _____

Please list your child's strong points as a reader and a learner:

List your child's interests and hobbies:

List what you and your child enjoy doing together:

Offer any tips or suggestions that might help me help your child learn:

When is the best time to call you?

READING STRATEGY INTERVIEW

Directions: On this paper, jot down notes as you converse with students.

Student's Name _____ Date _____

1a. How do you choose a book?

1b. How do you know that you can read and enjoy the book?

2. What do you do with the book before you start reading?

3. While reading, what do you do if you come across a word or section that you don't understand?

4. How do you help yourself remember the details of your reading?

5. When you complete a book, what do you do?

Strengths:

One or Two Goals:

Open-Ended Discussion Questions

Walk into any middle school classroom and you will find a class of 25 to 35 students whose reading levels differ widely. The questions that follow permit you to organize reading workshop around a theme, topic, or genre, and allow students to select books at their independent-reading levels that relate to the study.

The questions on pages 290–295, composed by my students, can be used when everyone reads different titles, when partners read the same title, or when small groups complete an author study.

Suggestions for Using Open-ended Questions

Place sets of these questions on index cards; create several decks for each group of questions. Partners or small groups can share a deck or students can select one or more cards to discuss. I like to color code my discussions cards, making Theme Questions pink, Character Questions green, etc. Some teachers also color code genre questions.

Sometimes, I invite students to bring in a free-choice library book and select a question for discussion. Groups of two, three, or four students discuss their completed book, using their question. This focuses the discussion, deters long retellings, and invites students to deepen their understanding of an aspect of their book.

Bind card decks with rubber bands and store in a shoe box or a plastic crate.

Note-taking Can Improve the Quality of Student Discussions

Before plunging into discussions, ask students to think about their question, skim their book for support, and jot down the ideas they've collected. Such preparation can create more thoughtful discussions.

QUESTIONS TO USE WITH FICTION

Questions That Foster Personal Connections

✦ How are your feelings and the feelings of a character in your book alike? How are they different?

✦ What feelings did you have as you read the story? Find some places that made you feel this way. Share and discuss these.

✦ What words does the author use that you might want to use in your own writing? Jot these down in your notebook.

✦ Have you had experiences similar to a character in the story? Discuss these.

✦ Select and read to the group a passage that you found meaningful. Explain why.

✦ How did the story change your thinking? Or can you show how it validated or affirmed your thinking?

Questions About Setting

✦ Where does the story take place? Discuss the important settings and explain why you believe each is important to the story.

✦ When does the story take place? Was it long ago, in the future, or the present? What did you learn about this time period?

✦ How much time passes in the story? Skim through your book and find places that show how the author makes time pass, and share these.

Questions About Characters

✦ Who is the main character? Why is this character important to the story?

✦ Are there words a character spoke and/or actions a character took that helped you learn what kind of a person he or she was? Find and discuss two important sections.

- Did any of the characters change? Pick one and discuss how an event, person, and decision changed that character.

- Discuss what you think the main character learned about himself, his family, or his friends.

- Describe a conflict between two characters. How was it resolved? What did you learn about these characters?

- Name one to two minor characters. Show how each affected the main character.

- Were there problems characters couldn't solve? Identify one or two and explain why you think they weren't resolved.

Questions About Structure

- What is the genre of your book? Give examples that support your decision.

- What literary techniques did you find? flashback? foreshadowing? figurative language? Find examples of two of these techniques, and share.

- Did the author create different moods? Find passages in the text that reveal two different moods, and share. Point out the words, phrases, and actions that helped create the mood.

Questions About Theme

- How does the title relate to the story?

- Discuss some points that the author is making about family, friends, feelings, nature, life experiences, or an historical period. Use details from the story that back up a point you're making.

- Discuss what the author might have been saying about family relationships and offer support from the story to back up your position.

QUESTIONS FOR BIOGRAPHY AND HISTORICAL FICTION

Biography, Autobiography, Memoir

+ Why is this person famous?

+ Discuss three to four personality traits that helped make this person achieve his or her goal.

+ What are two to three problems this person had to overcome?

+ What about this person do you feel enabled him or her to realize personal hopes and dreams?

+ Were there people and/or events that helped this person realize his or her dream? Select two and show how each influenced the person.

+ What do you admire or dislike about this person? Explain your position.

+ How are you and this person alike? different? Give specific examples in your discussions.

+ How did this person affect the lives of other people during his or her time? during our time?

Historical Fiction

+ What clues did you use to determine the time and place of this book?

+ What does the book teach you about family life and relationships between family members?

+ What does this book teach you about the role of men and women during these times?

+ What kinds of struggles and problems did the main character face? List three and explain how the main character dealt with and solved each one. If there was no solution, explain why you think the problem couldn't be solved.

+ Would you enjoy living during the time of this book? Explain why or why not.

+ What problems, conflicts does the main character face that you deal with in your life?

+ How do the main character's problems differ from yours?

+ How do people cope with economic problems such as scarcity of food? money? jobs?

+ How are minorities portrayed? Are they stereotyped? Offer examples.

QUESTIONS FOR FANTASY AND SCIENCE FICTION

Fantasy

+ What are the settings? Explain the elements of fantasy that you see in the setting.

+ How does the author enable you, the reader, to enter the fantasy world? Are there realistic elements? Discuss some of these and how they affect the story.

+ How do trips to other times and worlds help the characters cope with the present time?

+ Is there a struggle between forces of light and dark? Who wins? Offer support for the victory.

+ What special powers does the hero possess? For what purposes does he or she use these powers?

+ What does the hero learn about himself/herself? about life?

+ What personality traits do you have in common with the hero? Discuss two of these.

+ How do ideas and themes in this book connect to other fantasy books you've read?

+ Does the story deal with values and themes about death?

+ How has this book changed your thinking?

Science Fiction

+ What scientific advances do you see in the society? How do these advances in technology affect the characters' decisions and actions?

+ Are problems characters face in the story similar to or different from those people face today? Explain with examples.

+ Does the author deal with present-day issues such as population, food supplies, ecology, technological advances? Compare the author's views to your own.

+ Does the story offer hope for humanity or is it a warning? Explain your conclusion.

+ How do people fit into this futuristic society? Are they subordinate to machines? Has democracy vanished? See if you can identify the changes and offer reasons for each one.

+ Would you like to live in this society? Are there advantages and disadvantages? Offer reasons from the text for your decisions.

QUESTIONS FOR REALISTIC FICTION AND HISTORICAL FICTION

Realistic Fiction

+ What problems does the main character face? Do you feel these problems are realistic? Why? Why not?

+ Describe three or four settings and show how each influences the events and characters' actions and decisions. Would similar settings have influenced you in the same way? Explain.

+ What about the main character is realistic in terms of your experiences?

+ What about two to three minor characters is realistic in terms of your experiences?

+ What problems and conflicts in this book are realistic?

+ What problems do you and the main character or a minor character have in common? Compare the way you deal with those problems to the way the character dealt with them.

+ What are the realistic themes and issues in the book? Do they have to do with growing up, peer pressure, friendships, family relationships, survival, divorce, stereotyping? Discuss three themes the book explored.

+ In real life, events and people can change a character. How did an important event or person change the character at the end of the book?

Mystery

+ How does the author build suspense and excitement? Find two to three passages and discuss how the author accomplished this. Was it through description? characters' thoughts and actions?

+ What is the mystery that must be solved? How does setting affect the mystery?

+ What are some clues that the author includes to lead you away from solving the mystery?

+ What traits does the main character possess that enables him or her to solve the mystery?

+ Why did the main character become involved in the mystery?

+ How does danger affect the decisions and actions of the main character/detective?

+ At what point in the book were you able to solve the mystery? Why could you do this?

+ What part did you consider most suspenseful? Share it and explain why.

QUESTIONS FOR NONFICTION AND FOLK- AND FAIRY TALES

Nonfiction

✦ Why did you select this book?

✦ What new information did you learn?

✦ What questions did the book raise but did not answer?

✦ What did you learn from photographs? from charts and diagrams? from illustrations?

✦ Did this book change your thinking on this topic? How?

✦ Did the author weave opinions into facts? Can you find examples of each?

Folk and Fairy Tales

✦ Can you classify your fairy/folktale and explain why you selected the category? Was it a cumulative, circular, realistic, wonder, beast, numskull, giant, or quest tale?

✦ Does the tale revolve around magic numbers? If so, explain the role of these magic numbers in the story and how they affected the adventures and characters.

✦ Why must heroic tasks or deeds be accomplished?

✦ How do the adventures, the magic, and other characters change the life of the hero or heroine?

✦ What are two difficult decisions characters made? What influences these decisions? How do their decisions change their lives?

✦ What human characteristics do animals, flowers, and toys have? How are their qualities similar to yours?

✦ What is the clash and struggle between good and evil? Who wins? Offer support for your opinion on the victory.

✦ Who is the hero? The heroine? What qualities make him or her heroic?

Select a Quote

Name _____ Date _____

Directions:

1. Skim through your book and select a one- to three-sentence quote that made you pause and think.
2. On a page in your journal or on separate paper write the title and author of the book, then copy the quote and its page number.
3. Explain why this quote appealed to you. How did it make you feel? What did it make you think? visualize?
4. Then show how the quote connects to a theme, event, or character in the book.
5. Finally, try to connect the quote to your life or to another book.

Title and Author:

Quote:

The quote's appeal:

Connect the quote to a theme, event, or character:

Connect the quote to your life or to another book:

Think About What Characters Value

Name(s) _____ Date _____

Title and Author _____

Character's Name _____

Directions:
1. Divide your journal page into two columns.
2. Jot down notes under each heading.
3. With a partner, use this entry to discuss a character's values and compare them to yours.

What are values?	Where do values come from?
List of your values:	These values came from:
List the character's values.	These values came from:

Values the character and I have in common:

Note the key points of the discussion with your partner:

Problem, Actions, Results

Name _____ Date _____

Title and Author _____

Character's Name _____

Directions: Think of two major problems the main character faced. State the problems in the first column, write the actions the character took to solve the problems in the second column, and the results of the actions taken in the third column.

Problems	Actions Taken	Results
1.		
2.		

Inferring a Character's Personality From Events, Conflicts, Dialogue, and Decisions

Name _____ Date _____

Title and Author _____

Character's Name _____

Directions: Select a character from your book and think about how you describe that character's personality traits by studying an event, a conflict, dialogue, and decision. *Include implied ideas.*

Event	Personality Trait
Conflict	Personality Trait
Summary of Dialogue	Personality Trait
Decision	Personality Trait

Forming an Hypothesis About a Character and Proving it

Name _____ Date _____

Title and Author _____

Character's Name _____

Directions: To form an hypothesis about a character, create a statement that takes a position about a decision, an action or deed, feelings, interactions, or the personality of a character. Then find three pieces of support from the text to back up your hypothesis.

HYPOTHESIS	PROOF
	1.
	2.
	3.

TEACHER-STUDENT READING
CONFERENCE FORM

Name _____ Date _____

Topic to be Discussed:

Points Discussed by Teacher and Student:

Teacher Recommendations:

Actions/Goals Student and Teacher Negotiated:

Follow-up Conference Needed? _____ Date _____

Additional Comments:

FOUR-POINT RUBRIC FOR JOURNAL ENTRIES

The teacher or students can use this rubric to score journal entries. If the teacher scores the entry, use the rubric to comment on student's work. *Remember to start with positives.*

Score: 4 Points

+ Includes several supporting details from the text.
+ Makes personal connections and/or connections to other books.
+ Follows directions carefully.
+ Makes inferences using story details.

Score: 3 Points

+ Includes one to two supporting details.
+ Makes a personal connection.
+ Follows most of the directions.

Score: 2 Points

+ Retells the story.
+ Makes a personal connection.
+ Follows a few directions.

Score: 1 Point

+ Retells the story.
+ Does not follow the directions.

PARENT-TEACHER CONFERENCE FORM

Use this form to document a telephone or an in-person conference. Prepare for the conversation by listing the topics you wish to raise and discuss.

Child's Name _____ Date _____

Name(s) of Adult(s) Who Participated:

Topics the Teacher Wishes to Discuss:

Issues, Questions, Concerns Parent(s)/Guardian(s) Raised:

Recommendations and Goals:

Additional Teacher Comments:

BOOK CONFERENCE FORM

Document a one-on-one book conference with a student, using this form. The follow-up questions, in italics, will help students talk about their books.

Student's Name _____ Date _____

Title and Author _____ Brought Book _____

Why did you choose the book?

Is it a topic you love?

Did someone help you find the book?

What did you like about the story, a character, the setting?

Can you find a favorite part, read, it, and explain why you liked it?

Did you have a lot in common with the character? Explain what it was.

Did the author create suspense or make you laugh? Can you find a funny or suspenseful part and discuss it?

Can you connect the title to the story?

What about the main character was reflected in the title?

Were the words in the title used in the story?

How did the reading go?

Did you enjoy the book? Why?

Did you read with ease?

Were there any parts that confused you?

Was it difficult to stop reading once you got into it?

Did you learn any new words?

Any suggestions for the next book?

A CHECKLIST FOR MONITORING INDEPENDENT READING

Name _____ Date _____

Observations	Teacher's Notes
Book Log Entries Number of Books Variety of Titles	

Sustained Silent Reading
Selects books on independent level
Gets started quickly
Self-helps before seeking peer or
    teacher assistance
Shows pleasure in reading through
    journal entries, book talk, and projects	

Written Work Book reviews Critical paragraph essays Projects Response	
Oral Work Book talks Reading fluency Oral reading error patterns	

Additional Notes and Questions:

BOOK LOG FORM

Name _____ Date _____

TITLE, AUTHOR	DATE COMPLETED

PARTNER READING STRATEGY CONFERENCE

Directions: Converse with your partner to evaluate your use of a reading strategy. Then you and your partner, using your own forms, jot down notes under each question. Turn your evaluation in to your teacher.

This conference was held on _____ between:

Name _____

Name _____

What was the reading strategy you and your partner discussed?

How did the strategy help your reading?

What did you learn from your partner?

What other strategies did you use along with the one you practiced?

GUIDELINES FOR WRITING
READERS THEATER SCRIPTS

The Benefits of Readers Theater

Readers theater engages students in writing their own scripts from books and stories they've completed. In addition to learning how to script a section from a text, students work on fluecy and expressive reading. As they practice, their goal is to get inside a character so deeply that they project that character's emotional state and personality to the audience. It is a reading-writing experience that invites pairs and small groups who are reading the same book to integrate writing and drama.

Model the How To's For Your Students

First write a collaborative script, so students observe how you compose one. The guidelines below explain the process:

+ Tell students that a readers theater script always has one or more narrators and the characters from a selected passage.

+ Find a section, one to three pages, from a book or story that is rich in dialogue that presents and problem and/or conflict.

+ Show students how you assign narrative parts that offer background information, setting, and plot to one or more narrators. These sections can be shortened.

+ Take the exact words that character's say and write these in the form of a play.

+ Offer suggestions, in parentheses, for how the character speaks.

Setting Scripts Up

Narrator:

Emily: (sadly)

Reggie: (tense and tired)

Index

A

all-about-me letters, 92-93, 97-101
Analytical Reading Inventory, 248, 252, 253
Anderson, Richard, 14, 15, 30
annotated book lists, 235-36
    mini-lesson, 235-36
    guidelines, 235
assessment, interpretation, and evaluation, 243-79
    cueing systems, 249-51
    debriefing, 251-53
    definition, 243-44
    expertise in, developing, 246-48
    grading problems with, 272-73
    oral reading, 248-55
    possible assessments, 247
    reading strategies, evaluation of, 270-71
    reassessing, 255
    resources, 246
    self-evaluation, 259-70
    testing reading, 271-72
Atwell, Nancie, 31, 32, 67
author study, 192-95
author s chair, 24

B

Barr, Sadow, Blachowicz, 16
Bear, Invernizzi, Johnston, and Templeton, 251
bibliography
    children s books, 283-84
    professional books and articles, 279-82
Bomer, Randy, 32
book/books
    classroom library, 26
    conference (form), 304
    connecting students to, 183-200
    connections to other, 187
    core and extension, 193-95
    too difficult, 20, 184, 198-99
    discussion, 23, 37, 43-47
    listening to, 17, 37, 229
    log (form), 306
    novel studies, 192-193
    oral presentation, 162-63
    picture books, 180-81
    readability, 18, 190, 198
    school library, creating a, 19
    selecting, 20, 22, 73, 91-93, 190-98, 233-34, 237
    sharing, 20
    student choice, 23, 197-99
book review, 37, 38-40
brainstorm and categorize, 118, 119,132
    clustering, 127
    guided practice, 121, 122, 125
    guidelines, 124
    refining information, 125
    strategy lesson, 123-25
Brown, Day, and Jones, 15

C

Caldwell, JoAnne, 253
Calkins, Lucy, 67
categorize see brainstorm and categorize
cause/effect 178
    guided practice, 179
    guidelines, 177-78
    standardized test link, 179
    strategy lesson, 177-78
Clay, Marie, 13, 205, 276, 279
clustering, 127
comprehension, 12, 20, 116, 184
    repairing faulty, 16
    improve, 63

and read-alouds, 185–87
self-monitoring, 15–16, 66
and the senses, 156–58
conference
    book conference (form), 304
    getting-to-know-you , 88, 93, 103–107
    notes, 104, 104–105, 110,111
    one-on-one, 18, 23, 35, 211
    parent-teacher (form), 303
    partner reading strategy (form), 307
    peer, 37
    planning, 103
    teacher-student (form), 301
confirm/adjust, 66, 119, 214
    guided practice, 154
    guidelines, 155–56
    strategic reading group, 211–13
    strategy lesson, 154–56
context clues, 16, 225
    guided practice, 138
    guidelines, 137–38
    mini-lesson, 138–39
    practice using, 141–42
    standardized test link, 138
    strategy lesson, 137–39
    struggling readers and, 139–40
core and extension books, 193–94
cross-grade projects/experiences, 228–41
    annotated book lists, 235–36
    reading buddies, 231–34
cueing systems, three, 251–53

D
debriefings, 255–59
    productive, 256
    questions for, 256–57
    strategy in action, 257–58
    when to debrief, 256
Discover Your Own Literacy, 56
discussion groups, 24, 35, 43–47
    guidelines, 46
    management tips, 44–46
    planning suggestions, 48–49, 50–51

dramatizations, 37
during-reading strategies, 134–51

E
evaluation see assessment, interpretation, and
    evaluation

F
fast-write, 130–31
    guided practice, 130–31
    guidelines, 128–29
    strategy lesson, 130–31
Fielding and Pearson, 30
Flexible Grouping in Reading, 33
fluency
    developing, 17, 231
    prompts, 222
Fountas, Irene, 33, 205, 239
Fountas and Pinnell, 14, 33, 205
forms/information sheets/survey sheets
    book conference, 304
    book log, 306
    independent reading checklist, 305
    inferring about personality, 299
    forming an hypothesis, 300
    journal entries—scoring, 302
    parent information sheet, 287
    parent-teacher conference, 303
    partner conference, 307
    problem, actions, results, 298
    questions about reading, 286
    reading strategies evaluation, 269–70
    reading strategy checklist, 102
    reading strategy interview, 288
    reading survey, 285
    retelling: narrative, 249
    select a quote, 296
    self-evaluation—predict/support, 262
    teacher-student conference, 301
    what characters value, 297
    workshop goals, 260
free-choice time see independent-choice time

G

Grambell and Almasi, 32
gathering, 23, 26
genres, 25, 193-94
goal-setting, 21
Goodman, Kenneth and Yetta, 22, 251-53
grade-level readers, 90
grading, 272-73
grants for books, 26
graphophonic, 251
Graves, Donald, 56
grouping students, 27
    Flexible Grouping in Reading, 33
    guided reading, 18, 121
    strategic-reading groups, 23, 33, 35, 110, 202-17
    workshop, 30-37
guided practice/guided reading, 14, 18, 23, 31, 35
    brainstorming, 123
    budgeting time for, 77-78
    cause/effect, 177
    confirm and adjust, 154
    context clues, 137
    group, 18, 121
    Guided Reading: Good First Teaching
        For All Children, 33, 202-203
    implied meaning, 168, 169
    with partner, 120
    partner reading and retelling, 145-46
    personal connections, 74-75, 164
    predict and support, 119-120, 147-50
    and questions, 127
    read/pause/retell, 143
    resources, 76-77
    senses and comprehension, 156-58
    skimming, 76-77, 160-62
    in workshop, 31, 70-71, 78
Guided Reading: Good First Teaching
    For All Children, 33, 203

H

Holdaway, Don, 32

I

implied meaning
    clues, 174-75
    guided practice, 170-72
    and the inference game, 174
    strategy lesson, 164-66, 167-69
        See also inferences
In The Middle, 31
independent choice time, 23, 36-37, 42, 50-51
independent reading, 23, 26, 35, 36, 78, 122, 188
    choices, 195-97
    contracts, 198-99
    importance of, 30
    level, 190
    monitoring checklist, 305
Independent Reading Inventory, 229
inferences, 15, 164-76
    author's clues, 174-75
    and character's personality, 299
    inference game, 176
    prompts, 168, 221
    in read-alouds, 185-87, 188
        See also implied meaning
Informal Reading Inventory (IRI), 88, 92
interactive teaching, 276-77
International Reading Association, 82, 85
interpretation see assessment, interpretation, and
        evaluation
in-the-head strategies 59, 135-36, 185-87
        See also reading strategies

J

journals
    dialogue, 31
    keeping a, 124
    response. 23, 30, 37-39, 79, 112
    scoring entries (form), 302
    self-evaluating, 264-65

L

Lapp, Diane, 32

Leinhard, 30
Leslie, Lauren, 253
listening center, 17
literacy, exploring your, 56
literacy centers, 103
literacy folder, 92, 94, 105, 205
Literature as Exploration, 14
literature response journal see journal
Lytle, Susan, 67

M

magazines, 73, 195
metacognition, 135, 150
mini-lessons, 14, 18, 122
    adapting, 116
    annotated book lists, 235-36
    context clues, 137-39
    finding topics for, 68
    reading buddies (cross-grade experience), 229-32
    reading strategy, 61, 67-70, 78
    samples, 69
    three kinds of, 67
    workshop in, 26-27, 35-37
        See also strategy lessons
Minsky, Marvin, 14
miscues
    miscue key/code, 248, 257
    in oral reading, 252-54
modeling, 14, 21, 31, 135, 136
    during-reading strategies, 136-47
    with picture books, 180-81
    during read-alouds, 189-90
    three-part reading model, 61-62
Moe, Alden J., 248, 252, 253
motivation and involvement, 13, 19-22

Mc

Mclaughlin, 191

N

novels. 192-93

O

observation, 21-22, 77, 111, 203-204
    notes, 104-113, 202, 204-206
    systematic, 204
on-the-run strategies, 213, 217-20
Opitz, Michael, 33
oral presentation 162-63
oral reading, 14
    assessing, 245-50
    cueing systems, 251-52
    miscue key/code, 250, 254-55

P

paired questioning, 37
parent
    information sheet (form), 287
    parent-teacher conference (form), 303
partner reading, 122
    guided practice, 122, 145
    guidelines, 143-44
    strategy conference (form), 307
    strategy lesson, 143-44
Paterson, Katherine, 281
Pearson, David P., 182
    independent reading, 30
    reading strategies, 14-16, 76-77, 78
    skills vs. strategies, 59-61
personal connections/making connections, 62, 66, 116, 166
    to community and world issues, 163-65
    to daily living, 165
    guided practice, 72-74, 166
    prereading strategies, 116-17
    prompts, 166, 221
    and read-alouds, 185-87
    strategy lesson, 164-66
    supporting, 169
picture books, 180-81
Pinnell, Gay Su, 33, 205
plays, 231
poetry, 187-89, 231
post-reading strategies, 154-79

Powers, 22
predict and support, 16, 66, 119
    confirm/adjust, 117, 154-55
    degrees, 120
    forming hypothesis (form), 300
    guided practice, 121-22, 146
    guidelines, 145-47
    prompts, 221-24
    in read-alouds, 188
    self-evaluation checklist, 264, 265
    with strategic reading group, 212-16
    strategy lesson, 119-23, 145-46, 147
prediction log, 157
predictions *see* predict and support
prereading strategies, 118-19
prior knowledge, 12, 62, 63, 130
    activating, 14-16, 117-19
    lack of, 184
professional journals, 246
proficient readers, 90-91
purpose/importance of text, 15, 66, 22

Q
Qualitative Reading Inventory-II, 253
questions/posing questions, 16, 116, 134
    all-about-me letters, 96
    biography/historical fiction, 292
    debriefing, 255
    fantasy/science fiction, 293
    fiction, 44, 290-91
    folk/fairy tales, 295
    guided practice, 127
    guidelines, 128-29
    nonfiction, 46, 295
    open-ended, 44, 46, 129, 289-95
    paired questioning, 37
    read-alouds, 185
    about reading, 286
    realistic fiction/mystery, 294
    sample student, 126, 159
    self-evaluation of reading progress, 286
    self-question, 66, 220

    standardized test link, 130
    strategy lesson, 127-29
    in workshops, 35, 47
quote, select a quote (form), 296

R
read-alouds, 13, 23, 27
    choices for, 34, 35, 189
    in action, 187-88
    and in-the-head strategies, 185-90
    modeling strategies, 18, 186-90
    tips, 34
    workshop anchor, 33-35
read/pause/retell/read on or reread, 16, 36, 66,
    143-44
    guided practice, 144
    guidelines, 143-44
    retelling: narrative document, 249-57
    standardized test link, 144
    strategy lesson, 143-44
    what to look for in, 249
readers, kinds of, 88-92
    grade level, 90
    proficient, 90-91
    reluctant, 89, 102
    struggling, 82-84, 85, 102, 139-40, 198,
    229-42
reader's chair, 24-26
readers theater, 37
reading strategies
    applying, 14-18, 132, 204-207, 208
    content-area, 64
    demonstration, 79-81
    during-reading, 131-51
    evaluation (form), 270
    and faulty comprehension, 16
    and fluency, 17, 231
    guidelines, 81
    inferences, 15, 164-72, 174, 181, 223, 299
    key, 14-16, 66
    mini-lesson, 61, 67-72, 79-81
    modeling w/picture books, 180-81

monitoring progress, 267-70

on-the-run, 213, 217, 219-21

partner conference (form), 307

Pearson, 14-16, 79

post-reading strategies, 153-81

preparing students to read, 115-32

prereading, 116-17

prior knowledge, 12, 14-15, 62, 63, 116-119, 130, 184

prompts, 221-25

purpose of text, 15

and questions, 16, 96, 116, 135

and read-alouds, 185-87

reading strategy interview, 288

in a school year, 79-81

self-evaluation, 261-63

self-monitor, 15-16, 66, 135, 136, 152, 220

and struggling readers, 82-84

student checklist, 93, 101-105, 206-208

synthesize information, 15, 66

three-part model, 61-62

understanding, 66, 79-81, 209, 218

vocabulary, 16-17, 35, 137-42

vs. skill, 59-61

    See also in-the-head strategies

Reading: The Patterning of Complex Behaviour, 205

reading

experiences, 23, 198

guided reading, 18

independent, 23, 30

novels, 190

oral reading, 13

paired, 36, 110

poetry, 17

preparation, 116-32

program—defined, 13

questions about, 286

self-evaluation, 266-68

survey sheet (form) 285

testing students, 270-71

reading buddies, 231-234

organizing (mini lesson), 231-34

guidelines, 235

Reading Recovery Program, 13

recall, 21

recall and reflect, 136

Reed, Shallert, and Goetz, 22

reluctant readers, 89, 104

research, student, 37, 42

resources

assessment/evaluation, 245-46

books that hook readers, 240

content area reading strategy, 64

core books, 193

grants for books, 26

guided practice, 72-78

magazines, 197

novels, 192-93

observational notes, 105-10

professional journals, 246

read-alouds, 35, 187

short texts, 73

response journals *see* journals

retelling *see* read/pause/retell

Rosenblatt, Louise, 14

round robin reading, 13

Routman, Regie, 32

S

scaffolding, 84

Schallert and Reed, 19, 184

schema theory, 14-15, 117

creating a school library, 19

Schunk and Zimmerman, 19

self-evaluation, 27, 56-59

benefits of, 257-58

checklist (predict/support), 264, 265

journals, 266-68

reading progress, 266-68

reading strategies, 263

strategies, 21

workshop goals, 260-61

self-monitoring, 15-16, 66, 143, 152

prompts, 221

semantic, 249-51

senses and comprehension
    guided practice, 159
    guidelines, 158-59
    strategy lesson, 156-58

short texts, 73

The Shifting Sands of Factorland, 12

skill sheets, 13

skills vs. strategies, 59-61

skimming for information
    guided practice, 76-77, 161
    guidelines, 161
    strategy lesson, 164-66

SMOG (Some Measure of Gobbledygook)
        formula, 18, 191

standardized test links
    context clues, 137
    define terms (cause and effect), 177
    preview questions, 128
    rereading, 143-44

Steward, Ian, 12

strategic reading
    curriculum, 18, 86
    groups, 23, 33, 35, 112, 202-17
    guidelines, 81
    in middle school, 55-84
    practice, 37
    strategic reading groups, 202-26
    teaching, 13-18, 82-84
        See also reading strategies

strategic reading groups, 23, 33, 35, 112, 202-26
    changes in, 210-11
    "dynamic grouping", 204
    guidelines, 209-10
    on-the-run, 211, 217, 219-20
    predict and support, 215-17, 219-21
    research, 205-206
    responsive grouping, 203-204, 205, 224
    traditional grouping, 205
    transcriptions, 215-17, 217-18
    workshop, 210-12

strategy lessons
    brainstorm and categorize, 123-25
    cause/effect, 177-79
    confirm and adjust, 154-55
    making connections, 164-66
    using context clues, 141-42
    fast-write, 130-31
    framework of, 117
    implied meanings, 167-76
    partner reading and retelling, 145-46
    predict and support, 119-21, 147-51
    preparing students to read, 116-32
    posing questions, 127-29
    read/pause/retell, 143-44
    senses and comprehension, 156-59
    skimming for information, 160-61

struggling readers, 82-84, 85, 104
    choosing a book, 197-99
    context clues, 139-41
    cross-grade projects, 228-35
    reading strategies, 81-84
    timeline to support, 236-39, 240-41

student
    conferences, 18, 23, 35, 37, 86, 94, 103-107,
        110, 212, 301
    confidence, 21
    grouping, 18, 27, 32-33, 200-20
    knowing your, 22, 88-114
    oral reading, 13
    parent information sheet, 287
    parent-teacher conference (form), 303
    teacher interaction, 114, 203-204

summarize, 66, 222
        See also synthesize

Symbolic Book Talk, 162-63

syntactic, 249

synthesize information, 15, 66, 224
        See also summarize

T

text sets, 194-95, 196

text structures, 66

theoretical knowledge, 206, 209

think-alouds, 67, 70–72, 136–39

themes, 172-73, 193, 194-95, 221

three-part reading model, 61, 62

"tough" words, 136, 137-40, 223

V

visualization, 66, 185, 222

vocabulary

    building, 16, 35, 137–42

    integrating instruction, 17

    self-monitoring, 135

    "tough" words, 136, 137–41, 225

Vygotsky, Lev, 32–33

W

"What's Easy? What's Hard?", 92-97

Woods, Mary Lynn, 248, 252, 253

Woods and Moe, 248, 252, 253

word pronunciation, 225

Words Their Way: Word Study for Phonics,

    Vocabulary, and Spelling Instruction, 251

workshops, 13, 22, 29-54

    basic routines, 26-27

    behavior guidelines, 36, 41–42

    benefits of, 32

    calendar, 50, 54

    essentials, 35

    examining your, 28

    group work, 41, 43, 51

    grouping, 32–33

    guided practice, 31, 70, 78

    independent choice, 36–38, 42, 50–51

    and interactive teaching, 277

    managing, 36–42, 44

    organizing, 29-54, 188, 200

    read-alouds, 33–35

    sample schedules, 48, 49

    self-evaluation, 259-62

    setting the stage, 50

    strategic reading groups, 208-10

    with many students, 51-53

student research, 40

typical experiences, 23-27

writing, 31

writing

    brainstorm, 98-99

    journal, 23, 31

    about reading, 266

    workshop, 31

XYZ

"Zone of Proximial Development", 33